LEAF by LEAF

Adventures on four continents

The memoirs of

LEAF FIELDING

Part 2

Some names have been changed.

Published in 2016 by FeedARead.com Publishing

Copyright © Leaf Fielding.

Leaf Fielding asserts his moral right under the Copyright, Designs and Patents Act, 1988, to be identified as the author of this work.

All Rights reserved. No part of this publication may be reproduced, copied, stored in a retrieval system, or transmitted, in any form or by any means, without the prior written consent of the copyright holder, nor be otherwise circulated in any form of binding or cover other than that in which it is published and without a similar condition being imposed on the subsequent purchaser.

A CIP catalogue record for this title is available from the British Library.

The right of Leaf Fielding to be identified as the author of this work has been asserted by him in accordance with the Copyright, Designs and Patents Act 1988

Copyright © 2016 Leaf Fielding
Cover design by Sue Whatmough with photo by David Dukes

ISBN 978 0 9569240 2 5

Website: www.leaffielding.com

To Clive

To my wife
Sue
With all my love

love & peace

[signature]

via my beautiful
sister Judy

Also by LEAF FIELDING

'TO LIVE OUTSIDE THE LAW'

CHAPTERS

AFTERWORD

INTRODUCTION

Part 1 of my memoirs, *To Live Outside the Law,* opens with my arrest in Britain's biggest drugs bust: Operation Julie. The book covers my first thirty-three years on this beautiful and tragic planet, moving backwards and forwards between a prison cell and my earlier life.

I was six when the sudden death of my mother, in 1955, flattened me and was still reeling from the loss when my brother and I were packed off for ten rigid years in boarding school.

After my life-changing introduction to LSD in nineteen sixty-seven – the Summer of Love – my monochrome world was suffused with wild billowing rainbows: everything was drenched in colour, anything seemed possible. I dropped out of University and went on the road, travelling the hippie trail in Europe and Asia. It was a glorious decade of amazing adventures and narrow escapes, during which I met all kinds of extraordinary characters and some truly exceptional people.

My offbeat lifestyle led directly to my intimate involvement with the operations of the underground laboratory that produced the purest LSD the world had ever seen.

To Live Outside the Law ends with my release after five years in prison.

This volume carries straight on from its predecessor.

1. FREEDOM

If there's nobody to meet me outside the prison gate, I resolve, I'll just keep on walking. But three men are waiting, their breath hanging out in front of them in the cold morning air. My old pal Scooter stands with a hand resting possessively on a large Sedan. He's wearing a leather flying-jacket and has grown a beard. It suits him. Beside him is the ever-dependable Martin: my business partner, best man and best friend. Smiles, my blood brother through the long years in Horfield nick, beams at me, eyes alight. They hug me, one by one. More hugs all round – and then tears as they are overcome by their emotions. No crying from me – I can't stop grinning.

'Long time,' Martin murmurs, wiping his eyes.

Scooter turns on the engine. He opens the front passenger door and waves me inside. I wind down the window, look back and yell 'Fuck off Leyhill!'

We shoot away from the prison at top speed, hurtling down country lanes, heading to Reading. There are Saint David's day daffodils in the banks and on village greens. The air seems infused with a magical light. 'I'm free,' I murmur. The echo resounds ever louder in my head: Free Free Free Free Free!

Smiles taps me on the shoulder and whispers in my ear, 'I got out of the Moor a few weeks ago. Your friends are very glad to see you, no doubt, but I'm the only one who has the remotest idea what's going on in your brain.'

'Oh, man!' Joy makes me incoherent.

9

Scooter gives me a nudge and passes me a giant spliff. I light it, take a huge toke and hold it down for as long as I can. I take another and cough and choke. Smoke fills the car. Martin cracks a window to clear the fumes. I inhale a lungful of the fresh morning air and suddenly I'm flying, my head humming with a riot of thoughts that keep returning to the central, undeniable fact of this gorgeous morning:

I am free!

My five-year ordeal has ended. It's difficult to accept my time is done; it had seemed like it would go on forever. I keep saying to myself 'you did it, man, you got through. IT'S OVER!'

At the end of an excitable champagne lunch at Martin's house, I jump to my feet as I suddenly remember. 'Fuck! I'm supposed to check in with the parole service. I'm going to be late. Can anyone give me a lift into Reading?'

Scooter and I rocket down narrow lanes, through hamlets, past pubs and suddenly I'm in familiar territory – stuck in traffic at the Caversham Bridge bottleneck, cars and people everywhere. I stare out of the window, drinking in the riot of colour, looking hungrily at the young women, wondering what's coming up next.

The parole officer, rose to his feet as I entered his office. 'You're nearly half an hour late!' he spluttered.

He was younger than me. A short man with long fair hair, he was slim and casually dressed in faded blue denim. As I remembered, people who looked like that used to be OK, so I made a light comment, as I might do to a friend. 'I can't believe how quickly time goes by out here. Sorry I'm late - we got caught in traffic trying to get across the river.'

'It won't do, Fielding!' The parole officer looked petulant, as if he was going to stamp his foot on the floor. 'I won't have it happen again!' He banged his fist on the table to emphasise his words. 'It's a bad start, you know, a very bad start. You've only been out of prison for a few hours and already you've got a black mark!' He paused dramatically and took a deep breath. He was standing on his dignity – as though it would make him taller. 'Right. You're going to report to me every week, not every fortnight as arranged. And you'll report on time. On the dot!'

He jabbed the desk with his forefinger to emphasise his words and tried to give me the hard stare that minor officials use to intimidate those in their power. He looked rather pathetic. I wanted to laugh, but managed to keep a straight face.

'And you'd better keep me happy...' he added. His voice grew dramatically deeper. 'Because I have the power to send you back to gaol.'

I stared silently back at him until his eyes flicked away.

'Do what you like,' I said under my breath.

I'd relaxed my guard too soon. I might be out of prison, but until my parole was over I was still subject to the penal system. I resolved to move away from Reading as soon as possible. I wasn't going to be slung back inside by a pocket tyrant, masquerading as a hippy.

According to the terms of my parole I was supposed to be working in Reading Wholefoods, the health food shop that Martin and I had set up in the

11

mid-seventies. I turned up a few times but my heart wasn't in it. I didn't feel ready to deal with the public and didn't fancy spending my days in the stock room behind the shop, filling jars with sticky peanut butter and mixing dustbins full of muesli.

I was charged with stored energies, imbued with a force that can only be understood by people who've survived long confinement. I'd never been on such a wonderful sustained high. It wasn't worth the five years inside, but it was a sweeter compensation than I would have imagined possible. I had my life back, and I valued it in a way that cannot be comprehended by anyone who takes their existence for granted.

For the first time ever, I radiated a flame that attracted women like moths. I couldn't get it up with the first girl who dragged me into her bed: I wasn't in the sexual realm yet. The next time I was better prepared; I hadn't forgotten after all.

Just as prison closes over you, becoming the day-to-day reality to which you must speedily adjust, so it quickly drains away – most of it. A certain amount lingers for years and a small but irreducible residue can remain for life.

Every night in my dreams I was back inside. Part of me was still there. What a relief to wake up each morning and realise afresh that I was free. Every morning the prison images evaporated, but the next night they'd be back, the subordinate claws (sic) at the end of the long sentence.

Between getting the divorce and selling our house, Mary had put my things in storage with Jeff Wills, a friend from University days who was living outside

Henley. I'd been at liberty for a few weeks when Lewe, a pal from the early hippie era, offered to drive me over to pick up my gear. On the journey he plied me with questions about my years inside. It was ground I'd covered quite a few times since my release. A lot of people have an appalled fascination with prison.

Contemplating my little pile of possessions in Jeff's utility room was like looking through the wrong end of a time telescope. These things had once been important to me, yet I'd managed without them for years. I opened a suitcase. It was full of musty clothes: flared trousers, t-shirts and sweaters speckled with hash burns. My old Afghan coat had gone green with mould. The meagre wardrobe went straight into the bin, all of it, bar my once-worn wedding suit, which I donated to Oxfam.

'Jeff, please keep the fridge, cooker and other bits of furniture as a thank-you for looking after my things.' I didn't want to burden myself with stuff I'd only have to store again. Smiles and I had agreed long ago that as soon as our sentences were over, we'd travel round India. 'Could you take care of my books, my records and a few treasures for a while longer?'

'Sure, no problem.'

I thought I'd been dealing well with the echoes raised by the things I'd gathered in my earlier life. It hadn't occurred to me that not everything would be as emotionally neutral as faded clothes and old electrical appliances. I was fine until I came to the last item - a case of homemade wine. Lifting the heavy wooden crate onto a table stirred up deep memories from the sediment of the past – the years

13

with Mary. All at once I was falling apart: my eyes were prickly and wet, my unsteady legs could barely keep me upright.

I put the crate into the boot of Lewe's car and sat nursing my sad thoughts until we arrived at Martin's place. I lugged the crate into his kitchen, took out a bottle at random and set it on the table. My feelings were as twisted as the corkscrew I used to open that first bottle: dandelion wine. I could clearly remember the sunny summer afternoon Mary and I had spent picking the flowers in a huge meadow in Farley Hill. We'd gathered enough blossoms to make twenty-five litres of wine and fermented the must in a large glass carboy.

Over the next month, one by one, I drank these liquid memories of the life I'd shared with Mary. I hadn't wept in the five years I'd spent inside, but every time I drank the wine my wife and I had made together, helpless tears came spilling down my cheeks.

Martin clinked his glass against mine. 'It's all right to cry, Leaf. It's all right. Better to let your feelings out than have them going sour inside.'

'Thanks Mart.' I knew he meant well and I agreed with him in principle, but the crying just made me feel weak and useless. Cold winds of loneliness howled through the holes in my threadbare life.

As the weeks go by, I come to accept that I've spent too much time apart to easily reintegrate. Being among people whose lives have roots only emphasises my difference. Not connected to anything, I'm freshly transplanted, prone to wilting.

At the end of one particularly frustrating day when I have to see the parole officer, do some food shopping, take my dirty clothes to a laundrette and fruitlessly attempt to sort out some transport, I'm dismayed to find myself missing the uncomplicated existence of life in a cell. Then it hits me, like a punch on the nose: I'm damaged goods. Prison has warped me. Cell life has eroded what remained of my innocence and spontaneity. It has jaundiced my view of people and taught me to be suspicious, mistrustful.

I'd left the nick on a high, full of light and laughter, but snapping at the heels of euphoria came a rage at the years that had been taken from me. My thoughts were poisoned by the metallic taste of the feelings and emotions I'd had to suppress in order to survive the mangle of incarceration. I was still seething at the recent memories of being in open prison. Being considered tame enough to keep myself inside was humiliating. What made it worse was the knowledge that my gaolers had assessed me correctly: I'd been so emasculated by my time in nick that I'd stayed within the bounds of the imaginary walls when, at any moment, I could have just walked out across the fields and gone on the run.

I enjoyed the company of women, but I'd had enough of men with their bluster and bravado. I was fine with old friends, but with anyone else, unless I felt an immediate bond of sympathy, I just wasn't interested. I'd developed a tough carapace to survive the steely demands of prison life and I couldn't simply put it aside; it had become part of me. In bad moments – and I was having more and more of them once the initial novelty of freedom wore off – it seemed that all that remained of me was the hollow shell of the person I had once been. I spent days gazing sightlessly into the black hole into which the last five years had tumbled.

One of the lowest moments of my time inside had come just after my transfer to Leyhill open prison. I'd been assigned to work in the print shop - a building that reeked with the smell of toxic dyes. At the end of my first working day, I walked out into the extensive prison grounds and tried to clear my lungs of the poisonous fumes I'd inhaled. A squirrel crossed my path - the first wild animal I'd seen in years.

I looked at it, trying in vain to summon up some enthusiasm, or any feeling at all. And what I thought was: 'a squirrel. So?'

I sagged, floored by the realisation that the lifelong love affair I'd had with Nature was over. She meant nothing to me any longer. For years my only company had been two opposed sets of hard men: cons and screws. The need to successfully navigate this tense, potentially explosive environment had taken most of my energy. It had shrivelled my capacity to see beyond the rectilinear world of cell, corridors, workshops and exercise yards.

After the great burst of social activity in the first weeks of my release, I withdrew and spent much of my time alone, trying to relax enough to be able to re-establish my connection with the natural world. I was lucky that Martin had invited me to stay at his house. I couldn't have been in a better spot.

Martin's home was a tied cottage on a lane overlooking a bend in the Thames above Pangbourne. It was the perfect launching pad for a long walk in the Chilterns. The cottage backed onto a bluebell wood and the blue carpet had been laid in April.

Most days, with a bottle of water, a couple of sandwiches and some fruit in my shoulder bag, I'd set off looking for inspiration in the countryside. The first time I found it – in slanting sunlight, splashing on green beech leaves – I felt my eyes moistening and cried with joy. I sat down on the leaf-mould and followed the fortunes of a determined beetle, doggedly navigating the huge obstacles of the forest floor.

Feathers, spiders' webs, rock crystals, badgers at dusk, a crescent moon, tawny owls calling to each other under a canopy of stars... Nature's medicines slowly began to heal my invisible wounds.

A mile from Martin's house, deep in the beech woods, was an ancient stand of yew trees. I cut a dozen walking stick blanks from the straight branches of a fallen giant and spent my days working the handles into animal heads. In the evenings I talked with Martin, listened to music or sat on the bed in my room and wrote or read.

I knew I couldn't hide from people forever. Armed with a phony job contract, fixed up by a friend in London, I got permission from my parole officer to move to the capital. I'm sure he was as glad to see the back of me as I was to get shot of him. I took my suitcase of possessions up to Clerkenwell and moved into the flat I was going to share with Fifi, Sue and my old friend Caroline. The first thing I had to do in town was report to my London parole officer. I made sure I was on time for my appointment, but I needn't have bothered. After hanging around in the scuffed waiting room for over an hour, swapping stories with the crowd of bad lads on probation or parole, I was called into the office.

'Good to see you, Nigel,' my parole officer said. She had a pleasant smile. She stood and held her hand out across the desk. I shook it. 'Have a seat,' she continued. 'My name's Beverly Thatcher.'

'Is that Miss or Mrs?' I regretted the words as soon as they were out of my mouth.

'You're not the first to ask,' she said, still smiling. 'I wasn't born a Thatcher. I married one. Now, what about you? You've got a place to live and you've got a job. You're OK, aren't you?' She looked at me questioningly.

'Yes, I'm fine.'

'Are you short of money?'

'No, I've got money from the sale of my house.'

'Good. Well, as you can see from the waiting room, I'm up to my ears, trying to help people with all kinds of problems. I'm extremely busy and I don't need you cluttering up my office. Goodbye.'

'That's it?' I couldn't believe our interview was over so quickly. 'When do I have to report in next?'

'You don't need to report in. Ring for an appointment if your circumstances change or if you need my help. Here's my number.'

I took the piece of paper she was holding.

'I'll make a home visit to your address before long.' With that, my Mrs Thatcher rose to her feet and came round the desk. She rested her hand on my back, escorted me to the door and showed me out.

I liked the self-important swagger and bustle of London at first and explored the area around Holborn: a place steeped in history. But I've never been a big city person and, all at once, a great wave of revulsion for the endless milling crowds swept over me. I retreated to my room. The City was frenetically busy during the week but quiet at the weekends. Aside from our small block of Peabody Estate flats, the only residents of the area seemed to be the Italian shopkeepers and restaurateurs. Saturday and Sunday became my days for walking and for talking to the neighbours.

I'm sure my flatmates felt sorry for me; they couldn't have been kinder. They took me to the theatre one evening and suggested I accompany them when they went to the movies. Adorable Fifi made a Swiss patterned sweater for me on her knitting machine. Then she knitted me a matching hat. The pullover unravelled eventually, but I still have the Swiss bobble hat. Somehow it survived all the moves, all the ups and downs of my erratic life.

Realising that my room in the flat was in danger of becoming my new cell, I spent a few hundred quid on an old Renault 4. Now I was able to get out of the city whenever claustrophobia threatened to clamp its metal bands around my skull. I asked my Mrs Thatcher if I could take a short holiday in Ireland and she said it would be fine.

2. DÉJÀ VU

In the six months since my release from prison I'd been through an emotional cyclone. The euphoria of freedom recovered lasted for several weeks, but it was fairly quickly replaced by a deep depression. On release I couldn't stop grinning, now I couldn't stop crying. Anger followed the tears and it was only when I'd made my long overdue connection with nature that I began to feel like my old self again.

Every two or three weeks I got into the rattletrap Renault 4, drove down to Reading and called in on a few of my friends. My last stop was often with my old pal Lewe. We drank tea in his little kitchen and harked back to the heady days of the late sixties. As usual, Lewe moaned about the way England was changing.

'It's that wicked witch, the Thatcher,' he groaned. 'She poisons everything she touches. Don't get me started!'

'I didn't say a word. Tell me about the old crowd instead. Who's still around?'

'Most of the Reading people are. A lot of the students have gone. I'll tell you who else moved away – your old flame, Thelma. She's living in London.'

I turned this information over in my mind while driving back to town. Then I rang Lewe from the flat and got her phone number. I was curious to find out what the first girl I'd loved was doing with her life.

I kept putting off the call. I'd never enjoyed talking down the line to someone I couldn't see. I hadn't used the phone for five years and had hardly rung anyone since my release. Knowing my phone had been tapped before Operation Julie made my rare phone conversations short and strained. Who might be listening in, hoping to find clues to imaginary stashes? I was always itching to bring the call to an end and put the receiver down.

Eventually I nerved myself up and dialled Thelma's number. The phone rang and rang. I knew nothing of her current circumstances; I should have checked with Lewe. Just as I was about to hang up a man answered the phone. Her husband? Boyfriend? Too late to back out now. 'Hello. Is Thelma there?'

'Sorry, she's out,' the man said. 'Who shall I say called?'

'Leaf. I'm an old friend.' My voice was a little shaky as I left my number. Would she ring back?

She rang that evening sounding exactly as I remembered her. I wondered if she still looked the same. Eleven years had passed since I'd waved goodbye to her on the platform at Reading station, on my way to go adventuring in South East Asia.

We agreed we were glad to be talking to each other and that it would be good to meet. After some dithering, we settled on a time and place. I put down the phone, excited and apprehensive, wondering what I might be letting myself in for.

The vast London pub was packed and braying. I stood in the doorway, dismayed by the din, almost ready to turn tail. Reminding myself that I'd handled worse, I plunged into the throbbing heart of the beast, made myself slim and slid through the crowd.

Would we even recognise each other? I was waving a fiver, trying to snag one of the barmaids then realised Thelma was standing beside me.

21

'Leaf! you haven't changed at all,' she gave me a hug, then held me at arms length to check me over. She looked beautiful.

'Oh, thank God!' she said. 'I thought you were going to be fat.'

'Fat?' I had to shout to be heard through the storm of voices. London had turned the volume up while I was away.

'Yes.' She spoke in my ear. 'All that prison stodge and stuff...'

'I was the gym orderly,' I yelled. 'I did weight training, circuits... I could play badminton for hours. I've never been so fit in my life.'

She looked at me doubtfully. 'Hours?'

'It's true. Every night I did a hundred sit-ups, a hundred press-ups and a hundred squats in succession. It's very important to stay in shape.' Realising that I was boasting, I cut myself off before I got in any deeper. 'Enough of prison. What about you? What have you been doing?'

'I learned to play the flute and I've graduated from the Royal Academy. I'm an artist, Leaf. It's official, I've even sold some paintings.'

Her laugh rolled back the years. 'Tell me about the Academy. What's it like?'

Our words rained down into the bowl of the evening. Thelma was very much as I remembered: slim, long dark hair, loose, colourful clothes. She looked more assured, even better than I remembered: no longer the young girl I'd known, but a grown woman. After a couple of glasses of wine she took me to her flat in Knightsbridge.

I heard the sounds of rummaging. 'Close your eyes,' she whispered. 'Now breathe in.'

The scent of sandalwood whisked me to Singapore. For a fraction of a moment I was really there. Only the magic of smell makes time travel possible, even if it's just for an instant. I opened my eyes and took the box. It was the one I'd sent her from Indochina.

'I normally keep it closed,' Thelma said. 'Every time it's opened, a bit more scent escapes... it always made me think of you.'

'Who was the guy who answered the phone when I rang?' I tried to make the enquiry sound casual.

'That would have been Colin.'

'Is he your feller?'

'No, Colin's a flatmate. I haven't got a feller as it happens.'

'Fancy going out for a meal?' I felt very calm as I spoke. I could hardly believe how well our reunion was going.

'That's a lovely idea! There's a great Italian restaurant, just a few minutes walk from here. It's where I go when I sell a painting or if there's something else to celebrate.'

Eating, drinking, talking and laughing, we sailed through the meal. I held her hand as we walked back to her place. Did I feel I had something to prove? Of course I did. The simplest way to dispel the dismal memory of my earlier impotence with Thelma was by becoming her lover.

I'd fucked a few girls in my youth, but I hadn't fallen for them. First love had made me strangely impotent.

Now, over a decade later, lying in her bed in the afterglow, I had a clear picture of the young man I'd been, the romantic fool who'd walked into a room and fallen in love with a mermaid, curled up in a chair. I'd have given a lot to be that young man again.

It seemed, on that glorious day, that our young love might be rekindled. I would have liked nothing better.

We were soon spending a lot of time together and it was great, until I had a disconcerting moment of déjà vu, realising that I'd be leaving her to go travelling in Asia, exactly as I'd done eleven years before.

After hearing me talk about Smiles, Thelma was dying to meet him. I gave him a ring, fixed up a day and booked a table for three at an Indian restaurant. We fiddled with poppadoms and pickles and joked around, waiting for the main dishes to arrive. Thelma was telling us how the Royal Academy worked and what she'd been doing since she graduated. She came to a halt as waiters converged on us.

When they'd gone she blurted, 'You two are obviously very close. I can't help wondering whether you were lovers in prison.'

'What?' Smiles half-choked on his poppadom. I whacked him on the back. He coughed, drank water and laughed. 'Lovers? No we fucking weren't! We were mates, helping each other through a very bad time.'

Thelma and I took the ferry to Dun Laoghaire and hired an orange Renault 4 for our holiday. Orange wasn't a good colour in Eire, but it was the only car they had.

I was free to roam, but rather lost in Eire. Up to Operation Julie I'd been a psychedelic missionary, aiming to raise human consciousness. In prison my ambition had shrunk enormously, it had simply been to survive with my integrity intact.

I had to find my feet in this new and strange reality. At least I still had my cottage in County Sligo and friends nearby too. Maybe I could remake my life in Eire.

'Lets go up to Yeats country,' I suggested.

'OK, but first I want to see my brother. Paddy's in Dublin. It's on the way.'

Being in Ireland, after seven years absence, brought back some poignant memories.

~

In the early seventies, Mary and I had bought a tiny stone house, with two acres of land for just over a thousand pounds. My old friends Jack and Maureen had acquired seven acres and five ruins for the same sum. Four other friends had bought properties nearby in County Sligo and Leitrim.

Jack and Maureen in the woods near Sligo

The solicitors handling the sale were Argue and Phibbs. The manager of the agency was called Charlie Browne: it could only happen in Ireland.

It took a long time to finalise the acquisition of the property. Twice Charlie Browne lost all the paperwork. It had to be laboriously drawn up again.

I hadn't known that his wife had left him and he'd rather gone to pieces. Things happened slowly in Ireland, so taking the best part of two years to complete the sale hadn't seemed so unusual.

On the day we'd finally acquired the house, Mary and I had gone to look at our new property. We'd been put out to see a ragged man doing something obscure in our lower field. I'd walked across to ask him what he thought he was up to, but before I could speak he'd handed me an open newspaper, full of freshly picked mushrooms. 'Welcome home,' he'd said, disarming me completely.

~

We drove to Dublin and stayed with Thelma's brother Patrick, in the large house he shared with Donal, Declan and Davy from the band *Moving Hearts*. The place was awash with Guinness and poured with music late into the night.

Davy Spillane, the band's piper, had just returned from three days in the Wicklow Mountains. The mountain air and morning dew had made him as high as a skylark. His vibe and his playing were hugely attractive to Thelma: she came alight in his presence. For a while we listened to him, then she got out her flute and they made music together.

I love music, but I've never been able to sing in tune or play. I envied those lucky souls who, through their voice or an instrument, could give pleasure to others. I sat listening to the pair of them as they sounded each other out.

That evening we went to O'Donaghue's bar with Davy. He took along his *Uilleann* pipes for the Friday jam session. We sat at one end of the pub with the players. The bar filled as the musicians warmed up. Soon the place was packed and the band was hot. I was trying to keep my mind on the great music and away from the fact that the singer-guitarist was openly making a play for Thelma.

'How long, baby,' he crooned to her. 'How long must I wait? Can I have you now, or must I hesitate?'

Standing in the front row of the crowd were Mick Jagger and Keith Richards, getting off on the sublime jam like everyone else. I had a seat next to the band while Mick and Keith had to stand. So why was I the only person in the place who wasn't having a good time? I was seething.

After the gig, a crowd of musicians, actors and wastrels gathered at Paddy's house. Thelma sparkled. Paddy's shining sister was the new girl in town and she captivated them all.

I wasn't part of the musical circle that gathered around her in the parlour. I sat on the stairs, drinking black beer, thinking black thoughts. I had to squeeze to one side when human traffic wanted to pass. A few times I got splashed by a storm in a beer glass. Around three a.m. I staggered to my feet and shambled off to bed.

I woke with a throbbing head and a terrible thirst. Five o'clock. Where was I? The confusion cleared and I remembered. The day's events came back to me. Where was Thelma? The house was quiet. She'd either crashed out downstairs or... Ugly suspicions crawled into my mind. I dragged myself off the hard mattress and lurched into the corridor.

'Thelma!'

Blundering round the house, I found her sitting talking with Davy and slunk off back to bed. Hung-over, I brooded on it all the next day. She'd left me for a guitarist the first time around...

Dragging Thelma away from Dublin's rogue troubadours, I drove us across Ireland to County Sligo. There, on the beautiful west coast, we had moments when we were bathed in faery light: looking down on the glinting sea from Knocknarea, or walking on the strand under Ben Bulben. We had glimpses of sun, but it rained a lot between us.

We stayed with my London flatmate, Caroline,

and her man, Andy, in their cottage on the shores of Loch Gill. In rare evening sunshine I rowed Thelma across to the Lake Isle of Innisfree.

I thought it would be a wonderful experience, but I struggled with Andy's heavy dinghy. We zigzagged erratically towards our goal. When we finally made it to the legendary island, we found an overgrown tangle of vegetation. There were no beehives or linnets, but the isle was full of midges. They descended on us in clouds. We fled, slowly, unable to outpace the hungry biters.

I was hoping to see all of my Reading friends whilst in Eire, but Thelma didn't want to spend time with old hippies in the sticks. She made it plain she'd rather be in the city, jamming with musicians, hanging out with actors, artists and poets.

The day after the Innisfree misadventure, we went out to have dinner with friends near Coolooney. It was a grand evening and we didn't leave until the small hours. Driving towards the loch on deserted lanes at two in the morning, we came to a small collection of houses. In the centre of the hamlet, a dozen or more men were unloading long boxes from a lorry.

They all stopped to watch us go by. Intrigued, I slowed down, before speeding up frantically as it dawned on me that we were witnessing an arms delivery. My father was a Colonel: I knew what rifle boxes looked like. I glanced in the mirror. The men were throwing their arms around in agitated discussion. Several of them ran towards a car.

'Wow! Did you see that?' Thelma was looking out the back. 'Hey, they're coming after us. Get a move on!'

Moments later, there were headlights on the road

behind us.

'Who are they – IRA?'

'Must be.'

I was driving an orange hire car. At the start of the holiday we'd been joking about its unsuitability south of the border. Suddenly it was no longer funny. We were English, for Christ's sake – at least I was – driving past the delivery of an arms shipment in the middle of the night. I didn't fancy our chances if they caught us. I drove as fast as I dared on the narrow lanes.

'Speed up!' Thelma urged. 'They're getting closer.'

Of course they were closing on us. You can go faster with lights to follow. And they knew the roads: we were in their fucking territory! All this flashed through my mind in an instant. I just hissed 'I'm going as quick as I can!'

We reached the grassy triangle at the top of Andy's track with the car right on our tail. It tried to pass. I thought we'd collide, but I floored the accelerator and just made it ahead of them. After that the driver eased off the gas. The track was a dead end that led only led to the cottage and the lake. They would know we were boxed in.

'Caroline and Andy's drive coming up!' I barked, buzzing on adrenalin. 'Get ready. The moment I stop, run for the house!'

I swung round the corner, slammed on the brakes and doused the lights. We ran inside. I locked the door and we threw ourselves to the floor behind the bed. My heart was thudding so fast I thought it would burst. We lay still in the dark, listening. The other car stopped at the top of the drive. It stayed there for an eternity. Then the driver turned off the ignition. Silence crept around the house. We didn't dare move. After an interminable wait, we heard the engine cough into life and the car drove away.

In the morning, Andy listened to our story with an amused expression of disbelief. 'You're making it up, imagining things,' he said.

'No, I'm serious!' I insisted.

'How much did you smoke last night?' He laughed. 'Tell you what, I'm going into the village this afternoon, I'll find out what it's all about.'

Andy had the same look on his face when he returned. 'Just as I thought. A bunch of the lads had stayed up drinking. They figured it would be a laugh to chase an orange car. It was only a bit of fun.'

I knew it was the IRA but, not wanting to alarm Caroline, I said 'Sure,'and gave Thelma's arm a quick warning squeeze.

'Sure,' she agreed. 'Some people have such a strange idea of fun.'

The intrusion of the IRA into such a rural backwater woke me up. I'd spent the last week sleepwalking in a swirling cloud of emotion. Needy and insecure, I'd been getting myself in a state over Thelma.

The sudden danger jerked me clear from my mental fog. What had I been playing at? Soon I'd be off to India. I'd be gone for at least six months. How could I have tied myself in knots about a relationship we both knew had to end?

Mulling it over, I had a rare moment of insight: shipwrecked and stranded in prison, I was suffering from emotional starvation. I'd been clinging to Thelma like a drowning man. She must have thought she was in danger of being dragged under with me.

31

The spell broken, I drove her to the station and put her on a train to Dublin, where she wanted to be. I stood on the platform, waving goodbye, watching the train shrink to a speck and disappear.

Almost immediately I felt a whole lot better. A weight of expectation had been lifted from my shoulders. It was almost as if I'd got my old self back again. I stayed on near Sligo with Jack and Maureen, feeling incredibly light and free, as high as I'd been in the first weeks after my release.

My second time around with Thelma, brief though it had been, had given me a lot of things to think about. The start of our time together could hardly have been better, both of us were doing our utmost, but we were coming from totally different places. Our lives just didn't intersect.

There have to be positive reasons for people to choose to be together – and who in their right mind would want to share their life with me? If I looked squarely at myself, I had to admit that I was a mess.

Physically I was in good shape, mentally in turmoil, emotionally on the rocks: being pounded by the surf. Somehow I had to drag myself onto solid ground and get back on my feet.

How could I have even thought of sharing my life with another person? I'd hardly seen a woman for five years. Being with Thelma was enough to remind me how very different they are from men.

I'd need time to start getting used to them again.

I had my chance earlier than I could possibly have expected. By Rosses Point, I saw a lovely blond girl, pale, stretched out on the sand, sunbathing on the beach. As I walked past I said 'Hi'. She sat up and smiled. We got talking and clicked straightaway.

Swimming together, almost as one being, we rolled round each other like porpoises playing in the waves. It was fun. We were laughing and swallowing seawater. I realised I'd hardly laughed at all since arriving in Eire.

Gabriella and I had several wonderful days walking, climbing, swimming or just lying on the beach, arms around each other, talking. It was lovely, natural and undemanding.

I made picnics to feed us on the long walks we took, to the Doons, to Rosses Point and Knocknarea. Gabriella was German, beautiful in mind and body; I should have stayed with her for the rest of my life but I'd just regained my freedom and was going off to spend the next six months in India, where I hoped to piece together my shattered equilibrium.

When the time came to leave, I drove her to Dublin and took her to Thelma's brother, Paddy.

'Paddy, I have to get the ferry tomorrow, but Gabriella would like to spend some time in Dublin. Can you suggest where she might stay awhile?'

The guys came to meet Gabriella and fell over themselves offering her accommodation for as long as she wanted. I knew they would. Happy that she was in good hands, I returned to London to get ready for the trip to India.

I rang Smiles to bring him up to date with what I'd been doing. He had news of his own. 'Listen, mate, change of plan. My girlfriend's coming with us. I don't know how that stands with you, but Sally wants to come and I'm not leaving her behind.'

'Sure. No problem.' I was sounding like my dad: it was his favourite expression. 'What about getting together tomorrow to talk about the trip? I'm making a list of stuff to take.'

'We've done our lists. Got most of what we need.'

'Tomorrow, then, I'll come over.' I put the phone down and tried to think what effect this development would have on our plans. I soon gave up – too many imponderables. We'd just have to deal with things as they arose, and if three became a crowd... well, I was happy travelling on my own. I silently thanked the rash young man who'd overcome the terror of the unknown by crossing the Channel and walking and hitching to the Mediterranean. That solo journey, my first great adventure, had made all my subsequent voyages possible.

'Life is a gift', an inner voice had told me. 'Get out there and make the most of it!'

Another thing I'd learnt from my first solo trip: when you travel alone you meet more people.

The end of parole was close and thrills and tremors of anticipation were starting to run through me. Smiles and Sally were very much wrapped up in each other. I was glad for them, though I knew I would effectively be a singleton for much of the journey. We compared lists and went shopping for last details. I spent the final two days in the flat, taping the music I wanted to have with me on our travels.

Deep into a recording session, well-stoned and singing 'I shot the sheriff' at the top of my voice, I jumped at the ringing of the doorbell.

I cautiously opened the door. A woman stood in the entrance. A couple of seconds passed before I recognised my Mrs Thatcher.

'Happy Birthday!' said my parole officer. 'Any

chance of a cup of tea?'

'Sure. Come in.' I took her into the kitchen and told her about my travel plans.

I was thirty-four. The next day I would be free, whatever freedom meant. I'd done my time, whatever time meant... My ideas about the nature, the solidity, of time had been fractured beyond repair.

~

It was the summer of 1976. I'd awoken from a vivid nightmare and found myself standing on our bed, trembling, slick with sweat, sick with fear.

'What's the matter?' Mary asked sleepily.

'Just a bad dream. Go to sleep.' I went to the kitchen and shakily made myself a cup of tea. The details of the nightmare were absolutely clear in my mind.

I was in prison clothes, sitting in an armchair in the television building. The door burst open and the lights came on. I turned to see what had caused the disturbance. In the doorway stood three figures – a giant, flanked by two scrawny henchmen. The muscle man in the centre wore a coalman's sleeveless leather jerkin. He had curly black hair and a thick black beard. I stared at him in sick fascination. Radiating evil, he looked around the room and his eyes met mine. He smiled, licked his lips and pointed straight at me. 'You,' he growled. 'I'll have you!' Petrified, I escaped into wakefulness.

A year later I was arrested in Operation Julie. Inevitably I thought about the prison nightmare, but Horfield was nothing like my bad dream. Prisoners

35

didn't wear coalmen's jackets, the nick didn't have a building for the TV and there wasn't anybody who remotely resembled the black-haired giant.

Four years crawled by in Horfield nick and then I was transferred to Leyhill open prison for the last stretch of my porridge. I arrived with sixteen months of my sentence to run. It could be as little as eight months with parole or as much as four years with total loss of remission. I was uncuffed, processed into the nick, given my hut and cubicle number and told I could go. I stood by the door, waiting for a warder to unlock it.

'It's open,' the reception screw called out.

For a moment I didn't know what he meant. The only doors that I'd been able to open for the past four years were the half-doors of the toilets. I thought I'd kept myself together through the time in Horfield, but now I saw the truth: I'd been stunted by my confinement. The prisoner's mentality had stealthily covered me, like ivy creeping over a disused shed.

The screw must have watched this scene at the door many times.

'Hold on,' he said. 'Jones will take you up there in a moment.'

Jones, the reception orderly, was amiable and chatty. 'Part of the Julie mob, weren't you? Heard you were coming on the grapevine. First time in an open nick? You'll like it once you get used to it. The grub's a lot better for a start. And there are a lot of opportunities in a place like this, if you know what I mean. Only you've got be careful: Leyhill is full of grasses, see. Keep your business to yourself and you'll be all right.'

I was looking around, taking stock of the first

new place I've been in years.

'See those buildings...' Jones pointed to the right, 'they're the workshops. That's the Governor's office on the left. Straight ahead is the television building.'

As he said the final two words, three men appeared from behind the building. I saw, with utter disbelief, that the central figure was the giant from my five-year-old nightmare. He was flanked by his two scrawny henchmen. I'd forgotten about the prison nightmare, but it all came flooding back. It was unquestionably the same trio. The giant had black curly hair, a big black beard and wore a coalman's sleeveless leather jerkin. Every detail fitted. It was June, but I was shivering. The men from my nightmare waited for me outside the door of the television room. I forced my jelly legs to keep going. As we were passing, Goliath said 'Hi.'

He was addressing me. In total contrast to the dream, his voice was friendly.

'One of the Julie mob, aren't you? Heard you were coming. I've been looking forward to meeting you. I'm busy now but I'd like to have a talk later.'

Unable to speak, I nodded and moved on. I was frightened. A swarm of bees were inside my head, stinging me. I had no idea what Jones was saying as we walked up the corridor between the Nissen huts. I made it to my cubicle and collapsed. A huge hole had been punched in my reality.

Liberty and time: I'd taken these abstractions for granted until I'd had the ground whipped away from under my feet. I hoped the ancient wisdom of India would be able to give me some insights into the strange phenomenon of being.

~

I'd been overjoyed by the renewal of my young love with Thelma, then dejected when it didn't work out. Life on the loose was altogether a different proposition from festering in a cell. Freedom offered many more opportunities than prison, but it was a much more complicated proposition.

Institutionalisation is the longest word most cons know.

3. DHARAMSALA

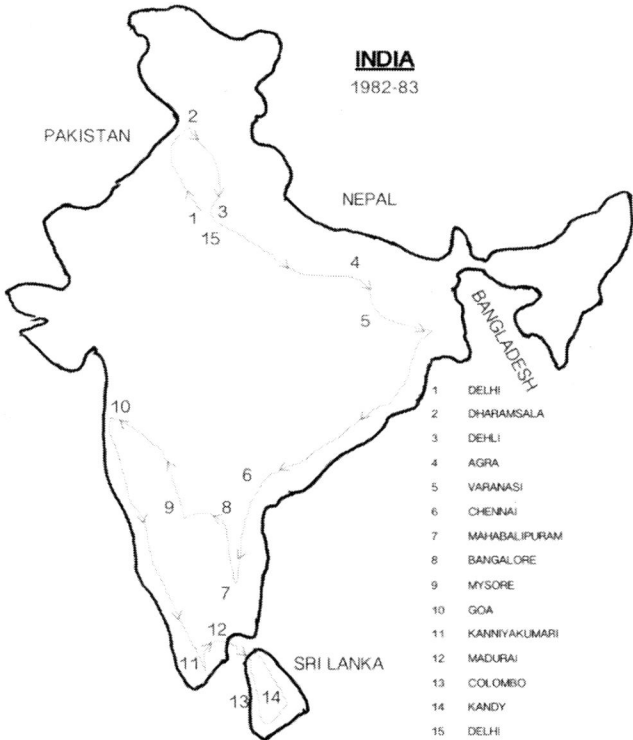

INDIA
1982-83

PAKISTAN

NEPAL

BANGLADESH

1	DELHI
2	DHARAMSALA
3	DEHLI
4	AGRA
5	VARANASI
6	CHENNAI
7	MAHABALIPURAM
8	BANGALORE
9	MYSORE
10	GOA
11	KANNIYAKUMARI
12	MADURAI
13	COLOMBO
14	KANDY
15	DELHI

SRI LANKA

Our journey round India and Sri Lanka

On parole in England, I'd felt like a marked man. I couldn't go anywhere without checking to see if I was being followed. I was unable to make or receive a phone call without wondering who might be listening in.

During the slow-motion months on parole there'd been weeks on end when I'd felt like one of those doomed figures in a Graham Greene story, limping around the fringes of life, disconnected, forever dogged by the ghosts of the past.

Now, at last, my time was done and I could go where I wanted without having to ask permission. My life was my own again. I was looking forward to escaping the oncoming winter, to travelling around India, being anonymous, off the radar.

I made a final check of the gear I was taking and packed it. After a last look around the bedroom, I hoisted my backpack and set off for the tube. Smiles and Sally were waiting on the platform. There was no need for words. I could see the excitement in their eyes. The train pulled in. We climbed aboard and sat in our seats, knees straddling our luggage, while we racketed down the rails towards Heathrow.

As soon as we were settled into our row on the plane, Smiles raised a hand to get the attention of the approaching stewardess.

'We're desperate criminals and we just got out of prison.' His huge grin belied his words. He winked at the hostess, leant forward and added 'Seriously, I want to drink champagne with my friends and we can't wait for takeoff – it's a very special occasion. Could you be a darling and bring us a couple of bottles of good bubbly? We'd really appreciate it.'

Smiles - a charismatic man - dazzled her with the famous smile that had given him his name and handed her some notes.

'I'll see what I can do.' She simpered and went off down the aisle, wiggling her bum. Moments later she was back with two bottles, three glasses and some change.

Smiles waved away the money. 'You keep it, darling. We won't want to be lugging English coins all round India.'

He popped the champagne when we reached the runway and filled our glasses as the plane began to move. On leaving the ground we drank to our unconditional freedom and celebrated until all the bubbles had burst. Then we crashed out. None of us had got a wink of sleep the night before.

I looked around blearily. Smiles and Sally were still asleep. My mouth was dry and my head throbbed. The plane droned on. Surely we couldn't be far away now, the cry from long childhood journeys came back to me. 'Are we nearly there?'

Smiles was snoring lightly. Wisps of blond hair had escaped from Sally's hairband; she looked younger and happier in sleep. I knew she'd been through a rough time, but didn't know the details. I still hadn't worked out what to make of her. I liked the way she spoke, in little bursts, waving her arms around, tossing phrases into the wind. I reckoned I was going to like her. She still seemed to be making up her mind about me. I imagined she saw me as part of her man's criminal baggage and potentially a problem.

I rang the bell. 'Can I have some water and an aspirin,' I asked the steward.

When the pulsing in my head eased, I fell to thinking about the book I'd been reading in the airport:

The cosmic cycle in India comprises four yugas, after which time and the world come to an end. They start over again as Lord Shiva dances existence back into existence. Each cycle lasts four million, three hundred and twenty thousand years.

We were going to spend the winter in India. With this new perspective on time, six months didn't seem like much at all. I was barely going to be able to scratch the surface of this large and complicated land, with its hundreds of languages and dozens of alphabets. So many alphabets! Europe manages on just two.

I was looking forward to learning more about the spiritual side of India. I'd had enough of the consumer mentality that seemed to have fixed its suckers onto England and was draining it of its lifeblood.

Most of the passengers on the plane were Indians, returning home after working in Dubai.

'Sir, please can you complete my immigration papers,' one of them asked me. 'I don't have writing.' Immediately all three of us were deluged with requests to fill in their forms. We'd done them all by the time we landed in Delhi in the early morning.

After chilly London, Delhi seemed hot, but not unbearably so. We retrieved our luggage and cleared Immigration, Health and Customs in an hour.

'That's got to be a record,' said the long-haired guy next to us in the queue. 'From now on I'm going to pick flights that land in the early morning. It takes four hours or more if you arrive during the day.'

There was a light tap on my shoulder. 'Excuse me, have you been in Delhi before?'

'Yes I have. I was here a few years ago.' I turned my head. It had to be the English girls. I'd spotted them at the beginning of the flight. Early twenties, I reckoned.

'It's our first time in India,' the girl continued, 'and it's all rather bewildering.'

'Yes it is confusing initially, but don't worry, you'll soon get used to it. You can come with us in our taxi if you don't mind squeezing in. I'm Leaf, by the way, my friends are Smiles and Sally.'

'What exotic names! This is my friend Alice and I'm Margaret.'

Alice nodded, but didn't speak. We piled into a ramshackle taxi and asked the driver to take us to Old Delhi. We drove past the encampments on the streets. At intervals the stench of shit filled the cab; open windows soon carried the smell away. The traffic was growing by the minute. We stopped outside a small hotel in a side street – Sally's choice, picked from the guidebook she'd brought.

The English girls seemed pretty blown away by what they'd seen and smelt. They appeared to be in shock.

'I'll book you a double room, if you like.' I volunteered. 'We'll all want to wash and sort out our things, so what about meeting in reception for a cup of tea in an hour or so?'

My room was a pale washed-out green. It hadn't been decorated for years. I looked around: a bed with sheets, a mosquito net, a chair, and a mat, nothing else. Dropping my pack on the floor, I went to freshen up in the bathroom down the corridor. Stripping off my travelling gear, I put on cotton trousers and a lightweight t-shirt. There was no sign of the others, so I went downstairs to the turmeric and cumin-scented lobby.

Under the fan seemed to be the best bet. I waited there, my drying hair stirred by the breeze, looking

43

at the bright posters of Shiva, Ram and Vishnu on the faded walls.

After we'd drunk *chai* with Margaret and Alice, Smiles said 'We're going to take a walk, stretch our legs a bit, come with us if you like.'

'Thanks, but I think we're going to have a nap.'

'Suit yourselves. I expect we'll run into you later.'

We set off on the short walk to Connaught Circus. We needed to move around after being so long in different forms of transport, and we wanted to have a look at Delhi in daylight. We'd only been going for a couple of minutes when Smiles suddenly exclaimed, 'Jake! It's been years, mate. What an amazing coincidence.'

We sat in a *chai* shop and drank tea while Smiles and his friend reminisced.

When we moved on, Smiles nudged me and opened his hand. In his palm was half an ounce of hash, a gift from his buddy.

'How about that! Is this a land of miracles, or what!' Smiles danced a few paces down the road, delighted at such an auspicious start to our winter in Asia. We went back to the hotel.

There was no sign of Alice and Margaret. I asked at reception and was told they were still in their room.

We went up on the flat roof, rolled and smoked a couple of joints and looked through Sally's travel guide. 'What do you reckon next,' I asked my friends. 'Chandni Chowk?'

'Sounds good,' Smiles replied.

We took two cycle rickshaws, one for them and one for me, and dived into the noisy muddle of the Delhi traffic.

'First time in India?' My rickshaw man wanted to know.

'No, I came here for my honeymoon, six years ago.'

'So where is your wife, then?'

Arrival at Chandni Chowk saved me from having to answer but it didn't prevent me from thinking of Mary. I wondered if we'd ever meet again. I knew the odds were heavily against it.

I gave the driver a good tip and, with a great surge of joy, shrugged off my Western paranoia and dived into the jostling throng that filled the cacophonous market street. I knew myself to be finally, unquestionably, away from the prying eyes and ears of enforcement agencies. I was high on the discordant sights and sounds, the swirls of garish colour, the cries of the market traders mingling with snatches of music, the chatter all around.

I walked among a dense crowd of strangers through an erratic succession of smells: frying, drains, incense, sweat, jasmine, wood-smoke, spices... The street was a mass of steadily moving people, faces of every shade, clothes of every hue and style. I turned round and caught sight of my friends a few paces behind. Smiles waved and yelled 'Woo hoo! What a buzz!'

I was laughing out loud in the crowded street. I felt I'd stepped back in time and was again dwelling in the uncomplicated territory of my youth. What a gas – free again!

Back at the hotel, I asked the receptionist if the English ladies had gone out. 'No they still haven't left the hotel,' she replied.

We didn't see them again. Perhaps they're still in Delhi, still hiding in their room.

I was idling on my bed when there was a knock on the door. Sally came in. 'Could you take over from Smiles for a while. He's in the queue at the railway station and he's dehydrating fast!'

'Of course. I'm on my way.'

I was too late: Smiles had made the train reservations by the time I arrived.

At first we did nothing much but wander around the city, picking up the vibes, looking at the sights and checking out the wares in the tiny shops. When we felt like a break from the heat and the crowds, we'd sit in a *chai* shop, sip tea and watch the brightly coloured world go by. We spent part of one afternoon coming to grips with the railway network: we were going to be making a lot of train journeys.

The day before we intended leaving for the north we went to a cinema to watch *Gandhi*. It was a long movie with an interval that occurred immediately after a graphic depiction of the Amritsar massacre, where British troops fired into a crowd of peaceful protesters, killing around a thousand men, women and children. The shooting and screaming died away as the lights came on.

The audience, distressed by the tragedy, talked loudly amongst themselves. The only white faces in the crowd, we drew the attention of those around us. Fingers were pointed, remarks made. The muttering rose in volume.

I whispered 'Stay in our seats, yeah?'

We sat with heads down. I quietly chanted '*Shanti, shanti, shanti,*' and tried to think peaceful thoughts. Finally, mercifully, the lights dimmed, the film resumed and I breathed a long sigh of relief.

We took the overnight train north to Pathankot, a military town near the tense border between India, Kashmir and Pakistan. Leaving the tanks, artillery and uniforms behind on the dusty plain, we climbed aboard an ancient bus and headed east. The winding, bumpy road led towards the Shivaliks, the foothills of the Himalayas. Our creaking transport seemed to be without springs and had wooden slats for seats. The bums of thousands of passengers had polished the hard slats. After five hours of arse-ache, we pulled in to Dharamsala, the home of the Dalai Lama and the Tibetan government in exile. Knackered, we shouldered our rucksacks and tramped uphill towards the house of a dear friend of mine.

Lyn turned men's heads wherever she went. Tall and slim, she had long black hair, the voluptuous figure of a fertility goddess and the mischievous face of a street urchin. When I first met her in Reading, in '68, she'd just been released from Borstal – on condition she take up her place in Reading University.

'I'm a bad girl trying to be good', she'd giggled, twisting a few strands of hair around her fingers.

Recently returned from Turkey, I was deeply sunburnt, had long tangled hair and was still dressed like an Albanian brigand. It was an exotic look that went down well with the wild girls. Lyn and I had got stoned, enjoyed a fun evening and spent the night together. We'd been good friends ever since.

She'd made the giant ACID banner that flew over our pitch at the Isle of Wight festival, Hendrix's last gig. She'd taken part in most of the jaunts, adventures, festivals and fun of the Reading days.

47

We'd corresponded while I'd been inside. It was her invitation that had brought us here. Years had passed, yet she seemed as lovely as ever.

'Leaf!' she exclaimed, as she threw herself into my open arms. 'At last! I thought they were never going to let you go.'

Aware of my companions standing behind me, I disentangled myself.

'Lyn, these are my good friends, Smiles and Sally.'

They shook hands and we all stood there for a moment until Lyn clapped her hand to her forehead and said, 'I'm so sorry! You must be exhausted. Please, come inside. Put your bags down. Are you hungry? Would you like some tea?'

'Thank you. A cup of tea would be perfect,' Sally replied. Smiles and I nodded agreement.

Lyn leant into the front room and called 'Arthur! Leaf and his friends have arrived. Come down and say hello.'

A voice floated down from above, 'Can't come immediately. I'll be with you in a while.'

'We have a friend of Arthur's staying over,' so I'm afraid you'll have to sleep on the floor of our spare room tonight. I hope that's OK.'

Smiles laughed. 'Don't worry about it. We'll be fine. We've survived worse accommodation, I can tell you.'

'It'll be rice, lentils and vegetables for supper tonight. Does that sound OK? Oh, one other thing,' she added. 'Each room has a house spider. They're here to keep the insects down. They're not in the least dangerous, but they are rather large. They live behind the paintings. You probably won't see them.'

We unrolled our sleeping bags on the packed earth floor. It had been a long journey. I'd hardly slept at all on the night train. I fell asleep as my head touched the pillow.

I woke in the night to the sound of a rhythmic crunching. The noise seemed to be not far from my face. I hauled myself up on one elbow, pulled my little torch out of my shoe and clicked the switch. A spider as big as my fist was methodically eating a giant cockroach. It dragged its prey out of the light. I turned the torch off and sank back to the ground. The size of my fist!

I thought I wouldn't be able to go back to sleep, but I remember nothing more of the night.

Lyn and Arthur had been in Asia for over a decade. They'd taught English in Teheran all through the revolution that overthrew the Shah's dictatorship. When their school closed they'd packed a couple of bags and left, travelling through Afghanistan, Pakistan and North-Eastern India, not stopping anywhere for long until they'd reached Dharamsala, the home in exile of the Dalai Lama.

The next morning Lyn and I went shopping. It was the first real chance we had to talk together. Once we were out of earshot she dropped the light chatter. 'Arthur and I are having to eat into our savings. It's putting a strain on our relationship. We'll be broke in two or three years. We've got to find work – but how can you make money in a town full of poor Tibetan refugees?'

She was baking wholemeal bread, making curd cheese and guava jam for the Westerners. They came to visit the old British hill station of MacLeod Ganj or to study Tibetan Buddhism at the home of the Dalai Lama. Lyn's work took hours and earned pennies.

'Know what?' she said. 'Money problems have been churning around inside me for a while. Now I've got someone I can to talk to, I feel a whole lot better!'

I was relieved to see the return of her cheeky grin. Lyn was a good friend. While I'd been in prison, she'd arranged – and paid for – a quartet of Tibetan monks to say prayers for the safe delivery from prison for Brian and I.

'I'd like you to meet the monks,' she said with a big grin. 'Don't look so serious. They're really nice people. Right now they're praying for the recovery of my friend's sick baby.'

We headed off, tracking a strange moaning sound back to its source. Four shaven-headed monks, dressed in red and gold robes, sat cross-legged on the beaten earth in front of a tiny bungalow. They each had a quarter part of the prayer book and sang simultaneously. Chanting, ringing a tiny bell at irregular intervals and beating a drum, they prayed all morning. One of them had a voice deep enough to make the earth quiver.

They followed their own part of the prayer and the sound wandered all over the place, but every now and then the four voices, the drum and the bell would come together in a spine-tingling climax of reverberating power.

At the end of their devotions I put my hands together.

'Thank you for the prayers you said for me.'

They bowed, and the bass voice rumbled.

'They're blessing you,' Lyn explained, 'for

50

giving them the opportunity to help their karma and get a better start the next time they step onto the wheel of life.'

We were sitting in a pudding shop, drinking tea and eating sweets made from walnuts and condensed milk. I broke the silence 'Are you still getting prison dreams, Smiles?'

'Yeah, most nights. It's a drag, but it's better than dreaming you're free, then waking up in a cell, as we used to do. Listen mate,' he suddenly looked serious, 'hanging out with Western Buddhists isn't our scene at all. It's India we want to see, it's Shiva I dig.'

We'd only been a couple of days in Dharamsala and my friends were ready to hit the road. We sat and talked things over. I was in no hurry to move on. I was enjoying Lyn's company and wanted to go hiking in the mountains.

'If you two would rather travel for a while, we could easily meet up in Delhi,' I suggested.

'Yeah, let's do that,' Smiles replied. 'We want to see Jaipur, Jodpur and Bikaner. Get out into the Thar Desert. Do the Lawrence of Arabia thing.'

'The lake palace at Jaipur sounds amazing,' Sally added. 'Smiles, tell Leaf about Bikaner.'

'Apparently there's a rat temple there, right out in the Desert. I've just got to see it. The Indians really are an extraordinary lot.'

We arranged to meet at our Delhi hotel in a month. The following morning they set off for the deserts of Rajasthan. Soon I would be going into the mountains with Lyn and Arthur and would finally get the huge vistas I'd long been craving.

4. MOUNTAINS

At the start of my time in the Himalayas

I had my heart set on spending time in the Himalayas. I've always loved high places. I'd never felt better than when I was in Cornwall, standing on top of Trencrom Hill, leaning into a westerly wind, speculating about the people who'd been in the exact same spot, several thousand years before me.

While in prison, I'd developed the notion that

gaining altitude would give me a better perspective on my existence. Cell life had made me short-sighted, only able to see what was right in front of my nose. What I needed was space. Lots of space.

For two weeks I walked the winding trails above Macleod Ganj, at around seven thousand feet. I was building up my strength and getting my body used to functioning in the thin air. For the first few days I had to keep stopping for a rest. Along with my packed lunch and water bottle, I took a pencil, brushes, watercolours and a sketchbook. I stopped to sketch and daub whenever I saw a particularly stunning view or a beautiful arrangement of natural objects. I rarely met anyone on my outings. Having spent so long in the ugly, crowded environment of prison, I was revelling in the solitude of my walks and the beauty of the landscape.

Three or four times I found myself shedding tears at the perfection of my surroundings. A couple of times the crying went on, as I wept for the five years of my life that had been confiscated.

In the evenings, Arthur studied Buddhist texts in his den, while Lyn and I smoked *charas*: pollen rubbed from the flowers of the living marijuana plant. To ready myself for the journey we were about to make, I adopted their routine of going to bed early and rising at first light. While we prepared the dinner, we reminisced about the past.

'Lyn, do you remember our dawn trips, when we poured out of Upper Redlands Road and went exploring by the lake and the standing stones at Wilderness Road?'

'I'll never forget the fox that calmly walked right

past us… he must have known we were harmless.'

'What about that time at the lake, when you suddenly appeared out of the mist? You were the lady of Shallot come to life. I thought I'd been taken to another universe! We lived through miraculous times.'

'We certainly did!' Lyn paused. 'But those days are gone,' she added sadly.

'True, but we may have more miracles in our path. Who knows what's going to happen in the coming weeks?'

Lyn, Arthur and I were going trekking together, as soon as I was acclimatised. The day before departure, we went down the hill to the market and bought the provisions we'd need for our four-day hike. That evening we carefully cleaned the rice and dahl, taking out the small fragments of stone that could break your teeth if you crunched on them.

'This is not a job to do on a mountainside,' Arthur said, 'when the light's fading and you're exhausted and desperate for something to eat.'

Arthur, tall, slim, broad-shouldered and po-faced, was an organised, methodical and somewhat dour man. He seemed a strange partner for a lady as volatile as Lyn. A native of Norfolk, deep into Buddhism, Arthur was a private guy who didn't reveal himself easily. It was some while before I discovered he played guitar in a rock band.

I woke early on the day of departure, full of a start-of-the-holidays feeling. The sun was just up when we set off and there was quite a chill in the air, but my t-shirt was soon drenched in sweat. Beyond Dharmkot, the last settlement, we came to a miniature Hindu shrine, dedicated to the goddess Durga. I crawled through the tiny portal and left a sweet as an offering. I placed a few flowers in a second shrine, a mile or so up the track we were following.

Religion is a palpable force in India. I'm not religious, but I see my life as a spiritual journey and was happy to pay respect to the Hindu pantheon. In their wild mountains, bears, big cats, poisonous snakes, avalanches, storms and landslides may all have to be reckoned with.

After we'd been climbing for four hours, we stopped for an early lunch then I had a nap while Lyn and Arthur went off to meditate.

Moments after they returned, a flock of birds came over a ridge and flew towards us.

'Luck,' whispered Lyn. 'Minivets. Don't move an inch!'

Forty or fifty scarlet minivets settled in a small tree. We stood frozen. The males were bright red, their mates yellow. The tree seemed to have been instantly decorated for Christmas by the wave of a fairy's wand. We gazed at the minivets in a trance, frightened to even swallow. When something finally startled them into flight, the tiny birds beat their wings and the tree appeared to burst into flame. Smiles had been right. We were in a land of miracles.

By mid-afternoon, Triund Ridge, our objective for the day, was in sight almost directly above us. My legs were feeling weak, my heart was pounding against my ribs and my breath came in tortured gasps. It had stopped being fun a while back. Arthur was striding ahead.

It was a male competitive thing; by leaving me struggling in his wake, he was seeing off a potential rival for his partner. I was determined to stay with him until he stopped... but he just kept on going, with an easy rhythm that made it look like he could walk all day. 'Is this just going on in my head?' I muttered to myself. 'I'm pretty sure it isn't. We males are a very competitive lot and none more so than runners, walkers and climbers.'

Though close to exhaustion, I forced myself to stick with Arthur. Then, just as I'd decided that I would stop and wait for Lyn to catch up, Triund came into sight again: this time tantalisingly close. Wheezing like an old man, I lurched the last few hundred yards and collapsed on the ground.

It was four o'clock and we'd been on the go for ten hours, but we didn't have long to stand and stare at the breathtaking scenery. We had perhaps an hour before the sun sank below the mountains. Lyn got the pots, pans, plates and food ready for our dinner in the little travellers' hut that perched on the ridge. Arthur went off to get water. I looked for firewood.

There were no trees on the ridge so I had to go down a couple of hundred feet to a straggly clump of Himalayan oaks on a near-vertical slope. I gathered an armful of dead branches and paused to rest, my back against a trunk, whispering to myself, *'I'm really here. This isn't a dream. I won't wake up in a cell. Life is good.'*

I humped the load back, stopping to rest every few yards. The final leg exhausted my last reserves of strength. I sank to the ground and watched while Lyn lit a fire and got our dinner under way.

To the north, a line of snow-capped mountains

towered over us. I turned to the south to see a vertiginous drop to the Kangra Valley, seven thousand feet below. Acutely aware of my tiny stature in this vast landscape, I left my body and soared. Looking down, I saw us as three ants on a pimple, on the southern fringe of a huge expanse of mountains. They stretched for hundreds of miles to the north and thousands of kilometres to the east. Then I looked south, trying to visualise a billion Indians spread across the vast sub-continent.

Arthur put a pan of water on the fire for the rice. My nostrils, catching a whiff of *dhal* and frying onions, brought me back to my body in time for supper.

We ate as the sun went down, keeping half the food for tomorrow's dinner. All at once the snowy slopes to the east turned a surreal salmon pink. The colour slowly faded then suddenly vanished.

At the end of the meal, Lyn made tea – our first hot drink since the morning. Instantly invigorated, we leapt about, gathering armfuls of firewood and breaking the branches up. We sat around the flames feeding the fire, replete, tired and happy.

'I've tried many drugs over the years,' I said yawning, 'but this is the first time I've realised what a strong hit you can get off tea.'

The moment the sun went behind the peaks, the temperature began falling. Layer by layer, I put on more garments until I was wearing every item of clothing I had. Lyn and Arthur went to bed, but I sat up, not wanting to miss anything: the night seemed pregnant with possibilities.

The moon rose – a full moon – and cast a wonderfully eerie light over the mountains and valleys. I took a walk to the end of Triund ridge. I was on a boulder-strewn grassy humpback that fell away steeply on three sides. All around me, lit by silver moonlight, smooth boulders were scattered in weird suggestive heaps: the sculptors' gallery of the night. Miles from anyone, I cupped my hands round my mouth and hallooed the peaks with all the force I could muster. I waited, listening intently. At length the mountains returned the whisper of an echo, reminding me how small and insignificant I was in this vast landscape.

In the morning I was shaken awake by a laughing Lyn. 'Cup of tea,' she waved it under my nose before putting it on a rock five yards away. 'Come on, lazybones. It's a lovely morning. Out of that sleeping bag. Get up!'

I groaned as I stretched my legs and felt the aches in thighs and calves. Then I rose and walked around, sipping my tea and trying to loosen up the knots in my muscles.

A big bowl of porridge set us up for the day. We washed the dishes, packed our bags, kicked out the embers of the breakfast fire and began the next leg of our journey.

We started off by going downhill, squandering the precious altitude we'd gained on yesterday's climb. The descent of the north side of Triund ridge seemed easy at first. We were heading towards a scattering of stone huts in a large green meadow that ran with dozens of streams.

'Laka,' Arthur murmured laconically, pointing to the buildings. 'Shepherds bring their flocks here for summer pasture.'

My legs were wobbly from the descent and we had all the climbing still to do.

We sat down to rest and refilled our water bottles from one of the streams that gurgled through the meadow. The water was icy cold and invigorating. I'd have happily sat there for a while, drinking in the mountains, but Arthur stood, stretched and slung his pack on his back. It was an unmistakeable signal. We followed suit and set our feet on the climb towards the Indrahar pass.

I was starting to really dislike Arthur.

Lyn broke the silence, 'I meant to ask you earlier. What's the news of Brian?'

'They haven't released him yet, but with any luck he'll get parole and be out within a few months.'

Our conversation petered out and we concentrated on putting one foot in front of the other. Grass gave way to bare rock and then we were scrambling across an area of scree – a landslide had obliterated the rough path we'd been following. A sudden explosion of movement made me jump and lose my footing as I recoiled from the lash of a large brown snake, dozing on the sun-warmed stones.

The snake, at least as alarmed as me, shot off at speed. Breathless, I stayed on the ground, getting over the shock. Gradually my pulse rate slowed.

'I don't get on with snakes. They give me the creeps. I'm OK now. Let's continue.'

I was quietly glad when Lyn overruled me and called a food halt. Lunch was a fistful of peanuts and raisins and two squares of Amul chocolate. 'Made with Class 2 preservatives' it boasted on the wrapper.

We kept climbing until I was drenched in moisture. By mid-afternoon the sudden gusts of wind grew colder and felt sharper. One moment I was sweating, the next I was shivering. I wanted something to chew on, to take my mind off my sullenly complaining legs, but forced myself to eke out my small bag of peanuts.

Our aim for the day was to reach a cave, three thousand feet higher than Laka and a couple of hundred feet above the snowline. The sun had gone behind the mountain by the time we arrived. We knocked the snow off our shoes and scrambled into the cave to get out of the biting wind. I heated our pre-cooked supper in the entrance with the scraps of wood we'd collected en route. Ravenous, we wolfed our food and then wriggled into our sleeping bags.

'How much further have we got to go before we reach the pass?' I asked.

'Not nearly as far as we've come today,' Arthur replied, 'but we'll be walking on snow from the start. The going will be harder.'

I wrote up my diary by the light of the guttering candle then blew it out and fell into a deep sleep.

We got off to a late start in the morning. None of us wanted to leave our warm sleeping bags. When we did get going, we had to climb using hands and feet, digging into the snow for purchase. A stretch of rocks, slippery and steep, was followed by another open snow scramble, more rocks, more snow. We inched upwards. Our progress seemed negligible. I was trying to stay positive, but every now and then a rebellious thought would sneak past my defences and ask me what the fuck I thought I was playing at. I could have been on the beach in Goa, or with Smiles and Sally at the Lake Palace of Jaipur. Instead of which I was wading through a foot or two of snow, over hidden rocks, any one of which could turn my ankle and make the descent a nightmare.

At a pause to get our breath back and eat a couple of squares of chocolate, we found that we all had chapped lips and runny noses. We were tantalisingly close to the pass, but we'd agreed we must reach it by one-thirty in order to get to the second cave before dark. Once we realised we weren't going to make it, we turned back.

Going down was easier on the heart and lungs, but after a while the effort of controlling the descent turned my knees to jelly and the rot soon spread to my thighs. We knew we shouldn't stop; we had to make it back to the cave while there was still some light. Even so, I couldn't resist calling to the others.

'Hey, come and look at this!'

I waved them over to the south-facing grassy slope I'd just discovered. We stood in open-mouthed wonder. The high meadow was a mass of flowers: small bright yellow ones, miniature purple irises, velvety anemones, sweet blue flowers and thousands of tiny wild strawberries. Hundreds of butterflies of all colours and sizes danced over the blossoms.

Back at Triund the following day, Lyn and Arthur did their *puja:* their prayers. I took off all my clothes and strolled along the ridge in the bright sunlight, enjoying the feeling of the breeze on my bare body. We hadn't seen another human for three days, so I was freaked when a man suddenly clambered into view, not ten yards from me. My hands moved reflexively to cover my genitals.

'Namaste.' He put his palms together in greeting. I did the same before quickly covering myself again.

You are wanting *chai*, sir?' his voice was so rhythmic he almost sang the question.

I felt stupid standing there with my hands over my prick, so I took them away, 'You have tea here?'

'Of course. It is my job to look after guests at the refuge. I am the *chowkidar*.' He rattled a big key ring, his badge of office.

'My friends are doing their *puja* at present. We'd like three *chais* when they've finished. But we didn't see you on our way up. Where were you?'

'Ah. I was called away on urgent business.'

I wondered what urgent business needed to be conducted on the ridge, but didn't ask. The *chowkidar* unlocked the storage bins in the hut. One of them contained wood, I noted with relief. I wouldn't have to carry logs uphill again.

At the end of another dinner of rice and lentils, I wandered along the ridge in the moonlight, scrambled up one of the boulders, sat down and listened to the night.

After a while huge moths with intricate mystical patterns on their furry wings filled the air around me. I felt myself expanding, my soul was full of joy. I was part of the natural world too. I promised myself my life would be spent in nature. I'd never be office-fodder, never be a city dweller.

It was time to move on. I was up well before dawn, my packed rucksack at my feet. I turned to Lyn. 'Goodbye. It's been great to see you. Thanks, thanks for everything'. I hugged Lyn and held her tight, not wanting to let go.

Arthur's hand was on my shoulder, sending me on my way. 'You don't want to miss the bus.' He said.

'See you in Goa at Christmas.' I hoisted my

rucksack and strode downhill without a backward glance.

At the station early, I stepped aboard the five a.m. bus to Manali, bagging the front seat, next to the driver.

In the dark, the bus toiled up zigzag roads and hurtled down the serpentine bends on the other side. The sky lightened in the east, feathery shawls in pinks and lemons. Then it was day.

We were travelling against the grain of the country. Each valley was a variation on the theme established by the first: huts, cooking fires, cows, clothes lines, a foaming river and boulders scattered as if they'd been thrown like dice from the hand of a god. Excited children and barking dogs chased the bus. Each ridge-top revealed astounding glimpses of the snow-covered Dhauladhar mountain range. My front seat vantage point had plenty of leg room and a magnificent view. It came at a price.

Every two or three valleys we had to stop by a river and let the boiling water in the radiator cool for a few minutes. Once it had gone off the boil the radiator could be topped up with melt-water. As front rider, I was the driver's assistant in this operation. He wrapped his hand in a filthy rag and wrenched off the scalding radiator cap; I poured cold water into the radiator from an oily plastic jerrycan.

Our first effort didn't go well. He burnt his thumb on the hot metal and dropped the radiator cap. Half the water I poured splashed over the radiator rather than going inside. I wiped the radiator cap clean, replaced it, and we set off again. We did better at the next stop and from then on we proved an effective team.

Several times through the day, at the bottom of ravines, I saw the rusty skeletons of buses that had plunged off the road.

It was dark when we arrived in Manali, the main town of the Kulu Valley. It had been drizzling for the last hour of our journey. Stiff, I climbed down onto the muddy ground and was immediately besieged by the crowd who flock around new arrivals at bus stations, selling produce or hustling for hotels and restaurants. I picked out a bright-looking kid and he drove the rest away.

My guide took me to a cheap hotel. I checked in, left my bag and went to have dinner at the *dhaba* next door. I mopped up the last of the greens with a *chapatti* and rose, ready to go back to my room and sleep.

'Hey, Leaf, isn't it? We met in Dharamsala a week or so ago.' The voice came from the shadows. A guy with long black hair and a thin face moved into the light. I recognised him but couldn't recall his name. 'I hope you're not here to buy,' he said.

'No, definitely not.' I'd been warned by Lyn not to score in Manali, a town full of Afghan refugees, informers and police.'But I wouldn't mind a smoke.

'Sure thing,' he said. 'Follow me.'

'You've to be careful here,' the guy muttered as he skinned up in his room. 'It's not cool. Anyway Manali dope isn't very good. The best *charas* comes from the Parvati valley – that's where this is from.' He took a long toke and passed me the glowing joint. I had a couple of hits before passing it back. By the time he handed it back to me my head was full of fireworks: rockets, sparklers and soft Bengal lights. I decided to go to Parvati to score.

5. PARVATI'S RUBIES

Beneath a startling blue sky, under dazzling snow-clad mountain peaks, great swathes of the forest were turning red and gold. The thin mountain air made the colours preternaturally vivid. Our bus ground slowly uphill, making disturbing noises of complaint. The Parvati valley grew narrower, it turned into a gorge and the road came to a sudden end. The driver swung his vehicle into a parking bay carved out of solid rock. He spun the wheel, reversed sharply and slammed on the brakes again.

I waited for the passengers near the front to get off, then stood, stretched and looked down through the window. The back of the bus was hanging over the gorge. A great void gaped beneath me.

'Fuck!' The river was a narrow ribbon, a dizzy distance below. Freaked, I grabbed my gear, scrambled to the front of the bus and stepped onto solid ground. The driver yelled something, waved and then sped off, all but scraping the wall of rock as he shot downhill.

Mountain shepherd: Himachal Pradesh

65

Along with the few remaining passengers, I continued on foot along the uneven track, looking where I was placing my feet, but also glancing across the gorge. Manikaran, the hot springs village on the other side of the river, was alternately revealed and concealed by shifting clouds of water vapour.

The only way to reach the village was by walking across a swaying bridge of old planks, tied together with rope. I watched the other passengers nimbly start across before setting foot on the bridge. The backpack changed my centre of balance. The planks sagged and bounced unpredictably; the footsteps of the other travellers were sending ripples and counter-ripples up and down the span.

'This is nuts,' I said to no-one in particular. 'One false step and I'm just a red smear on a rock.' The white-green river roared beneath me as I staggered and lurched across. Heart pumping, I stumbled onto the ground on the far side and found myself at the entrance of a stone temple. My glasses steamed up in the heat and my nose wrinkled at the sulphurous smell.

A figure, clad in a sheet, materialised out of the mist. He put his palms together in greeting.

'Welcome to the temple baths,' he said in good English. 'The ladies pool is to the right. You may not go there. This is the men's bathing area. You can put your clothes by the side of the pool while you enjoy the waters.'

I wasn't sure whether or not to mention money… 'Er, do I need to pay to use the pool?'

'It is not necessary,' he said. 'With the Gods' blessing we stay warm all winter. Those who visit may share our good fortune.'

The men's bath was around the length of a cricket pitch and half that in width. Billowing clouds of steam swirling around the pool made my estimate a mere guess. By screwing my eyes up I could make out some stone pillars and carved seats. Slow-moving bathers and waders came into and out of vision.

Hot water continually gushed into the pool from a pipe. It flowed out through a spout in the wall behind the columns and poured into the river below.

I dropped my rucksack, stripped down to my underpants and made a bundle of my clothes near the water's edge. After soaping my body, I tentatively eased myself into the super-hot water. Soon my eyes grew accustomed to the surroundings. Immersed in steaming mineral water, I soaked away the aches of the journey – the perfect way to relax after a scary bus ride.

Refreshed, I dressed and went to look around. There was hot water running in stone channels all over the village. In the centre stood a raised stone platform, waist high, some twelve feet square, with a six-inch lip. The water flowing in the channel was boiling.

While I was eating the picnic I'd bought with me, several women arrived and put their pots of food to cook in the constant stream of scalding water. They joined the group chatting happily on the benches while small children played around their feet. It was an idyllic scene. I'd arrived in Shangri-la. It wasn't a legend, it *did* exist and I was in it.

There was no hotel or guesthouse in Manikaran. The village's one shop only had cauliflower for sale. I asked the shopkeeper if there was anywhere I could stay, miming sleep to make myself understood. She called over a lad lounging by the entrance and issued a series of instructions. The boy nodded. Beckoning me to follow, he led me to a small house on the edge of the village. I gave him a rupee for his help.

The house belonged to an old couple. Tiny and deeply wrinkled, they showed me a small musty-smelling room with a thin mattress on the floor.

'*Tin* rupees,' the old man said, holding up three fingers. Three rupees came to about twenty pence. I nodded my acceptance. His wife pulled at my sleeve to get my attention and mimed eating. '*Tin* rupees.'

'*Accha*,' I replied: OK, good.

Pleased at my attempt to communicate in Hindi, grandma patted me on the arm and went off chuckling to herself. I unrolled my sleeping bag on the thin mattress and jotted down the impressions of the day in my notebook. I was dozing when she woke me and beckoned me to follow. The smell of cooking lentils made me realise just how hungry I was. She fed me a dinner of *dhal*, green leaf vegetables and *chapattis* - plain food but it tasted great. Her husband pointed to a basket of apples and indicated I could help myself.

Before I had a chance to take him up on the offer, his wife returned, bearing a small wooden bowl full of honey. A couple of chunks of honeycomb clung to the side of the bowl. '*Tin rupees*,' she said. '*Accha.*' I smiled, nodded and took the wooden spoon she held out. Bed and board had cost me about fifty pence. After the delicious honey I was too full to eat any apples, but I thought I'd take two or three when I went walking in the morning.   The sun had set, but there was still enough light to see, so I went for a stroll, to have a look around and help my dinner go down. Back at the house, as the light faded, I was given a candle. I expected to be asked for three rupees, but there was no mention of money.

I cleaned my teeth, undressed and got into my sleeping bag. My rolled-up jacket served as a pillow. I put my glasses in one shoe and my torch in the other. Blowing out the candle, I lay down and watched the images of the day replay themselves in front of my closed eyes.

I was in another world. I'd come from frenetic London, a city where millions of people live in close proximity and ignore each other wherever possible. I'd arrived in a place where life was unhurried, people were kind and friendly, and children played happily with homemade toys.

When I went out in the early morning it was cold and the puddles were rimmed with ice. On my way to the square I ran into a wild-haired young guy. 'Hi. You speak English?' he asked.

'Yes, I do.'

'Hey, good to meet another European,' he said, smiling and holding out his hand. I shook it. 'You're the second foreigner in the village,' he continued. 'I'm Andreas, from Switzerland. You?'

'My name's Leaf. I'm English.' I looked at his deeply tanned face, his laughing blue eyes and asked, 'What brought you here, Andreas?'

'The same as you, I expect.' He chuckled, pulled a *chillum* from his waistcoat pocket and started filling it. 'I didn't want to do military service so I left my country. What about you, Leaf?'

'I needed a change of country too. I was involved in a massive acid bust in England and spent five years in prison. I just had to get away.'

'Five years! That must have driven you crazy.'

'It drove me half crazy at least. I've come to India in search of my sanity.'

Andreas was friendly and helpful, telling me where I could get food in the village and how to go about scoring. He intended to get enough *charas* to see him through the winter in the tropics. He'd been in the valley the year before and knew his way around.

'There are a couple of dealers in Manikaran,' he said. 'But the way to find the best and cheapest *charas* is to buy directly from the people who rub the plants. They go up into the high mountains: the greater the altitude, the stronger the dope – more ultraviolet, I suppose.

You'll meet the rubbers on the trails, heading towards the village as they bring their fingers to market.' His sudden grin took years off his age and made him look a teenager. 'Have a very good day.'

'Thanks. Maybe I'll see you up the valley.'

In the square I bought *chapattis* from one woman and eggs from another. She showed me a few wrinkled apples in a woven basket, but I'd already got enough fruit from my hosts. I put the eggs in a plastic bag, immersed them in the steaming water in the square and went to fill my water bottle from a cold tap.

When the eggs were ready, I lifted the bag from the water and gave them time to cool before wrapping them in a handkerchief. I put them in my *jhola* – my shoulder bag – and set off to explore.

I ambled uphill, exulting in the brilliant blue of the November sky. By late morning the sun was hot, but the air stayed cool. The autumn colours were at their absolute peak. It was a perfect day for being outside and walking with no particular destination in mind.

A lot of the time, when not in company, I have a tune running through my head. That day it was a Beatles song. I never sing in public but, as there was nobody around, I began to croak out loud: 'Good day, sunshine...'

The sun was in my face. The Kulu cap I'd bought in Manali had no peak. At first I had to use my hand to shade my eyes, but the higher the sun rose, the easier it was to see.

A young man emerged from a green side valley. Way behind him in the distance a long waterfall was tumbling silently to earth.

I paused to get my breath. As he neared I put my palms together and greeted him. '*Namaste.*'

Stopping in front of me, he opened his hand. It held four sticks of *charas*, hand-rubbed cannabis resin, each one roughly the size of my little finger. I examined one and warmed the tip with a match to check the purity. It smelt fresh, aromatic, wonderful.

'*Tis* rupees,' he said, holding out his sticks. He had a cast in his eye; it seemed a common problem in this part of the mountains.

Thirty rupees, a couple of quid, for over an ounce of dynamite dope sounded like a good deal. '*Accha,*' I replied, pulling out my roll and giving him the money in return for the fingers. '*Chillum*?' I asked.

He laughed, whipped out his pipe and handed it to me. I sat down on the ground, in the shade thrown by a tree, and put a little tobacco in as a plug. I heated the end of a stick and crumbled a generous sprinkling of resin into the pipe. The aroma making me salivate. He held the match while I fired up the *chillum*. We shared it, taking turns to draw in a lungful of smoke and hold it for as long as we could.

When the *chillum* was finished, he tapped the ash out of the pipe, wiped the inside with a grubby cloth, rose to his feet, waved farewell and carried on downhill. I sat cross-legged beside the track for some time, unable to stand: totally out of my box.

Later in the day I came across a couple of other grass rubbers. They both showed me their wares. I warmed the fingers, smelt them and bought them too. When I headed back down towards the village, I was carrying something over three ounces of the strongest dope I'd ever smoked – as good as the Buddha grass I'd got in Thailand in the seventies.

The following day was virtually a re-run of the first. The young men I encountered stopped to greet me and show me the little black sticks of *charas* they'd rubbed from the wild marijuana plants, high up on the slopes of the mountains. The dope was always very good and I bought all they had for sale. I was building up a collection of sticky fingers.

In the evening, when I went to bathe in the temple, the water in the pool seemed even hotter than it had been the day before.

'Is it my imagination,' I asked the temple attendant. 'Or is the water hotter than yesterday?'

'Indeed you're not imagining it. The water temperature rises and falls all the time.'

By the end of the week the pool was too hot to swim in.

Diary: November 1982

72

Forests, waterfalls and snow-capped mountains make a stunning backdrop to my wanderings in the valley. But more than once I find I've retreated into myself, lost all awareness of my surroundings. My body might be in Shangri-la but my mind is all over the place, churning out spiralling thoughts within thoughts, trying to work out what I'm doing in the Himalayas and what the fuck existence is all about. What am I to make of my seesaw life and what's coming next?

I'd had thousands of hours of reflection in my cell in Horfield prison and had convinced myself that I was pretty together. Now I saw that my thoughts had been utterly distorted by the reducing-lens of prison. All I'd been doing was keeping my head above the sea of shit. I was free, at last, but also somewhat lost.

I needed to learn how to relax, down through all the levels of my tensed-up mind. The psychic muscles I'd developed to survive prison were now a big hindrance. I'd come to India to be far away from the people who'd put me inside. I needed space to get a perspective on my time in jail. Most of all, I had to learn how to unilaterally disarm myself.

'How would you describe yourself in a hundred words?' I ask. Like many people who live alone, I've got into the habit of talking out loud.

'I'm loyal to my friends, fairly intelligent and can be amusing when I get into my stride in good company. I love nature, books and music, loathe cruelty, capitalism and the screech of opera sopranos. I can become sharp when irritated or hungry and peevish if I don't feel well. I tend to postpone unpleasant decisions, hoping they'll go away; sometimes they do. Honesty is very important to me but, if I'm being entirely frank, I have to say my honesty is too often trumped by polite insincerities, the common coin of my middle-class upbringing.' I surprise myself by chuckling.

'At least you can laugh.' It seems a good sign, so I carry on. 'My greatest asset is the ability to know instinctively who my friends will be and whom I should avoid. I've spent the free part of my life in congenial company. Life is good among friends. Outside of institutions, my experiences have been mostly positive and, as a result, I'm mostly positive.'

Looking back to my beginnings, I saw that my life had started with six very good years. I'd been loved, cared for and felt secure. The abrupt end of the good times brought a lost lonely year of mourning for my mother, followed by ten years of struggle in an authoritarian male-only boarding school. My release from that straightjacket was succeeded by ten wonderful years of hippie freedom, of internal and external exploration. That, in turn, led to five years in another male institution, where everything was either compulsory or forbidden. My sentence was now over, but I wasn't yet over it.

My life has never followed a predictable path. Intuition and adventure sit in one of the pans of my scales, reason and logic in the other. Rational processes had dominated during the struggle to survive prison. Here in the mountains I could feel the balance shifting. A little speck in Shiva's cosmic playground, I was ready to believe almost anything.

Sitting by the Parvati river one day, I realised I was looking into the island of my past, into those dreadful times following my mother's death.

6. MISSING MUMMY

Richmond, Yorkshire. July 1955

Roger gave me his big brother look and said, 'Home without our Mummy isn't home any more.'

He was right, so we agreed to run away to a desert island.

Mummy's sister, Auntie Con, was looking after us. She'd brought our cousin Stephen with her. Stephen was seven, a year older than me. He was blond and wore specs that make him look like The Milky Bar Kid.

'Please, please can I come too,' he begged us, when we told him about Roger's plan. Stephen was troubled by warts, but he knew all the ways of getting rid of them, from new pennies, to stolen bacon and things you could only do by moonlight, so we agreed to let him come.

We got up before dawn, crept out of the house and crossed fields wet with dew. When we got to the River Swale we walked along the bank to the spot Roger had chosen as our new home. It wasn't far from the place where we fished for sticklebacks at the weekends. We crossed the plank that linked the island to the rest of the world, then Roger threw it into the river. We watched it float away downstream.

It grew light enough to see that there wasn't a lot on our desert island: rocks, gravel and small bushes. There were no coconuts or bananas. It wasn't a proper desert island at all!

'Where's our breakfast?' I demanded. We'd

forgotten to bring it and I was getting hungry. Now we were marooned, like Robinson Crusoe. We'd probably starve to death.

I was glad when the policeman arrived. He waded across to the island, picked me up and carried me to the shore. I stood shivering on the riverbank while he fetched Stephen and then Roger. In ominous silence he took us to the police station, put us in a cell, locked the door and went off to change his trousers. We were in terrible trouble...

Daddy arrived, talked to the policeman and took us home. We thought he'd rescued us. Years later he told Roger and I what had happened. Finding us gone, he'd alerted the local bobby and told him to lock us up if he found us first. This would give us such a fright that we'd never do anything that would get us locked up again.

It seemed a bizarre idea to me, but I must admit that it worked for Roger and Stephen.

I never fully got over my mother's sudden death; I don't see how a young child can. It knocks an enormous hole out of the middle of your life – and nothing can ever put your life back on its old course.

If your mummy can suddenly be gone, then nothing is secure. Nothing in life is solid or certain.

I sat looking out of the window of Nanna's front parlour waiting for our Mummy to come back to us. I only looked downhill: Broomhill Road is a cul-de-sac. I constructed all the scenarios I could think of that would allow her to still be alive. The line that held out most hope was that she was doing secret work for the government, protecting us against the Communist menace.

At the first Assembly of the school year, the Headmaster announced 'Boys, you must all be kind to the Fielding brothers. They've tragically lost their mother.' Disregarding his own words, he beat me a few days later: four strokes with a long, whippy cane, for the crime of using the wrong flight of stairs.

From the moment of the Headmaster's opening remarks, Roger and I were marked out as freaks: boys without a mother, siblings to be whispered about. Maybe they feared our condition was contagious. To begin with, nobody was sure how to deal with us: everybody had a mother.

My only female contact in the first year at prep school was Maisie, a big sunny Suffolk lass who helped the little ones bathe. I was in love with Maisie. She was the only one who was natural around me.

~

A voice dragged me out of the depths of my childhood and dumped me back in the present. I turned, instantly on guard, and tried to dry the tears that had been running down my face and dropping off my chin. A smiling shepherd, dressed in sheepskins, handed me a small black stone.

'*Dhanyabad,*' I muttered. Thank you.

He put his hands together, bowed and wandered away with his small flock, leaving me to my thoughts. I blinked to clear my still swimming eyes and wiped away the tears with the back of my hand. The stone bore the clear imprint of a flower. Looking up from examining this extraordinary gift from a total stranger, I noticed a small area of the sandy riverbed had a pinkish tinge.

This stretch of the Parvati River was broad and shallow. I took off my shoes, rolled up my trousers and waded in. The river – melt-water from the glacier at the head of the valley – was icy cold. I plunged my arm in, picked up a handful of the sand and sorted out a number of tiny red stones. Rubies. I'd found Parvati's rubies!

In India, the Gods are the superheroes of the comics lying around in the *chai* shops and barbers. In Delhi I'd read the story about Parvati's ruby necklace: Lord Shiva and his consort Parvati had quarrelled. Angered, Shiva grabbed at his wife's necklace, the string snapped and the precious stones tumbled into the water. It hit me yet again. I'd found some of Parvati's rubies. I wrapped them in my handkerchief, stowed them in my pocket and headed back to Manikaran.

I awoke from a bad dream of a huge black presence, a string of human skulls hung around her waist: Kali, the Hindu Goddess of time. She'd plucked me from my bed and popped me into her mouth – a snack to be sucked dry later. It was cold in the room, but my sleeping bag was drenched in sweat. What on earth had I been thinking? It made no difference that they were so small as to have no commercial value; I'd taken Parvati's rubies from her river. What an idiot I was!

My watch showed three a.m. – the middle of the night. I felt very alone. Surely I should put the rubies back. I rolled a little spliff and thought about it while I smoked the joint. Then I had a clear moment of inspiration and knew with absolute clarity what I had to do.

7. BUST AGAIN?

Andreas was having breakfast in a *chai* shop. I went over to say hello. 'Hi man. I've got to catch the bus to Kulu tomorrow. I'm going down to Delhi to meet up with my friends. But I could do with picking up another twenty or thirty *tolas* of *charas* before I go. Any idea who I should talk to?'

'Sure. There's a woman who buys from the country people up the valley,' he replied. 'I want to score too. She has kilos to sell... only I've dealt with her before. The negotiations will take all day.'

'Shall we make a start, then?'

'Yes. Oh, I forgot to say, she's the boss of the house. Mountain women are strong. Her husband does what he's told.'

Her house was one of the biggest in the village. A tall man opened the door in answer to our knock and invited us inside. The room was spacious and gloomy. There were no open windows and little light penetrated. We took off our shoes on the outside step, entered and sat on carpets on the floor in front of a low table.

Behind the table sat a silver-haired woman. She must have been a real beauty when young. She still had a strikingly handsome face, full of character, though now fissured with deep lines. Something about her regal presence made me want to hear about her life story but I reminded myself this wasn't a social call; we were here on business. Her man came in with lit candles. He placed them on the table, served us with tiny cups of tea and small sweet cakes.

She told him to bring us some samples. We rubbished the first dope, so he was dispatched to bring something better. Shaking our heads and chuckling, we shrugged that off too. She joined in the mirth, with a loud coarse laugh, and sent for the next grade. This was better but old and dry. I broke open one of the crumbly fingers. She remonstrated with me angrily.

'She asks you not to do that,' her man said diplomatically.

'Please tell her,' I said, 'that we need to see how fresh it is. Let's not go through all the grades. Just show us your best *charas* and, if we agree a price, we'll buy.'

We drank more tea and smiled at the lady. Her man went off to get more samples. He returned with a package wrapped in several layers of material. This looked more promising. At her invitation Andreas filled a *chillum*. I held a lit match for him while he got it going and took a blast when he passed it to me. I offered it to her man. He smoked and passed it on. She threw out her high-volume laugh and spoke to him.

'What did she say,' I asked.

'She said after the chillum I won't be good for anything today.' He got a fit of the giggles.

We were infected too. The dope wasn't bad. She spoke some more.

'Twenty-five rupees a *tola*,' he informed us.

A *tola* is a little over eleven grams, but had been decimalised down to ten for foreigners like us.

'Too much,' I said.

'You want cheap?'

I was surprised. She did speak some English.

She sent her man off. He came back with a bag of dry old Nepalese temple balls. 'You want cheap?' She cackled, offering me the Nepalese. 'Eight rupees a *tola*.'

Andreas and I had a quick whispered conversation. He nodded agreement.

'We might pay twenty-five rupees a *tola* for something better.' I said.

After another round of tea and sweets she finally agreed to show us a kilo of the best. She spent ages unravelling the seven layers in which it was wrapped. We smelt it, smoked it and got thoroughly wrecked. Laughing wildly, we tried to focus on sorting through it, for every finger is different and there was the odd dud one. Finally we both had what we wanted, thirty *tolas* apiece: some three hundred grams each. My legs were beginning to ache from sitting cross-legged for so long.

'Twenty-eight per *tola*,' she said.

'No,' I replied. 'That's too much. Twenty-four.'

After an age we admitted to twenty-five and she conceded twenty-seven. My legs were killing me. We munched sweet cake, drank more tea and smoked a chillum for inspiration.

'Ok, twenty-six,' I said finally, ready to close the deal.

'No, twenty-seven,' she insisted.

We were stuck. She wouldn't come down and we weren't going to go up twice running. We made the next gambit in the bargaining game: we rose to go. Regretting that we'd been unable to do business and thanking her for her hospitality, we hobbled out of the house.

'She'll get him to call us back,' Andreas

whispered as we limped off, trying to look as though we didn't care at all.

'You can bank on it,' I said.

She didn't. We slunk back to the village having spent the whole day failing to agree on a deal... and I was leaving in the morning.

That evening I packed away the dope I'd already bought. I got up early and went to see if I could score a few more fingers before catching the bus. I met up with Andreas. We'd passed the old lady's house when a boy came running after us.

'Come, come!' he said.

'Something new.' The dealer lady smiled and opened a big bag we hadn't seen before. It was the tops, better than the dope she'd showed us yesterday.

'Twenty-seven,' she said firmly.

'OK,' I agreed instantly. There was no more time for haggling. I needed to pack the *charas* away and get to Kulu in time to catch the weekly bus to Mandi.

To leave the valley, I had to re-cross the river on the swaying rope bridge. In the middle I threw some fingers of *charas* into the green rushing waters of the river Parvati – an offering to Lord Shiva for a safe journey through his land.

The British never conquered this part of the Himalayas. Nor did anyone else. The Maharajahs of Kulu were one of the world's longest reigning dynasties, a single family's unbroken governance stretching back thirteen hundred years.

Kulu's self-rule ended in 1948, when newly independent India absorbed the princely states. Ringed by enormous mountains, twenty thousand feet high, the Kulu valley was easy to defend, impossible to capture. There was only one entrance: through a road cut into the side of a great vertiginous gorge, several miles long and at least a mile deep.

That made things easy for the Indian police, who stopped the Kulu-Delhi bus and took the Europeans and their baggage off to be searched. I had close to a pound of *charas* on me. It wasn't for dealing. The dope I was carrying was to be our private supply for the six months Smiles, Sally and I were going to be in the sub-continent. If the search uncovered my stash, I'd have no chance of convincing them it was for my personal consumption. I wasn't feeling great but, for once, my prison experience came in handy. I was able to appear relaxed, though I certainly didn't feel it.

The foreigners were inspected in pairs. The odd man at the end of the line, I was last to be searched. The policeman missed the dope I'd hidden in walnuts in my rucksack. He failed to find the fingers concealed in a packet of ginger biscuits in my *jhola,* my shoulder bag. Then he held out his arms, and mimed tapping me down.

Not having had time to properly stash the sticks I'd bought that morning, I'd made a flat pack of them and put it in my money belt round my waist. Still trying to appear nonchalant, I raised my arms. He began with my hair before moving his hands to my shoulders. The smell of spices in his mouth didn't cover the rotting-tooth stink of his breath. Gagging, I turned my head sideways to get a clean lungful of air. From the armpits he moved down towards my waist until his questing fingers reached the hard pack of *charas*.

'What is this?' he asked, tapping the edge of the

bulky money belt.

For the second time in my life, I experienced the meltdown moment of being bust. For an indelible instant I had a vision of life in an Indian prison. 'Not again,' I swore to myself. 'Not again'.

Doing nothing more than playing for time, I reached into the pocket of my jeans. I was still acting Mr Cool. My fingers closed on my Swiss army knife. Pulling it out, I said 'It is this.' I opened the corkscrew and handed him the knife.

He took it and inspected it with interest. First he opened the large blade, then the small one, the bottle opener and the screwdriver-cum wire stripper.

I showed him the thin gouger blade he hadn't discovered, followed by the toothpick and the mini tweezers. Then I closed everything up, put the knife back in my pocket, picked up my bags and got on the bus. Paralysed, the policeman stared at me, a baffled look on his face. I looked back as we drove away. He was gazing at our departing bus, still in a trance.

Thank you Shiva. *Bom Shankar!*

8. THE LENGTH OF INDIA

Apart from buying the *charas*, I'd spent next to nothing in Kulu, so I celebrated my narrow escape with a night at the Mandi Palace hotel, where I had one of the best meals of my life and slept like a Raja in a four-poster bed.

In the morning, I got on a bus and made the Delhi rendezvous with Smiles and Sally.

'How was it in the mountains?' Smiles asked. 'We had an incredible time. You really should have come with us.'

'The Lake Palace was unbelievable,' Sally added. 'Leaf, you don't know what you missed!'

'I've had the most extraordinary time too. I've climbed mountains and visited places and seen things I would never have imagined. It's been a wonderful month. And I've got our stash for the winter. I think you'll find it very interesting.'

The three of us spent the rest of the day swapping Himalayan and Rajastani experiences. I didn't mention the rubies. I was keeping them as a surprise.

We walked down to Delhi's main train station, and spent eighty dollars each on First Class Indrail passes. They gave us two months free train travel anywhere in the country – as long as we'd booked the day before. First class wasn't as grand as it sounded. It had been devalued, rather like the English football league, where the old Third Division is now called League One. First class was really third class, ranked below the two air-conditioned classes. It gave us plenty of leg room – important on long rides – but we sweated just the same as the people packed in fifth class.

Our first ride was to Agra, to see the Taj Mahal. We'd timed our visit to coincide with the full moon.

The Taj Mahal

We strolled around the city in the afternoon and then headed towards the Taj. As the sun sank lower in the sky, the parrots in the trees set up such a shrieking din that we had to shout at full volume to be understood.

I'd heard so much about the Taj Mahal over the years that I fully expected it to be a big let-down, but it wasn't. The mausoleum was magnificent, the gardens exquisite, the whole experience inspiring.

Around the three nights of the full moon, visitors were allowed to stay until ten or eleven. Glutted, we'd been sitting quietly, watching the dusk fade into night, slowly digesting our rich experience. A woman glided by in front of us and sank to the ground, perhaps fifteen yards away. Unaware of our presence, she sang a haunting song of unearthly beauty. India is full of unexpected magic.

The following day, the Taj was closed to the public for the visit of the Indian and French Presidents. The air filled with the throb of helicopters as the bigwigs arrived. We set off in the other direction, to find the government hash shop in the old city.

Most of the larger towns in the north of India had a government hash shop. An overweight greybeard presided over the Agra branch. We had a hilarious time with him. We retired to his office where, between blasts on a *chillum,* he told us that he'd been the customs controller of Bombay until his retirement.

'Then how did you come to be in this business?' Sally asked, in her light innocent voice.

'I paid for it, of course. I had to stump up a *lakh*, a hundred thousand rupees, for the concession. That's over seven thousand pounds in sterling.'

'Why that's a fortune in this country, isn't it?'

He nodded, smiling.

'Your English is excellent. Have you lived in Britain?'

'No, my dear, I just had a good education.'

'Was it worth it – the hundred grand?' Smiles wanted to know.

'My god, yes it was!' He got an attack of the giggles, 'This *charas* is super strong. Where's it from?'

'Fresh from the mountains,' I told him.

'Aha! That explains why it's so much better than anything I've got here. Vijay!'

A young man put his head round the door.

'Vijay, you're in charge for the afternoon. We'll be in my quarters. Get the boy to bring us *chai* and *barfi* and make sure we're not disturbed.'

I left a stick of Parvati *charas* with him when we moved on. He gave me a small sphere of opium in return. I stashed it away, to use in case of the runs.

Sally insisted we take a short detour to visit the ghost city of Fatehpur Sikri, built in the reign of the Emperor Akbar. The architecture was simply stunning. In the sixteenth century the city had been the capital of the Mughal Empire, but it was abandoned after fourteen years when the water supply dried up.

The few visitors were heavily outnumbered by the hoopoes that strutted on the walls and pecked at the ground, raising and lowering their impressive crests as if in salutation.

Blond hair damp with sweat, fanning herself against the fierce heat, Sally stood in the shade and spoke with passion.

'The thing you've got to understand, guys, is that the whole place was built to a grand plan. Architecturally it is one, a masterpiece, all done in red sandstone. The scale is staggering.' She waved her arms around, encompassing the buildings. The air of smiling vagueness Sally often wore was gone. So was her reserve.

'Imagine the place swarming with people – soldiers traders, travellers, urchins, cobblers, thieves... Europe had nothing like it. See that mosque over there,' she pointed to one of the buildings in the distance. 'It housed ten thousand worshippers, all on their knees, stretching their hands towards Mecca. Ten thousand, just imagine!'

Inevitably, Sally and I had been weighing each other up. I still wasn't sure how she really felt about me. New partners sometimes want to close the blinds against their loved one's past.

In the middle, Smiles managed a balancing act. Librans all, we were weighing the scales, trying to find a triangular equilibrium.

At Varanasi we spent several days wandering around the markets, the temples and the *ghats*, waiting to receive the lightweight clothes we'd ordered. On our way down to the river Ganges before dawn one morning, we took a short cut and found ourselves lost in an area of wood-yards. Nobody was around to give us directions. A huge, half-starved dog slunk into view, its ribs standing out through the taut skin. Several more followed it.

'God, that leader's a big brute!' Sally gasped.

'Keep moving steadily,' Smiles said calmly. 'If they sense we're afraid they'll be on us.'

We angled away from them, not sure where we were heading. Silently they followed at a distance, but gradually they were edging towards us, until they were close enough for us to see their drooling jaws. Were they desperate enough to rush us? Dressed in light cotton, we didn't even have belts to defend ourselves. Smiles whipped off a sandal and faced the pack. 'Come on then, you bastards!' he yelled, waving a fist at them. 'Want some leather do you?'

The dogs retreated a few paces. For a moment it was a standoff – then the leader took a step towards us. The pack followed. I clenched my fists: the only weapons I had to defend myself...

A bicycle rickshaw miraculously materialised out

of a side alley. We ran for it and squeezed in.

'*Chalo*!' we chorused, laughing with relief. 'Let's go!'

There were crowds of people by the river: begging, bathing, washing clothes, offering to clean our ears or give us a massage, practising yoga, selling food, jewellery and trinkets... Some of them were just hanging out, like us.

Varanasi is India's holiest city, its *ghats* washed by the waters of Mother Ganga. It was packed with pilgrims and full of old women: widows who'd come to this holy place to die, in the hope of a better rebirth. They held their hands out to us in supplication. We gave them our change and small denomination notes, wishing we could do more. But there were thousands of them and, no doubt, many thousands more, converging on this auspicious spot by the sacred river Ganges.

There were plenty of children hanging around, waiting for a chance to carry someone's bag, bring them fruit or do anything that would earn them a few *paise*.

'Hey, come here.' Smiles beckoned a young lad over. 'Speak English?'

'Oh yes, Sahib.'

'Good. We want bamboo sticks, OK?'

'OK. Come.'

We followed the youngster to a bamboo seller and bought two walking-stick lengths. Then we got the boy to take us to a metalworker and had the sticks shod with a disc of lead.

We paid the metal man and gave the lad a few *rupees*.

'Thank you *Sahib*, thank you a thousand times!'

He raced off, skipping for joy.

'If we're going to travel all over this country, we should be prepared to defend ourselves...' Smiles squared his shoulders, puffed his chest out and banged the metal-tipped foot of his cane on the ground, reverting for a moment, into the young, strutting Mancunian squaddie he'd been in his teens.

After travelling all night, our train pulled into Kolkata. We disembarked, stretched our legs and picked up peanuts and a hand of bananas from one of the fruit stalls. There was just time for me to have a shave before we hopped aboard the Chennai train for a thirty-hour ride down the Coromandel Coast.

'Thank you, that was delicious.' Sally said to the waiter at the end of another *thali* lunch. 'I just can't believe how good these meals are,' she added to us.

'It's lucky we got our Indrail passes. Can you imagine how difficult travelling would be without the trains?'

'Yes,' Smiles said. 'It was an excellent move.'

On long journeys, a waiter would come and take orders for the next meal. At the following stop he'd telegraph the orders ahead. Our meal was delivered to us down the line. It was freshly cooked and piping hot: the system worked perfectly. We always got exactly what we'd ordered. It was invariably delicious and inexpensive. Our diet wasn't a problem in this country; the majority of Indians are vegetarians.

Tamil Nadu was hotter than the north. The people darker and jollier, the food more watery and fiery. We went to visit the Coromandel Coast and have a look at the ancient cave carvings of Mahabalipuram.

A lonely seventh century temple, covered in intricate carvings, lay on the beach, listing slightly, radiating sadness, helplessly waiting to be consumed by the waters of the Bay of Bengal.

We didn't hang around in Chennai, but took a few train rides to get to the sandalwood city of Mysore, with its palaces, formal rose gardens and temples. We were all getting on well and everything was going fine until we were on board the train to Goa. The first symptoms erupted suddenly.

'Oh my god!' I moaned as knifing pains sliced through me. My midriff was disintegrating. Swaying down the corridor, I just made the toilet in time, dropped my pants, sat and relaxed my sphincter muscles. Half of me seemed to be going down the pan: the little that was left was dissolving. I ached, moaned and groaned: 'Mysore arse.' My strength ebbed away so alarmingly, I didn't know if I had the energy to stand.

I stayed in the loo until the opium I'd been carrying since Agra soldered me shut and took away the pain. I must have picked up the bug after eating dates from a street stall. I was still shivering when we pulled in to Margao station, in southern Goa. We took the shortest route to the sea, landing up in the village of Benaulim.

I could hear the crash of waves breaking from my mattress on the floor of the dormitory in the Bar Pedro, but several days passed before I made it onto the beach and into the Arabian sea.

Travelling in India was often gruelling: Bus and train journeys were long, hot and crowded. We'd covered thousands of kilometres in a few weeks. What a pleasure it was swim, sunbathe and relax.

In the green paddy-fields behind the beaches, tiny children perched on the necks of giant water buffaloes, controlling the great beasts with gentle nudges from their knees.

We bought fruit and veg in the market in Margao and visited Anjuna flea market in the north. Anjuna was full of old hippies and freaks like us. It felt like we'd stepped back in time to the colourful years of the late sixties and early seventies.

Smiles on the beach: Goa 1983

Relaxing in Benaulin: 1983

93

9. PRISON PSYCHOLOGIST

Christmas came and went. By the New Year I was feeling well again… until I saw the Horfield Prison psychologist sitting in Pedro's bar in Benaulim.

Dressed in Hawaiian shirt and Bermuda shorts, he looked quite different from the man who'd interviewed us in Bristol and turned us down for our second parole application. But it was him; the massive facial tic removed any doubt.

Head reeling, I retreated to my hammock. The dam holding back my prison paranoia burst and it all came flooding out. Surely the authorities couldn't still be keeping tabs on us… or could they? Did they really think we were still dangerous? What was going on?

Free for less than a year, prison was never too far below the surface of my mind. I often woke from dreams, sweaty and afraid, with fading memories of cells, screws, searches and stashes.

Smiles erupted onto the verandah. 'You won't fucking believe who I've just seen!' he snarled. He looked as agitated as I felt.

We kept changing our minds about whether or not we should challenge him.

'It's got to be coincidence,' said Smiles.

'Come on man. You don't really think this is an accident. What are the odds of that?'

'You're right. Naïve to think there's an innocent explanation. So, what's it all about? Are they still keeping tabs on us, following us around the country?'

'Search me. You know it could just be a coincidence, the poor sod's got to go somewhere for his holiday and Goa is a popular place.'

Our thoughts chased their tails until our heads were spinning.

I said. 'Let's have a cool drink and think about this.'

We sat in silence for a moment then Smiles said decisively, 'We'll confront him!' He slammed the little round table with his fist and made my banana *lassi* jump. Gobbets of the thick liquid leapt into the air and oozed down the side of the glass. 'Let's settle this once and for all.'

'OK.'

We went looking for him, but the man was nowhere to be found. Maybe he'd recognised us and fled.

Sally looked at the two of us, put her hands on her hips and said, 'Time for a change of scene.'

'You're right, girl.' Smiles clapped his hands together. 'The vibe's been fucked up. We're out of here.'

Quiet Goan Beach

95

10. PARVATI'S NECKLACE

I was ready to move on. It was time for me to head south and fulfil my promise to Parvati. We boarded the overnight bus to Mangalore.

I can never sleep on long bus rides. I doze and come to, aching in bum, leg or neck, shift to a new position and repeat the cycle, ever more frequently. I surfaced as we were taking a ferry ride across a river. The reflection of the moon rippled across the black water. The riverbank was drenched with the heady perfume of queen-of-the-night.

For mile after mile, I stared sightlessly through the bus window, dark memories of Horfield prison running through my mind. Suddenly a double file of forty men appeared in the headlights, jogging towards the bus.

They were carrying a massive tree trunk between them, chanting as they ran. The night swallowed them up. Another forty men came lumbering past, with another giant tree. Twenty or more trunks were carried past my wondering eyes. A thousand singing men, running giant trees through the jungle at four in the morning?

Life is a conundrum.

From Mangalore, we continued down the Malabar Coast to Trivandrum and then on to Kanniyakumari, the southernmost tip of the sub-Continent. We booked into a hotel and went onto the balcony to check out the view. A naked trio of ash-covered *saddhus* were coming down the road, taking it in turns to thrash each other with whips.

'Jesus! Look at that,' I gasped. 'One of them's a woman!'

Kanniyakumari was packed with pilgrims. Indians go on pilgrimages as easily as Europeans go on package holidays. We were as far south as it's possible to go and still be in Mother India.

Our erratic, wandering journey of over three thousand miles had taken three months. Now it was almost at an end. I bought a tube of glue and a framed picture of Parvati, about the size of a large hardback book. In my hotel room I carefully fixed a string of rubies round her neck with tiny glue spots. She looked great. The goddess beamed at me. I winked back at her.

I couldn't keep my secret any longer. 'Have a look at this,' I said to my friends.

Some time before, I'd mentioned finding rubies in the Parvati river, but I hadn't shown them what I'd done with the tiny jewels.

'Oh Leaf, that's lovely!' said Sally. 'What prompted you to do it?'

'Kali. She came to me in a dream – a nightmare really. She popped me into her mouth and then let me go. I knew it was about the rubies. I either had to put them back or do something special with them. I decided to take them to the other end of the country.'

'Let's have a proper look,' said Smiles, inspecting the picture carefully before handing it back to me. 'You did the right thing, mate. It's always a mistake to cross Kali. That string of skulls she wears should make it plain to anyone.'

'Would you like to come with me to the temple?'

'Thanks, man, but this is your trip, isn't it?'

Sally nodded. 'You should go on your own.'

I held the frame carefully in both hands. Surrounded by other pilgrims, I walked the last two kilometres barefoot. Direct contact with the Earth seemed of prime importance.

Taking great care to avoid being jostled, I glided over the ground, approaching the culmination of the journey that had taken me the length of India.

My happiness swelled with every step I took. By the time I reached the temple I could barely contain my joy. I slipped into my sandals and approached the dignified priest who seemed to be in charge of the reception of visitors. I explained my purpose.

'This Hindu temple,' he replied. 'Not tourism.'

My journey couldn't peter out like this. 'Not tourism,' I said and tried again to make him understand. I managed to convince him to call another priest.

This man spoke good English. He waggled his head and clapped his pudgy hands with delight at my story. 'From the Himalaya to Kanniyakumari you have brought Parvati's rubies! May I see?' I unwrapped the picture and showed it to him. He waggled his head again and said 'Come with me'.

I kick off my sandals and follow him into the temple, through a maze of corridors and tunnels, thick with worshippers, heavy with incense. The past and future have disappeared: I am entirely in the present, more alive than I've felt in years.

In the temple there are countless shrines to the hundreds of members of the Hindu pantheon. The priest leads me to a small Parvati shrine where I dedicate the goddess's rubies and leave the framed picture as an offering. I strew the floor with flower petals then I kneel, put my forehead to the ground and thank Parvati and her consort, Lord Shiva, for our safe journey through their miraculous land.

At the beginning of my time in India I'd been wondering what my life was all about. Now, I realised I'd been asking the wrong question. My life wasn't 'about' anything. It was an ongoing process.

Everything I'd said, felt, done, been or imagined was in the past and unchangeable. Life was moving forward of its own accord. My job was to enjoy the ride whenever possible and try to endure it without complaint when times were bad.

I'd made a breakthrough. Thanks to Lord Shiva and Parvati, I'd signed a peace treaty with myself and was at rest, for the first time in years.

Temple on beach: S.E India.

11. EATING GOLD

In Kanniyakumari, a handsome young man rode through town on a white horse. His pink silk suit was plastered with banknotes. Seeing us in his path, he stopped and invited us to his wedding.

We accepted, of course, and sat with a hundred or more guests in the reception room, looking at the happy couple facing us. It felt very hot in the room, and I was only wearing light cotton.

'I feel sorry for the bride and groom,' I whispered to Sally.

'So do I. It must be murder under all those heavy clothes.'

Dressed in their weighty finery, the newly-weds looked hot, tired and very embarrassed. Their ordeal went on for over an hour before they were allowed to retire. That was the signal for conversation to begin. We all sat at long tables and began the wedding feast. Waiters with long rubber aprons, carrying a bucket in one hand and a cup in the other, came whizzing down the aisles. The first doled out a dollop of rice, the second a splash of a watery vegetable dish.

'It's a bit too hot for my taste,' Sally grimaced.

'We've eaten better in a simple *Dhaba*, and this family is obviously rich.'

'But it's a wedding gift, Smiles.' The food was fiery and welcome, so I accepted seconds when offered.

That meant I was already quite full when the real feast began. Course followed elaborate course until I lost count. In order not to be rude to my host, I had to eat at least a little of each dish. I've never, ever, been so stuffed. The wedding dinner finally came to an end with sweets decorated with gold leaf. It was the only gold I'd ever had in my life – and I ate it.

The holy city of Madurai, in the South of India, is second only to Varanasi as a place of pilgrimage. An elephant ambled through the crowded streets, accepting gifts of buns from the pilgrims, taking them with its trunk and delicately popping them into its mouth. The gentle giant's rider sat right up on its neck, directing the great beast with light pressure from his knees.

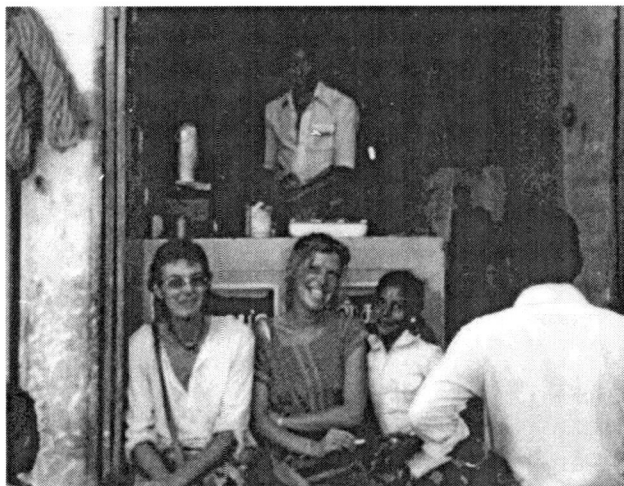

With Sally and Issy, taking a break in a chai shop.
Issy was a sweet girl who'd attached herself to Sally.

Madurai is famous for its extraordinary temple carvings. While my friends were off exploring the town, I got talking to a resident scholar at the temple.

At his invitation, I climbed one of the four towers. All were covered fine stone carvings, life-size or larger.

In a tiny room at the top of one of the towers, the scholar spread a large ancient linen sheet before me, It contained a hundred or more squares of pigment. Each square had some miniscule writing beside it.

'Every colour has its own special attribute,' he told me, 'be it earthly, watery or divine. What is your colour? It will tell me a lot about you.'

I immediately pointed to the sky blue square, my favourite colour for as long as I can remember – the colour of Manchester City, the football team I've supported since I was five.

'Excellent!' he said, obviously pleased. 'This is indicative of a strong spiritual nature. Now, if you had chosen this -' he pointed to a translucent violet, 'you would assuredly be reborn at a higher level.'

Getting ready to leave India behind, we moved on to Rameswaram, to take the ship to Sri Lanka.

Although we already had our tickets, we arrived at the port with hours to spare: Smiles preferred queueing to rushing. We waited among a large and ever-growing crowd to get into the harbour. Impelled by pressure from behind, the throng surged towards the gates and were beaten back, with appalling ferocity, by a line of khaki clad policemen wielding *lathis*: long truncheons.

'Two of the many faces of India,' Smiles' voice was harsh. 'Spirituality and savage beatings.'

We hadn't been directly affected by the police brutality. The sticks had fallen on the heads of the poorest people, travelling in steerage, but the violence sickened me. Had it been possible, I'd have left, but as we were now inside the port, that wasn't an option. We had to hang around for a couple of hours, waiting for the lighter to take us to the ship, anchored in the roads of the Palk Strait. Once aboard, we marked time for several hours while the lighter brought more and more loads of passengers to the ship. Surely there were too many people being allowed on the vessel.

'Do you remember those little three-line stories about ships in the Indian Ocean?' Over the years I'd seen quite a few in the press: 'Overloaded ferry sinks in the Bay of Bengal. Seven hundred passengers missing, feared drowned.'

'Don't,' Sally was upset. 'It's bad enough seeing those poor people getting thrashed.'

The sea stayed calm, the journey itself was uneventful but the three-hour crossing became a fifteen-hour nightmare, at the end of which hundreds of people were held on board for hours, in sweltering heat, without access to any sort of drink.

'I've got some water left in my bottle,' said Sally offering it to Smiles. 'Shall we share it, or hang onto it until we're desperate?'

'I think we should keep it as long as we can. You OK with that, Leaf?'

'Yeah, I'll be fine for a while.'

Eventually we were all jammed into the oven of the Singhalese immigration hall. Wedged back to back, face to sweating face, we were unable to move and were kept that way for over an hour.

'Shit! I've lost one of my fucking sandals!' I moaned.

'Don't even try to look for it, man. Once down on

103

the floor, you might never be able to get to your feet'.

When the door to Customs was finally opened, the crowd became an ugly mob, flailing to escape. Things calmed down once the first few hundred people had fought their way out. We walked under a sign that said 'Welcome to Sri Lanka' and joined the queue at the Immigration desk.

A scowling immigration officer inspected my passport. He called over a senior official who looked through my passport with a frown. 'You are a writer,' the man said accusingly 'A journalist perhaps?'

I grasped that investigative journalism was not welcome in this country and replied, 'No, not at all. I write science fiction.'

'Ah. Arthur C Clarke. An excellent writer. He has a house here.' The officer stamped my passport, handed it back and said I could enter the country.

The island was a place of extraordinary beauty. The jungles were lush, the fields fertile. Food burst out of the ground. The south coast had a string of perfect beaches, full of tide-pools and bays, brimming with bright ocean life.

It was a physical paradise, yet the tension in the air was electric: Sri Lanka had such a screwed-up vibe. I changed a hundred dollar traveller's cheque into Sri Lankan currency in a bank in Colombo. The teller counted out my notes, giving me ten dollars worth of Sri Lankan rupees. I was furious at this blatant attempt at a ripoff. His reaction, when I demanded the missing ninety dollars, showed he hadn't made a mistake – he'd just been caught.

'Get me the manager!' I demanded.

'Leave it, Leaf,' Sally's voice was soothing. 'You got the right money in the end.'

'Yeah, come on, man, we don't want to waste our time arguing in sweaty offices.'

In stark contrast to Indians, who freely express their views on any subject, the Sri Lankans were afraid to talk about anything to do with the government.

The only political conversation we had was with a teacher in the botanical gardens in Colombo. Although we were sitting in the middle of a large lawn and there wasn't anyone within earshot, he kept looking around nervously. 'Democracy is dead, my friends,' he uttered in a depressed tone. 'There have been some killings and disappearances. The opposition is intimidated and there's about to be a war with the Tamil separatists: Civil War. God help us all. I must go now. If I'm seen talking with you I'll be in trouble.'

Colombo was hot, sticky and oppressive. The army was out on the streets. Squads of armed young men in uniform guarded every major street intersection.

'They look like children,' Sally commented.

They were stinking, drenched in adrenalin, looking around nervously, with itchy fingers on slippery triggers.

'They're armed and frightened,' I told her. 'That's a terrible combination. We should get out of here as soon as we can.'

We left first thing the following morning. Heading south, we took a bus down the coast to the small town of Unawatuna, where we booked into a beachside restaurant with a handful of palm-frond chalets.

The owner was a large man in a *lungi,* with a vast stomach and an insincere smile. Great tufts of black hair sprouted from his nostrils.

'Help yourself to whatever you want from the fridge, we'll settle up when you leave,' he said.

Swimming in the ocean, looking in the rock pools at the rich marine life and watching the woodcarvers at work was fine, but after three days we'd had enough lazing around. We got up early, ready to head inland for the major festival that was coming up in Kandy.

Our sly host presented us with a huge bill.

'Hold on,' I looked him straight in the eye. 'You've charged us for five nights with dinners when we've only been here for three. And you've put us down for forty-two bottles of Coca cola.'

'None of us drink coke, ever.' Smiles stared with his bright blue eyes at the dishonest bar owner.

The fat man crossed the drinks off the bill, then started to dispute the number of nights we'd stayed.

I cut him off, saying 'We'll pay what we owe, but if you want to argue, I'll call the police.'

I've never called the police and don't suppose I ever will, but my bluff worked.

We left for Kandy, in the mountains, for the festival of the Buddha's Tooth. The city was packed, half of Asia seemed to be in town. The first resthouse we tried was full, so was the second and the next.

'We should have come earlier.'

'But Smiles, we didn't know it was going to be such a big deal.'

'Well, we're here now,' Sally said. 'I think we should take the first place with a room.'

Eventually we found a house that had a spare room. It was a utility room, not a bedroom, but we couldn't drag our luggage any further, so we took it and slept on the floor.

On the great day, when forty-nine elephants paraded the holy relic around the town centre, we were upstairs, trapped in a restaurant, unable to leave because the streets were solid with people.

'I'm not bothered that we're stuck on the first floor,' I said. 'We've got food and drink, a toilet if we need it and we couldn't have had a better view of the elephants' parade. This is a day to remember!' Smiles clinked his glass with Sally's and then with mine. 'Here's to the elephants. May they live a long and happy life.'

Towards the end of the festival, two bright sparks had the idea of following close behind the truck that trundled along after the last elephant. All the animals had defecated at around the same place, below our window. The undercarriage of the lorry spread their waste into a sheet, around a foot thick.

The unsighted guys jogging along immediately behind the vehicle weren't able to stop themselves in time. They ran straight into the shit, skidded, lost their balance and, to the huge amusement of the watching spectators, toppled into the muck.

As soon as the show was over, tens of thousands of visitors poured out of Kandy like water from a colander. We trickled along in their wake.

In the morning, over breakfast, Smiles said 'We've had enough of this so-called tropical paradise. It stinks at so many levels. Sally and I are going back to India, where people are at least free to say whatever they think and don't just see you in terms of the money they can screw out of you.'

I know what you mean, but while I'm here I want to have a look at the East Coast. I've heard some great things about it. Anyway, you need some space on your own, I guess, and maybe I do too.'

Travelling as a threesome wasn't always easy and, in the tense atmosphere on the island, our tempers had grown a little frayed. We agreed a date to meet in Delhi and went our separate ways.

I boarded a bus bound for Trincomalee on the East Coast. The sinuous road wound through jungle-covered mountains and past beautiful waterfalls. When the driver had to brake sharply, to allow a troop of monkeys to cross in front of us, I spotted the rusty wreck of a bus, almost entirely swallowed by vines and vegetation. Suddenly we drove into a snowstorm of white butterflies.

'Close the windows!' the people at the front screamed. 'Close the windows!'

We failed to shut them in time. The bus filled with thousands of butterflies. They were everywhere, on my arms, legs, lips and glasses... The poor creatures were flapping in my hair and clinging to my ears.

Unable to see his way out of the white cloud, the driver panicked and turned on the windscreen wipers, smearing hundreds of bodies in an arc of yellow pus. We blindly inched forward and finally emerged from the living storm. The conductor stepped down and cleaned the windscreen. In deathly silence we continued the journey. Not a word was spoken: we were all in shock.

Among the last to leave the bus at Trincomalee,

as I got off, I turned to take a look inside. The interior was shrouded with winged corpses. What a sad contrast to the mystical night I'd had with the giant moths on Triund ridge in the far north of India. A huge feeling of depression settled on my soul: Sri Lanka was getting to me.

Trincomalee has one of the best deep-water harbours in the world. It was packed with warships and crawling with troops. The teacher had been right: war was coming.

I couldn't wait to get away and left alongside Kristina, a radiant Swiss traveller I'd met, who felt the same way I did. We stocked up on food and took a bus ride up the coast to the fishing village of Nilaveli.

We stayed for a week with a fisherman's family, sleeping on the sand in their hut. We shared the food we'd brought and they cooked for us. Each day we walked, swam and imagined we were on a desert island, hundreds of miles from the nearest humans

My time on the island was running out. Knowing Smiles and Sally would be expecting me in Delhi, I said goodbye to my new friends, caught the ferry back to India and endured the long train ride to the capital. There I met up with my travelling companions. It was time to return to Britain.

In the UK, I'd have to come to terms with a very different reality: Thatcher's hard-hearted world of market forces and Falklands task forces.

I carefully packed my fragments of coral and scraps of driftwood. 'I'll be back,' I promised any gods who may have been listening. 'I'll be back.'

12. GLASTONBURY PRETENDERS

Britain seemed a cold, unwelcoming place after the warmth of India. I wasn't pleased to be back in Blighty. The country had a leader who was excited by war and found the environment a humdrum issue. Bellicosity and ignorance of this order was really depressing. It wouldn't have been so bad had she been out on a limb, but her views were popular. I was the one who wasn't in touch with the mood of the times.

I don't enjoy being out of step, but sometimes you just have to be. I fell out with a few people about the direction the country was headed. La Thatcher was ace at polarising opinion. I might have sunk into a trough of cold cynicism, had I not accepted an invitation to visit Meg in Somerset.

We'd first seen each other when she and her daughter, Jess, travelled to Horfield Prison to visit Smiles. I'd also had a visit that day. Smiles had pointed me out to them and they'd waved to me. I saw them again in London on the weekend home-leave I was given shortly before my release.

'Come and visit us in Frome when they let you out,' Meg had said at the end of my home-leave, when I had to return my body to the prison.

Meg was tall, slim and self-effacing, one of those rare people who looks after everyone else and puts her own needs last of all. The centre of her life was her six-year-old daughter, Jess.

They made me welcome in their house in Somerset. I was happy to stay. It was April and buds were swelling and blossoming. So was my relationship with Meg. Ours wasn't a grand passion, love at first sight. It was more the coming together of two people who needed some rest and comfort after having been battered by the contrariness of life.

At first I made a point of not taking sides in the differences between mother and daughter, but inevitably the time came when I intervened in one of their disputes.

'Look, it's way past your bedtime Jess. You've been messing around for the last half hour. It really is time you went upstairs.'

'Yes, go on, darling,' Meg added. 'Do your teeth. I'll be up in a minute to read to you.'

'You can't tell me what to do!' Jess screamed at me. 'You're not my Dad!' She was furious and crying as she ran out of the living room and up the stairs.

Her words echoed in my head long after she was asleep. I kept on thinking about our situation. Being with Meg was great; the better I got to know her, the more I liked her. I realised I had to come to terms with my new position in their household.

I well remembered what it was like, having a stepmother. Now I appreciated the difficulty of being a step-parent. For the first time, I understood how tough it must have been for Katie, taking on two teenage boys and a girl of ten. But knowing the thanklessness of that role I was determined not to repeat the terrible mistakes Katie had made.

Although over twenty years had passed since our wicked stepmother had erupted into our lives, the boy I'd been still lived within me. I knew how it felt to live under a dictatorial regime, your own home an enemy-occupied zone. The last thing I wanted to do was to inflict anything like that on Jess; I already loved this delightful little redheaded scrap. She liked me too. She'd danced for me the first time I'd gone to their house: Jess lived for dancing.

Midsummer approached. Meg and I got our supplies in readiness for Glastonbury festival, just down the road. A couple of days before the music began, we drove to Worthy Farm with Meg's friend Ann and her daughter, Flora, and set up our campsite.

The next day people were pouring in by the thousands. This was going to be a big affair. I kept being reminded of my first massive festival: the Isle of Wight. The similarities were obvious. The differences, though less apparent, were salient.

The merchandising of hippy paraphernalia made the crowd appear more homogenous, but Glastonbury lacked the unity of spirit that had made the Isle of Wight festival – a gathering of half a million people – seem like a people's parliament, an assembly for determining the future course of events. Those times were past. Our revolution had petered out. For most of the current generation of festival-goers, Glastonbury was an opportunity for a long weekend of sex, drugs and rock 'n roll. Then back to work

Drugs of all types were on sale. I was sitting around a campfire with my old cellmate Eric and Louise, his wife, when a guy came up offering hash for sale.

'You must have heard of Operation Julie' he said. 'I was a big man in the acid gang. I knew Henry Kemp and Richard Todd and all the top people.' Eric and I looked at each other quizzically.

'I thought Richard Todd was an actor,' I said to

Eric. Simultaneously we burst out laughing.

'What's so funny?' The dealer was indignant.

Neither of us deigned to reply to the lying git, but Smiles' ex, Mary, was with us. She didn't let the pretender off so easily. 'You're talking to the wrong men. You might convince a lot of people, but these guys…' she pointed at Eric and me, 'really were bust in Operation Julie.' After a beat she added 'And you weren't.'

The imposter, his disguise stripped from him in a flash, slunk naked into the night.

Extraordinarily, the next day we met another fantasist who also asserted he'd been part of the Julie Mob… Who were these sad pretenders who'd want to claim membership of our burnt-out shooting star?

Meg, Jessie and I hadn't gone to Glastonbury just for fun and music, we were trying to earn a crust, doing breakfasts. The sign at the entrance to our encampment read:

£1 BREAKFAST
Fried egg sandwich
Real coffee

The smell of freshly made coffee drew more custom than we could easily handle. The line of people waiting to eat never seemed to diminish. We worked flat out until midday – buttering brown bread, frying eight eggs at a time in two large saucepans and making endless pots of coffee. We thought we'd brought enough for the weekend, but we ran out of supplies after a few hours. I spent a good deal of time getting out of the festival grounds, buying huge amounts of bread, eggs and coffee in

Glastonbury and getting back into the site.

We only worked in the mornings. The rest of the time was ours to do what we liked. As the sun sank down towards the horizon on the second day, we ate some festival food, listened to a band then sat around a fire with Eric and Louise, smoking and joking with friends and passers-by. The evening was carried off by the night and we got to bed somewhere around three.

At seven in the morning, I staggered out of our tent, half asleep, bursting for a pee. A queue of thirty-odd dishevelled people stood waiting for their egg sandwich and coffee. They all stared hungrily at me.

'I'll be right back,' I promised, and hurried off to splash water on my face and have a quick slash.

Smiles, Sally and I had made plans to return to India in the autumn. Meg and Jess would be joining us. The winter holiday was going to take another chunk of the money I had left from the sale of my house, but I tried not to think about that too much.

I really wanted to have another crack at crossing the 14,160 feet Indrahar pass and reaching Chamba, so I suggested that I go ahead on my own. They could follow several weeks later. There was no way either of them would have made it over the mountains. Meg didn't really like my plan but reluctantly agreed. I'd have a few weeks in the Himalayas then travel down to Bombay to meet their plane. Together we'd take a boat ride down to Goa for a lengthy beach holiday.

Before a long journey I always experience a mixture of elation and apprehension. I was excited by the prospect of returning to the mountains but not

114

looking forward to the flight to Delhi. My first jaunt in a plane to the Isle of Man had been a thrilling affair, but flying had stopped being fun long ago. Reminding myself that I'd never let my fears prevent me from doing what I wanted to do, I sat down with Meg to work out our departure dates. I bought my ticket to Delhi and theirs to Bombay.

My packed rucksack was standing by the front door.

'I'll see you in Mumbai,' I said to my girls. 'We must try to remember to call it that.' I gave them both a hug and added 'I'll be waiting for you at the airport. I'll ring you the day before your flight. See you in India!' Feeling excited, nervous and a bit of a rat, I set off on the next leg of my search for myself.

The flight to Delhi was uneventful – which is the best you can hope for in the air. I spent the night in a cheap hotel in the capital and the next day took the twelve-hour bus ride up to Dharamsala.

Lyn and Arthur had split up. Lyn was clearly suffering. She put on a brave face each morning, but every now and then the mask cracked and her anguish came pouring out. I did what I could to cheer her up, but it wasn't a lot: I couldn't do anything about her underlying grief. The only practical thing I could do was make her surroundings a bit less dismal by painting the walls of the little shack she was renting.

'You're better off without him,' I said as we sat eating dinner. 'Can't you see he was a control freak, always holding you back, preventing you from bursting into flower. You'll get over him. At first it seems like things won't ever improve – I've been there, I know – but you will get through it. And when you do, all your friends will be delighted to see the return of the wonderful woman we all know and love.'

'Thanks Leaf,' she said sadly, laying a hand on my shoulder. 'I know you mean well, but you don't know the half of it.'

'So tell me.'

She shook her head and whispered 'It's not found in words.'

'Let's go walking for a few days then. You need a change of air. I remember you telling me that troubles seem insignificant when you're standing on top of a mountain. Let's climb. I want to have another go at getting over the Indrahar pass. Come with me.'

'I'd only carry my problems with me and bring you down.'

'You'd never bring me down, Lyn.'

I tried a couple more times to get her to go climbing with me, but nothing I said could persuade her to leave the town. She wouldn't even join me on the short scoring trip I made to Kulu. This time, learning from my last journey there, I paid a Gaddi to carry my *charas* through the checkpoint. The police only searched the foreigners.

13. SLEEPING IN CAVES

In a *chai* shop in Dharamsala bazaar I fell into conversation with two young Australians, Peter and Rose. They were keen to go trekking in the mountains before winter closed the passes. They had a refreshing openness and a gleam in their eyes that made me think they'd be good company.

'Last year I went with a pair of friends,' I said. 'But we turned back just short of the Indrahar pass that leads to Chamba.'

'Chamba is where we were thinking of going. Our aim is to get to the temples at Brahmaur.'

'I've got a map that shows a couple of caves you can sleep in for the first two nights,' I volunteered. 'It's only a rough hand-drawn thing, but I know for a fact that it's right about the first cave. I tell you what, I thought I'd be going back up there with my pals, but they've split up and both are busy trying to reorganise their lives. Maybe I could come with you.'

'Hey!' Peter exclaimed, glancing at Rose, 'I was just about to ask if you wanted to.' He turned to his lady.

She nodded. 'It'd be great if you came with us,' she said.

We spent the next few days walking on the slopes above Macleod Ganj, getting used to the altitude as well as finding out more about each other. Peter and Rose were straightforward people who said what they thought. I liked them from the start. In their twenties and fit, I reckoned they wouldn't have any trouble getting over the Indrahar Pass.

On the chosen day, the three of us headed off into the mountains. Lyn had told me about Brahmaur with its thirty-odd temples and its proximity to Mount Kailash, the home of Shiva. The idea of walking there really appealed to me.

We hiked to Triund and spent the night on the ridge. The next day we crossed to the Dhauladhar range and began to climb. Our second night was in the cave I'd slept in the year before, above the snow line at around twelve or thirteen thousand feet. In the morning, we set off towards the Indrahar pass. The air was thin and the going was hard, but after three hours of slow progress, with lots of stops for breath, we were joined by a local, a young *Gaddi* named Mahmud, on his way to his village. He reduced his pace to ours so we could walk together. He knew the way, which was a big help. Two more hours of hard slog saw us exhausted but triumphant at the top of the fourteen thousand foot pass.

The Indrahar pass, 14,160ft. I'm on the left, Rose in the middle, Mahmud on the right. Photo by Peter

Getting to the top of the pass gave us the most wonderful feeling of achievement.

'Whoopee!' Peter yelled at the top of his voice. Rose and I joined in. We were higher than kites, literally. We could see the big birds circling way below us.

'The view is stunning in every direction.' Peter spoke in a little above a whisper. We took photographs of each other, of the Kangra valley, where we'd been and the High Himalaya, where we were headed. We each put a stone on the cairn that marked the low point of the pass.

'We should eat something, keep our energy levels up.' I passed around a bag of peanuts and raisins. We chewed and gazed in awe at the amazing world that lay all around us.

The strong wind made it too cold to hang about, so we took the first steps of the descent into Chamba. Having seen us to the top, our companion, Mahmud, carried on and soon left us far behind, but not before he'd given us an invitation to stay with him and his mother when we reached their village.

Crossing the pass gave me a real sense of achievement. My expectations of life had been eroded by imprisonment, but getting over the Indrahar pass gave me such a lift. I'd had some low moments when I feared my active life was over, but I now knew I wasn't finished yet, far from it.

I inhaled the icy air and felt myself expand. What I do with my life is in my own hands, I realised.

In the late afternoon, we found the second cave on my hand-drawn map. I lit a fire with the sticks I'd been carrying and brewed up. The tea gave us an energy boost.

After we'd eaten, we crawled into our sleeping bags.

'What a day, hey!' Peter was on a high. 'I wasn't sure we were going to make it, until Mahmud turned up. That was a piece of luck.'

'Ow! I've just been bitten.' Rose exclaimed.

'So have I.' The more I wriggled, the more I got bitten.

We didn't get much sleep; the cave was full of fleas. They kept us scratching and swearing through the long hours of darkness.

We were now hiking in the wild mountains, in an area of self-governing valleys where the people lived without vehicles, roads, money, shops or police.

Mahmud was there to greet us when we arrived at his village.

'First I will take you to my mother's house,' he said. 'Then you can meet the other families in the village.'

'You speak good English, Mahmud. Where did you learn?' I asked.

'In Macleod Ganj. It's important for someone in the village to speak English and I was chosen. I wanted to learn so I could help our people.'

Mahmud's mother was short. She had a serene face and a warm smile. A little girl clung to her skirt and looked at us with wide staring eyes. Rose bent down to say hello to the tot. She hid behind her grandmother but kept peeking out to look at the strange foreigners. We dropped our backpacks in Mahmud's entrance, then went around the other houses so Mahmud could introduce us to all the villagers; everyone greeted us warmly.

Two years had passed since the last outsiders had turned up, Mahmud told us. The pair of young German hikers had stayed a night and continued on their journey, but the people in the next valley knew nothing about them. They disappeared without trace.

'It's lovely here in late autumn,' Rose commented. 'But what's it like in winter?'

'Winter is very hard,' Mahmud replied. 'The snow can be ten to twelve feet. Sometimes hungry bears come into the village looking for food. If they get into the snow tunnels we make between the houses, we shoot them with our long muskets.'

The small village temple, a Shiva shrine with a palpable savage power, was adorned with tridents, each strung with bear's claws and teeth. The temple looked as though it hadn't changed since medieval times.

'The wood and stone houses are so beautiful and so sturdy!' Rose turned to me. 'I don't know why, but I thought they'd be living in huts or something.'

'This is where we thresh our grains,' Mahmud said, pointing to the large slate-flagged courtyard. 'Mountain springs give us clean water. We have apple orchards and grow lentils, beans and vegetables. The children collect honey. Our flocks of sheep and goats supply us with food, drink, clothing and some money. In the autumn we make apple wine to drink in the winter, when we mostly stay inside and smoke the plants given to us by Lord Shiva.'

The major excitement during our visit was an upcoming wedding. Though the big day was three months off, the women gathered each evening to make plans and talk while they prepared the bride's trousseau. Their singing and ululations could be

121

heard from afar. The tangible air of expectation in the village took me right back to the precious days of Christmas as a child with magic in the air.

We ate with our young friend's family. At the end of dinner, I gave Mahmud's little sister a bar of chocolate. She'd never had one before. She spent that evening just savouring the smell of it.

Exhausted, overwhelmed with impressions of the day, I went to bed, wrote a few lines in my diary, blew out the candle and fell fast asleep.

In the morning, Rose joined the gathering by the stream, where the women washed clothes and nattered. Peter and I sat with Mahmud and the men, grouped around the blacksmith on a hillock, forty yards away.

The blacksmith's anvil was a three-inch square chunk of steel, embedded in a great block of wood. His charcoal-streaked assistant squatted by the fire. Dressed entirely in stinking goatskins, working bellows also made from goatskins, he was a figure from pre-history.

'Some of these men are from outlying farms and villages,' Mahmud told us. 'A few of them have walked for a day or even two to get their axes and mattocks fixed.'

The men sat around the smith, smoking *charas* and drinking *chai*. For the most part they talked amongst themselves, but at times banter flew back and forth between the men at the fire and the women by the stream. The young children ran around by their mothers, playing a game of tag with a goatskin ball. Their laughter rang on and on in the clear mountain air.

On the evening of the second day in the village, the little sister carefully opened the bar of chocolate. She took out one square to eat and put the rest away.

I thought of all the waste and extravagance of the rich western world and compared it with the frugality of our hosts.

'Are we more contented than these mountain people, do you think,' I asked my Aussie friends.

'No,' Peter replied. 'Not at all. It's just the opposite. We're drowning in our abundance, clutching at straws that might make our stressed-out lives a little more meaningful.'

Had it not been for the rendezvous I'd made with Meg and Jess, I would happily have stayed on with our hosts and maybe never left. But the new factors in my life meant that I could no longer think only about myself. I had to consider my girls.

After three nights, we left these hospitable people in their isolated valley, crossed another watershed and started to descend. Clouds covered the sun. Around noon it began to spit, soon it was drizzling, then raining, pouring, pelting and finally bucketing. We plodded on for the rest of the day, squelching through the liquid world. When we arrived at the next village we were soaked to the skin and so cold that shivers were wracking our bodies.

Spotting a small group of *saddhus* sheltering on a porch, sharing a *chillum*, I went over and said hello. The cone was passed to me. It warmed my cupped hands. I touched it to my forehead, cried *'Bom Shankar!'* inhaled, and passed the *chillum* on.

I put my hands together, turned them sideways and laid my face on them to mime sleep. An old *saddhu*, with infinitely wise eyes and grey-white hair that cascaded to his waist, called over one of the kids who were hanging around goggling at the *feringees*: the foreigners.

The youngster was back in a moment, with a smiling young man who greeted us and said, 'I am the miller. Please come with me. You will be our honoured guests.'

The young miller and his even younger wife took our sodden garments from us and draped us in blankets. The miller's wife sat us in front of a roaring fire and put our clothes on a line to dry. Then she began cooking. Over three hours she fed us six or seven tiny courses of spicy vegetable dishes. Each delicacy came with hot *chapattis* and each time the *chapattis* were made with a different freshly milled flour.

'What an amazing meal!' Peter exclaimed. 'I've never had anything quite like it.'

The miller and his wife were such a sweet couple and so much in love they touched each other tenderly whenever they thought we weren't looking.

'You will sleep in our bed tonight,' the miller stated firmly.

'What? No, no!' I protested. 'The floor will be fine. We've been sleeping in caves.'

The miller's wife made an imploring speech.

'My wife is saying you must have our bed, and I agree. I insist,' he added, with tears springing into his eyes. To refuse would have been to belittle their generosity.

We thanked them and squeezed into their bed. They slept on the floor.

In the sunny morning, after a breakfast of freshly

made spicy *chapattis,* we hoisted our packs onto our backs and began the next leg of our trek. After a couple of hours we stopped for a break.

'Check this out, guys!' Rose exclaimed showing us the bag the miller's wife had pressed on us. It was packed with hardboiled eggs, crisp apples and *chapattis,* stuffed with mixed vegetables. 'What lovely people!'

Tramping up the slate road into the temple town of Brahmaur, we came on a teenager in T-shirt and shorts standing under a stream of icy water.

Two men stood in the dry, holding fistfuls of notes, betting on how long the youngster would be able to stand it. The lad's body was juddering and his brown skin was developing a blue tinge.

'Let him stop,' I called to the man urging the youngster on.

'No,' he replied. 'It is a discipline he practices. He can stand some minutes more.'

Brahmaur, with its thirty-odd temples, is close to the foot of Mount Kailash, a holy peak sacred to four religions: Buddhism, Hinduism, Jainism and Bon, the pre-Buddhist religion of Tibet. In Hindu mythology, Shiva's home is on Kailash. That was where Rose and Peter were heading.

The small town is a place of pilgrimage. The most extraordinary buildings dated from the ninth century. Shaped rather like the Cucumber, but made of ribbed stone and sporting a straw hat with a bobble on, the temples had a weathered yet jaunty look. They'd been there for well over a thousand years. They'd seen it all and were still grinning.

Ninth Century temples at Brahmaur

At the parting of our ways, I hugged my travelling friends and said goodbye with genuine regret. Peter and Rose had been great companions on the road, never complaining, always cheerful, even when cold, fleabitten and soaked to the skin.

I would've loved to go on with them to Mount Kailash, but it was time for me to head south to meet my girls. I shouldered my rucksack and started walking towards Chamba, my first stop *en route* to Mumbai, a thousand miles away.

The four-day journey, gave me time on my own, precious time to reflect between lifts. I was a stranger to the friendly people who stopped to pick me up. They talked, smoked and offered me food. My lifts took me any distance between two and two hundred miles and gave me the feeling that anything was possible.

14. PELTED BY MONKEYS

Jess couldn't get over the moustache that had sprouted under my nose. I was dismayed by the loss of her long red hair, cropped for the tropics. In the packed rugby scrum of Mumbai's airport lounge the three of us tried to adjust to the changes that six weeks apart had made.

'Come on, then,' I said after a while. 'Let's get a taxi into town. We've got a cabin reservation on the boat to Goa in a couple of days. I couldn't get one earlier, so I've booked us into a hotel.'

Our cab faltered on leaving the airport, then picked up speed and raced along for a while until a series of agonised metallic squeals from under the bonnet signalled its demise. The moment we came to a halt, the flow of air ceased. The heat was a hammer, raining relentless blows on us. Leaving the baking taxi, we stepped into a stinking outdoor furnace. We were in the city dump. A vast sea of suppurating rubbish stretched to the horizon in every direction. Thin children and skeletal adults were picking over the garbage. Meg looked at me questioningly. I knew what she was thinking. After all I'd told them about the magic of the East...

Luckily we didn't have to wait long in the stench. I flagged down another cab and soon had my girls under a fan in our hotel room. We took it in turns to shower and change into fresh lightweight clothes.

Jess fascinated the Indians: a seven-year-old stick insect with a carrot top and a face that refused to tan.

Everywhere we went in Mumbai, people wanted to sit her on cushions and feed her cold drinks and sticky sweets while they drank in her most un-Indian features.

'What is the matter with his face?' Meg kept being asked.

'Nothing. They're just freckles.'

'Why do they think I'm a boy?' Jess was indignant.

'It's because you've got short hair, darling.'

'That's right, Jess. Indian girls have long hair.'

The ferry to Goa took around twenty-four hours. We'd gone on board and were just settling into our cabin when there was a knock on the door. I opened it and was confronted by a long-haired, overweight white man.

'Hi, the name's Willy. We're neighbours for the journey so I thought I'd come and say hello.' He sounded American.

We shook hands.

'What brings you to this part of the world, Willy?'

'I love it. I've been coming here for years. I'm a ship's cook. I work seven days a week for seven months, then I get five months off, I spend my holidays relaxing on the beach in Goa.'

'Do you like chocolate?' He asked Jess.

'Mmm,' she nodded enthusiastically.

'Good. Then come with me.'

We squeezed into his cabin. Two huge suitcases took up most of the space.

'Apart from chocolate, what do you reckon is in the trunks?'

'Clothes?' Meg ventured.

'Nope.'

'Medicines?'

He dismissed my suggestion with a wave of his hand. Willy couldn't wait for any more guesses. He opened the cases. They were packed with food. 'Help yourself to the chocolate, eat as much as you like. I expect you think I'm nuts, bringing my own food along. But apart from the chocolate, which won't last long in this heat, the rest is all herbs, spices and the bases for the sauces that I make. I buy all the fresh ingredients in the market and, with my essences, I can recreate the cuisine of just about anywhere in the world.'

Whistles and the sound of the ship's siren signalled our departure from port. 'Got any dope with you?' Willy asked, once we were under way.

'Sure,' I replied.

'Make us a strong one, could you? Then we'll get the munchies and be able to eat this chocolate before it all melts.'

Andy and Sally, good friends from the Sixties who lived near Glastonbury, arrived in Goa soon after us. We'd been expecting them, having spent much of the summer hanging out together. Andy was lean and carefree, his habitual expression a sunny smile. Sally was short and sweet. She did the worrying for both of them.

We took things easy for a couple of weeks in the little village of Benaulim, while my girls weighed up their new surroundings. Although unlike anything they were used to, Goa was much more familiar than any other part of the country would have been. A Portuguese possession for over four centuries, the enclave had only been part of India for twenty-one years. It was a tolerant, place. People were mostly Catholic in the towns and villages of the coastal plain. In the hills they were Hindu.

The beaches of Goa were home to a sizeable winter population of freaks and resting travellers. You could have fish and chips and banana fritters in a beach restaurant and finish your meal with a Kingfisher beer and a *chillum*.

Unusually for India, the Goan beaches were clean. We frolicked in the water, played on the sand or hung out in beach bars.

'Mum!' Jess ran up to us excitedly. 'I've got a new friend! He's English and his name is Joe. He's got freckles, just like me! Please can we play in the water?'

'Of course you can, darling, but don't go too far out. I'll be keeping an eye on you.'

Jess and Joe played together on the beach, looking for shells, making sand castles then knocking them over. They were having a lovely time in the warm waters of the Arabian sea.

At Anjuna flea market we met up with Lyn and Arthur. They hadn't got back together, but had agreed to spend Christmas in Goa, as they'd done for several years. Lyn seemed in good heart and high spirits. She'd been a party girl before taking up Buddhism. At heart she still was. With plenty of old friends in the northern resorts, Lyn sparkled in the great social mix that was Goa in winter.

In the New Year, we took some hair-raising motorcycle taxi rides to the markets on the northern beaches and we did some exploring inland. 'Shall we go to Bondla Wildlife sanctuary,' I asked.

'Have they got monkeys?' Jess wanted to know.

'Yes, I think so.'

'Goody! Can we go, Mum?'

'Yes, if you like we can have a look.'

The wildlife sanctuary turned out to be little more than a small zoo. The monkeys were the only sizeable creatures on show. They were listless and looked sad. It was very depressing.

'I don't want to go to any more zoos,' I heard Jess say.

'Hey, come and look at this!' I called the girls over. We couldn't help laughing at a big sign that proclaimed:

BONDLA WILDLIFE SANCTUARY
NO INDECENT BEHAVIOUR IN
FRONT OF THE ANIMALS.

We were in the Bar Pedro, full of lunch. I was nursing a kingfisher beer and staring at the breaking waves. 'Are you up for some exploring?' Andy asked me.

'Definitely. You can only laze on a beach for so long then it gets boring.'

'Good', Sally chipped in. 'It's time for a change of scene. Have you found out about the bikes yet Andy?'

'Yes, I've bought one and borrowed another. You can hire them from the shop next to Sad Guru.'

'That's a strange name,' said Meg.

'Sad Guru is the barber,' I told her. When we leave, I think I'll stop shaving and grow a beard.'

'Don't,' Meg said. 'It'll make you look older.'

We went shopping in Margao, the nearest sizeable town, and stocked up on the things we'd need for a few weeks off the beaten track. We'd heard tantalising tales of remote beaches in the south of Goa that hadn't been overrun by Westerners.

I hired two more bikes. With Jess perched on the back of mine, the five of us set off southward down the long straight beach, cycling on the firm sand by the water's edge. After ten miles, we came to the mouth of the Betul River and negotiated with a boatman to ferry us across the turquoise water.

With the five of us, and all our gear on board, the small motorboat was overladen. Andy and I were busy using large rusty cans to bail out the water that kept slopping into the bilges.

'Keep baling,' Andy urged when I paused for a rest. 'We don't want to capsize and lose our gear!'

On a headland on the far side of the river, we found a place to camp for the night. We collected some brushwood, lit a fire, made supper and ate as the sun went down.

Soon after dark we saw the lights of a small fishing fleet, coming in from the sea. The boats slowly beat their way upstream, engines straining to make headway against the strong river current. Andy enlivened their passage by letting off a few fireworks. The fishermen cheered, whistled and shouted. Andy had lit up their evening.

We were woken at dawn by a fearful racket. A troop of furious monkeys were screaming with rage and pelting our camp with coconut husks and cashew fruit.

'We must be in their territory.' Sally squealed as

a cashew fruit whizzed past her head. 'We should move on. For goodness sake Andy, stop winding them up!'

He was lobbing fruit and husks back at the monkeys.

'Come on, Andy. I'm leaving!'

The sun was in a hurry. It soared into the sky and glared down at us. Our progress was slow and sweaty. Carrying the cycles for much of the way, we inched round the jungly headland. In the fiery afternoon, scratched to pieces, dog-tired, insect-bitten and hungry, we blundered into a perfect bay.

Andy in the cave on Zurim Beach

Zurim beach was about a quarter of a mile long, bounded by two rocky headlands and backed by cliffs. Coconut palms leant over the white sand. The stream that bubbled out of the coconut grove and onto the beach ended in a little freshwater lake that soaked into the sand, a few yards short of the Arabian sea.

The first night we all squeezed together into a

small cave. The following day, at the north end of the beach, I strung rope between coconut palms to make a frame and wove in palm fronds for the walls and roof of a little shelter. Andy and Sally put together a similar structure two hundred yards away. Our shelters were very simple. Their function was just to keep off the morning dew.

The only other people on the beach were a pair of Goan families, who lived in a two huts by a stream at the south end of Zurim.

'Look what I've got,' Andy said, returning from a walk with something hidden behind his back.

'What is it?' Meg asked.

'A present from our new neighbours.' Andy produced a bottle with a flourish. 'Moonshine *feni*.'

'Is that a good idea, Andy?' Sally was disapproving. 'You know full well that whole villages have gone blind after drinking homemade *feni* at a wedding.'

'I'll take my chances.' Andy laughed off his wife's concern. 'Our neighbours have their own still. They make the *feni* and drink it. They seem fine.'

'What's *feni*,' Meg asked.

'It's a spirit,' I told her, 'distilled from the sap of the coconut palms or from cashew fruit. Do you want to try some?'

'Are you going to?'

'Sure. I'll have a swig… after Andy.'

Life was simple on the beach. Shrugging off the complications of civilisation, we wore next to nothing – a thong or a *lungi* – and went barefoot. The birds and the growing light woke us at dawn. We rose and swam before a breakfast of tea and porridge. The only things we needed to do were fetch water from the stream and collect enough wood to cook our food.

Each day one of us scoured the cooking pots with sand and ashes. Someone else shook out the *lungis* and mats. The rest of the time we were free to do whatever we wanted. We mostly beach-combed and played in the water. I regretted not having a brought a Frisbee with me, but the curve of the bay made waves which were perfect for bodysurfing. We surfed until exhausted, four or five times a day.

In the heat of the afternoon, we lolled in the water or lay in our hammocks under the coconut trees and chatted or dozed. Jess wrote up her diary. The days were blending into each other. Soon I lost track of time.

In the late afternoon it was time to light a fire. In the evenings we smoked a *chillum* and watched the sun plunge into the Arabian Sea. We ate our rice, vegetables and *dhal* whilst the sunset glowed and faded, then we'd stroll down to the sea for our evening's entertainment. We swam in the warm black soup and slapped the surface of the sea to make the phosphorescent sparkles in the water that echoed the stars above and prefigured Andy's nightly display.

While the rest of us had brought food, cooking pots and practical things like rope, candles and matches, Andy had filled his rucksack with fireworks. He gave us a small show each evening, spraying the night with baby rockets, golden rain, Bengal lights, roman candles and Catherine wheels.

Once a week Andy and I lugged our bicycles up the cliff to the road and cycled for a very pleasant hour through banana plantations and cashew forests to the nearest food shop.

'This is about the closest we can come to paradise.'

'Yes, it doesn't get much better than this, does it. Aren't we lucky.'

'It's not entirely luck, Leaf, as you know full well.'

At the shop we stocked up on vegetables, rice, lentils, lemons, tea, sugar, biscuits and cigarettes. The fruit and veg would go in our *jholas*. The other purchases were poured into paper cones – sheets torn from a child's schoolbook, rolled into shape and bound with cotton thread.

Back at our camp, we hung the provisions in bags strung from ropes stretched between coconut palms – our attempt to keep our supplies out of the reach of the large red ants that continually quartered the grove, looking for food.

Our kitchen was at the base of the cliff, under a great lump of rock five metres high. I lit a fire one afternoon and put a pan of water on to boil. I was squatting down to add more wood when something soft and heavy landed on my head and slid onto my shoulder. A large black snake slithered down my arm and wriggled away into an area of scrub and broken rocks.

'Oh my God!' I ran out of the grove and onto the beach, gibbering with fright and shock.

'What's up?' Sally called out to me. 'Are you OK?'

'A snake. A great big fucking snake just landed on my head!'

'You're not bitten or anything, are you?'

'No, thank God.'

'I expect the smoke you made disturbed it and made it fall. It was probably as frightened as you.'

That night my dreams were full of serpents in Paradise.

On the day of the Spring equinox full moon, I took a trip, my first for some time. I thought it would be interesting to look back over the whole experience of the heady hippy decade, the prison years and what had been happening in the eighteen months since my release – I decided to view it from the perspective of acidland.

LSD is unpredictable stuff. Instead of thinking about the past, I found myself irredeemably in the present, perched on a rock, totally focussed on the waves of the Arabian Sea, each one essentially the same as the one before but different in some subtle aspect of foam, spray, spread, colour or character. Even waves have character on acid.

The tide of a thousand hissing advances and sucking, dragging retreats continued through the day. Finally, under my fascinated gaze, great chopping waves began taking bites out of the sand. The beach was being eaten foot by foot. The water reached our shelter and the waves munched the sand in front of it. Watching the ocean methodically remove the beach was an awe-inspiring demonstration of the power of water. Rapt, I gazed as our home for the past month sagged and leant before dramatically collapsing.

I became aware of Meg, screaming in my ear, trying to be heard above the sound of the sea.

'Leaf! Our passports!'

Fuck! Our kind neighbours had told us in mime that the Spring high tide would remove the beach that night. We'd stashed our few possessions on a ledge halfway up the track to the cliff-top. But I'd forgotten to retrieve the bag that held our passports and traveller's cheques. They were buried in a cloth bag, under a foot of sand, in the place where we slept.

'Idiot, fool!' Cursing my erratic memory, I jumped down to the wreckage of our beach shelter and scrabbled under the spot where I thought our pillows had been. I found the passport bag just before another breaker smacked against my legs and removed a foot of sand from beneath my feet.

That trip reminded me of my long journey of exploration with acid and all the joy and trouble it had brought me. What an adventure it had been though: a well-meant attempt to bring the people of the world to a higher level of consciousness.

I'd resolved, during my final days in prison, to write my memoirs. I decided to make a start, to get it all down before I forgot or muddled the details. I thought it was a story that needed to be told. At the same time, I hoped that putting it all down on paper might help me get some kind of perspective on my life. Who knows, it might even make a writer out of me and finally justify the empty boast in my passport that had so worried the Sri Lankan officials.

After a wonderful month on Zurim beach, we returned to Benaulim. Each morning after breakfast at Pedro's Bar, Jess and I would go to our beach hut and write. She was keeping a diary of her Indian winter. I was filling notebooks with the strange and extraordinary stories of the acid years.

Jess had changed a lot in our four months in

India. At the start of the holiday she'd been a frail and delicate child. By the end of our time here, she'd become almost sturdy. Running and playing in the sand, with her friend Joe, had built up her strength. She'd learnt how to swim and ride a bike. She knew how to split a coconut, tie a *lungi* three different ways and do a number of things unknown to the Somerset primary school to which she now had to return.

It had been costing us next to nothing to stay in India. Back in Frome, even though we lived simply, my money was going at an alarming rate.

At Glastonbury festival that summer, we sold the earrings and pendants we'd made from Shiva's eyes, the shells we'd collected on the beach in Goa. It kept us for a few weeks, but it wasn't enough.

Life with my girls was a different proposition to being an itinerant loner. I loved the warm feeling of being in a family with Meg and Jess and their dog, Savage. I thrived in their happy home. The India trip had cemented our relationship, but what were we going to do next?

Quite by chance, I ran into the old friend who'd taught me the painting trade in Reading, in the seventies. 'Stuart! Great to see you! What are you doing in Frome?'

'Working, same as ever. We live near here now.'

'How's the family?'

'Lorraine's fine. The boys are growing fast. What about you?'

'We're not long back from India. England's expensive. My money's evaporating like water in a heatwave. Stu, I need to find some painting and decorating work. Got any suggestions?'

'You're in luck, Leaf. You always were a jammy bastard.'

'Not always.'

'Yes. True,' Stuart admitted. 'Anyway, this is your lucky day. I've got the contract to do a council estate and I'm already overworked. You can paint some of the houses if you like.'

'That's brilliant, Stuart. Thanks.'

Andy and Sally came back from India a few weeks after us. Andy was a painter too. As there was plenty of work, we all made good money for the rest of the summer. Then the weather turned.

Painters in Britain have a hard time of it during the long unforgiving winter. When there was no indoor work, I'd sit and write by the stove in the living room, trying to knock into shape the account of the acid years that I'd written in Goa.

But, try as I might, I couldn't find the right way to tell the story. I was still too close to my experiences to be able to get a handle on them.

I was writing other stuff too. occasionally I'd come up with something I thought was worth keeping. Politically, I was as disillusioned as I'd been since the swinging sixties gave way to the selfish seventies. Ecologically, I was angrier than ever about the way we were destroying our home, our beautiful planet.

THE ACCOUNT OF MAN

Kill the krill, cull the gulls, empty the teeming plain,
Snuff the choughs, stab the stags, spray herbicide
like rain.
Croak the frogs, waste the whales, go persecute the
hares,
Club the crabs, skewer the skuas, gas badgers in
their lairs.
Poleaxe the polecats, poison les poissons, batter the
butterflies,
Take out the tapirs, strangle the swallows, pollute the
land and sky.
Fell the forests, oil the oceans, make the earth
beneath you groan.
Hey! You with the soul, mow down that last mole…

Now man, you stand alone.

15. BARCELONA

In a book of Victorian games I picked up in a jumble sale, I found three intriguing puzzles and decided to make one of each. I tried them out on our friends and they went down well, so I decided to go into production in Meg's tiny garden shed.

I enjoyed making the puzzles but flogging them was another matter. It takes a born salesman or woman to persuade strangers to buy something they don't need: a puzzle is never a necessity.

We did well at Glastonbury Festival, where loads of people were looking for a small unusual present to take home, but selling to retailers was a hard slog.

For the month leading up to Christmas, we rented a street pitch in Bath. Hands tucked under our armpits, Meg and I stamped up and down by our little stall, trying to stay warm while we knocked out our puzzles to the present-buying public. A deep chill seeps into you when you spend all day on winter streets.

I was irresistibly reminded of my pavement drawing year with the Electric Eel, as we travelled southwards through France and Italy. However fast we travelled, the cold weather kept up with us.

I wondered where the Eel might be now. I hadn't seen him for years. The last time had been at the end of a festival, here in Bath. Someone had told me they'd clocked him at a gay encampment. I went over to see if I could find him.

The guy I asked said, 'Yeah, he's here somewhere.' He shook a recumbent form in a sleeping bag. A bleary Eel poked his head out.

'Wha'?'

'Great to see you, man,' I said, squatting down beside him and giving his shoulder a squeeze. 'How are you doing? It's been a long time.'

'Hey, Leaf. Too much!' He could hardly keep his eyes open.

'You OK? How are things?' I asked.

'Oh wow, man, I haven't slept, like, days... What are you doing here?' His eyes closed.

I tried a couple more times to get through to him then left him to rest. When I returned, a few hours later, the gay gang had struck camp and the Eel had gone with them.

Just thinking about those frozen months on the road with the Electric Eel was enough to make me feel I had to get away from the UK. Bloody winter – it was the bane of my life.

'Let's move to a warmer country,' I suggested with a heartfelt sigh. 'I'm fed up with living indoors for most of the year.'

'So am I,' Meg agreed.

We cleaned up in the panic buying of presents in the fortnight before Christmas, but in January we couldn't sell a thing. I was back at the beginning: all my travels in foreign countries had ended with me having to return to the UK to make money.

On a trip up to London, I called in to see Dave Tomory, a guy I'd first met in Dharamsala who'd become a good friend.

'Wherever I go, I always end up having to come back to bloody Blighty,' I moaned.

'So go for an EFL qualification.'

'A what?'

'EFL. It's a teaching qualification: English as a Foreign Language.'

'Forget it, Dave. I vowed I'd never be a teacher!'

'How old were you then? You were probably still at school.'

'I was, it's true.'

'Then maybe you should give it a go. I did the course and enjoyed it. It was good fun.'

'But you're not teaching…'

'Indeed.' Dave chuckled. 'The training was fine, but teaching didn't suit me. I got a job in Oxford, doing a summer course for a group of rowdy Italian adolescents. They didn't want to learn our language. The only thing they aimed to do was fuck English girls. I'm not judging them – I was like that at their age, but it was tedious trying to get them to focus in class, so I quit.'

'I don't blame you.'

'But Leaf, just because it didn't work for me doesn't mean it won't be right for you. If you're serious about getting away from the English winters, you should give it try.'

Desperate to move to a country where the winters weren't so long, bleak or cold, I let myself be persuaded and signed up for an International House EFL course in London.

I went home to Somerset at the weekends, but stayed with Dave during the week for the month-long intensive course. He was a brilliant host. Knowledgeable, amusing and an excellent cook, he made us a delicious dinner each evening.

Not having to feed myself gave me enough time after the classes to assimilate the ground we'd covered that day. The course was demanding and very stimulating. I was surprised to find I really enjoyed it. I worked hard at the lessons, learnt a lot, had a great time, passed the course and left with a basic qualification to teach English as a foreign language.

I was midway through my first intensive course for foreign students in Bath. My pupils were a dozen French adolescents and two Italians, fifteen to eighteen year olds, all abroad and intent on having fun. It was exhausting work, but once I promoted the chief troublemaker and put him in charge of making a news programme, he got all the others in line. We had a lot of fun and they picked up a fair amount of English. It was good preparation for the profession I was going to be practicing – if I could land a job.

One night, on my way to bed, the phone rang. I picked up the receiver.

'Leaf? Dave Tomory here. Listen, you'll need to brace yourself. I've got some very bad news: Lyn is dead.'

'Oh no! What happened, Dave?'

He took a deep breath. 'She went on a retreat involving a meditation on fire in Bodh Gaya. At the end of it she doused herself with petrol and lit her own funeral pyre.'

I was stunned, reeling. 'Thanks for letting me know, Dave. I can't talk any more right now. Another time.'

'Sure, I felt the same. I only found out yesterday.'

I hung up and stared into emptiness.

'Oh, Lyn!' I couldn't stop thinking about her. I kept wondering what more I might have done when she needed help. I cursed myself for having swanned off into the mountains when I should have kept her company. I should have seen through the bright mask she wore in Goa.

Why had she done it? Had she simply had enough

of life, or was she purifying herself through fire, to emerge like a phoenix from the ashes?

I can see her face in front of me to this day: it's burnt into my brain. I think of her whenever I light a fire and stare into the flames.

In the summer there were plenty of English teaching jobs being advertised in the educational supplements, most specified experienced teachers. I sent off dozens of job applications to language schools in Southern France, Spain, Portugal and Italy. I decided to accept any teaching post and stick it for a year, whatever it was like. After that I'd be a teacher with experience, able to pick and choose.

Responding to an advert in the Times Educational Supplement, I was called to a UK interview for a job in Spain.

Godfrey, the owner of the school I was hoping to join, was short and scruffy. 'How would you explain this to a first year student who knows no English?' He put a vase on the table and looked at me enquiringly.

'I'd draw a picture of a vase, say the word and mime pouring.' He set me a few more questions which weren't too difficult to answer. It was the first career interview I'd ever done and it went off very well. Within the opening minutes I knew I'd be offered a job. I was and I took it. The pay was poor, but Godfrey assured me that Spain was a cheap country to live in.

I told Meg and Jess the good news about the interview and said I'd go on my own to Spain in mid-September and, provided everything went well, they could follow after a month or so.

At the end of the second week of the intensive training course for new teachers in El Vendrell, Godfrey offered me the post of senior teacher at another of his four schools: the College Academy in Vilafranca del Pénedès. My pay would be the same as the rest of the staff, but I'd have fewer teaching hours. I accepted.

When I arrived in Vilafranca, after the end of the course, I learnt the previous term had ended in disaster. One of the teachers had died in a car crash, returning to Vilafranca from a late class on the coast.

In front of a knot of grieving teachers, Godfrey had snapped 'The stupid bitch! How am I going to get someone to cover her classes at this time of year?'

Disgusted by his callousness, the entire English staff had handed in their notice.

I was wondering uneasily what I'd let myself in for. I'd had an 'Introduction to Spanish' course at school and was frantically re-learning the little Spanish I'd once studied.

All the English members of my staff were new to Spain and new to the profession. I was the only one with any hands-on practice at all: my three weeks intensive course in Bath.

The school was in a complete muddle. There were no class materials for the teachers and no teachers' books for many of the courses. The Director of Studies – whose task it was to sort all this out – hadn't returned from Africa...

My job had fiasco written all over it.

The saving grace of the school was its remarkable secretary. Ana was a tiny ball of high energy from

Màlaga. She handled the parents and public with great flair, giving out information, enrolling students and keeping the entire administrative side together. Her steadying presence enabled the staff to concentrate on preparing their lesson plans.

The teachers rose to the challenge. They were a good bunch, all conscientious people. We'd developed a rapport through the fortnight's training, reinforced by the week we'd spent together in the large flat Godfrey had rented for us.

'OK.' I said at the beginning of the meeting I'd called. 'We know we're in a mess, but we've all done our EFL training, so I'm sure we can think of things to do with the classes until the rest of the books arrive. Ask me if you're short of ideas.'

Dominique, the jolly French teacher, stated confidently 'Now that the school fees are in, we'll be able to get the rest of the books'.

'How do you know that?' I asked.

'Ana told me. She also said that the school no longer has credit with the booksellers. We must pay cash for anything we want to buy. Ana has the money and the shopping list. Someone needs to go up to the bookshop in Barcelona to pick up what we need. I'll do it if you like.'

We all pulled together, pooling the knowledge we'd picked up on our training courses, sharing ideas and lesson plans and telling each other what had or hadn't worked well in class. For the first month virtually every moment of our waking lives was occupied with the job of keeping the courses going. When the rest of the teachers' books arrived, life became a little less hectic.

One by one we found our own flats in town, but

in those crucial first weeks we were in close support of one another. Gradually, steadily, we grew more confident about what we were doing.

In November, I rented a house in Sant Père Molanta, a village a couple of miles out of town. Meg let her house in Frome. She drove down with Jess at the end of the month, in a large estate car packed with their essentials.

In the Seventies, she and her husband, Mac, had run a ranch in Almeria for a couple of American millionaires who liked playing cowboys. Meg spoke reasonable Spanish and felt at home in the country.

Jess was a big hit in the little village school. The only foreigner, she quickly made friends and swiftly began picking up Castillian and Catalan.

One December evening, shortly before the start of the Christmas holidays, I asked my girls, 'Do we want to stay or return to the UK? We've been here for quite a few weeks so we should all have a good idea of where we'd rather be. I know what I'd prefer, but first I'd like to hear what you think.'

'Please can we stay?' Jess said immediately.

'Yes, I like it here,' soft-spoken Meg murmured. 'Let's not go back.'

'Good. We'll stay then.'

'Hooray!' Jess leapt to her feet and danced around the table, stopping to kiss her mum then me on her way past.

I knew this was a place where we could enjoy life, and that was even before my small group of students from Freixenet, the largest of Catalunya's *Cava* makers, presented me with a dozen bottles of their bubbly at the Christmas break. I used the

149

bottles of fizz to kick off the New Year's party I gave for the school's teachers.

We'd made a great start in Catalunya. After the initial problems, the school was running well, everyone was so friendly, the winters were sunny and Mediterranean beaches were only half an hour away. The list went on: Barcelona, one of the world's great cities, was just up the road, we'd made some good friends, the cost of living was low and property was cheap...In January we began to look for a place to buy.

'Moving here was such a good idea,' Meg said over our Christmas dinner. When Jess went to wash her hands, she continued. 'I hated it when some of the people in Frome started talking about your past and calling you a dirty drug dealer. This is your chance to put all that firmly behind you. Nobody here knows about your history and there's no reason why they should ever find out.'

16. CAL XAIU

Cal Xaiu was a derelict farmhouse a mile up a dirt track on the edge of the Pénedès valley. We first saw it on a cold, clear, February afternoon, floating in a sea of pink and white almond blossom. With the house came a couple of acres of terraces, a score or more almond trees and a wonderful view across the Pénedès valley to the fairy-tale mountain of Montserrat.

'What do you think?' Meg glanced at me. I could tell she liked the look of it.

'It's just what we're looking for,' I replied, 'but there's no way we can afford fourteen thousand pounds.'

'Let's have a word with Richard and Jane,' she suggested. 'Just the other day Jane was saying they're fed up with the all noise in town and they'd prefer a place in the country.'

'Even if they want to come in with us, I couldn't

manage seven thousand. Five max.'

'My mum might help out with two thousand. First we'll check it out with them. If they're interested I'll talk to her.'

Richard and Jane lived and taught in a town twenty kilometres away. I rang them to ask if they wanted to have a look at Cal Xaiu. We drove up there together at the weekend. They loved it too and offered to go halves on the farmhouse. As it split pretty well into two we agreed to become joint owners.

Richard was tall, straight-backed and curly-haired. He'd worked in the City until the craziness became too much. They'd moved to Catalunya so that their two daughters could grow up in a more relaxed environment. Richard's habitual expression tended to be on the worried side of neutral, but when he forgot his woes he had a very sweet smile.

'Shall we have a barbeque to celebrate?' Jane had large sparkly eyes. She was short, pretty, had a mass of curly black hair and a great laugh that bubbled up from somewhere deep in her stomach. I liked her immediately. Two or three weekends each month they'd come up with their lovely daughters, to picnic and party.

We moved into our side of Cal Xaiu in April. We were camping really, washing outside in a bowl and going to friends' flats in Vilafranca for showers. There wasn't any electricity, so our evenings were lit by candlelight. We had no plumbing, but could get fresh water from a spring, a hundred yards up the track. Cleaning our teeth at night, we looked up at the stars and listened to the nightingales singing their hearts out. The little darlings had us surrounded.

152

There were six or seven of them, moving us with their heartrendingly beautiful mating calls.

As spring swelled, our terraces filled with poppies, margaritas and irises. Summer and autumn in Cal Xaiu were full of wonder too. The days were hot, the nights warm. Chirruping flights of bee-eaters passed overhead and swifts quartered the sky. Most days we heard golden orioles, but we rarely saw them. Hoopoes bobbed around the fields, reminding me of the ghostly grandeur of Fatehpur Sikri and of the marathon tour of India with Smiles and Sally.

We'd have loved to stay in our house, but to spend the winter in a place without electricity or water would have been too much for my girls. We harvested and dried five sacks of our almonds, then took a winter let on a flat in Vilafranca.

'Hasn't the year gone well,' the French teacher, Dominique, said at the end of the summer term. 'I was really worried at the beginning.'

'So was I. Early on I thought it was going to be a complete fiasco.'

'Really? You never gave that impression.'

'That's because I didn't want to demoralise the staff.'

Nearly all of the teachers had stayed on, making the start of the Autumn term a completely different proposition to the previous year. It wasn't long before the school was running smoothly and I was able to spend time on the work that needed doing at home.

Cal Xaiu was a typical Catalan farmhouse with thick walls and small windows, designed to stay cool in summer and warm in winter. It had been empty for eleven years; the walls and roof were good, but the floors were shot.

All our money had gone into the purchase. My wages were just enough to support us, so we had to make economies to be able to buy tools and building materials. Power tools were out of my reach. I used a lump hammer and cold chisel to make ten holes through the fifty centimetre thick wall. The work took weeks and left me with a lifelong ringing in my ears.

I rounded up a few helpers from the school to help me fit the upstairs beams. Half a dozen of us finished the work in an afternoon. That evening we gave a party for our team of volunteers.

We often had big barbecues with our friends. We'd set light to great mounds of vine cuttings and prepare the vegetables. When the fire had burnt down to a large glowing pillow, we'd bake potatoes in the base and barbecue aubergines, peppers, artichokes and *calçots,* a type of onion, on top. We'd eat our outdoor feast with rough bread and *romesco*, a Catalan sauce of roasted almond or hazelnut paste, tomatoes, salt, olive oil and garlic. The food was all washed down with litres of our neighbour's good red wine from the barrel. It was cheaper than milk.

On weekday afternoons and evenings I taught English and made sure the courses kept running smoothly. The rest of the time I worked on the house, the land and my command of Spanish. By the following April, when we returned to Cal Xaiu, I'd put in the floors, made two bedrooms and a landing, prepared a vegetable patch and planted a dozen young fruit trees. That summer my old pal Scooter came down to help us for a while and wired the house for me. I built a brick-lined septic tank and began work on the bathroom extension.

Following our move, Jess had been enrolled in the Sant Martí Sarroca School. Meg and I figured she'd find her feet and make some friends before long, but she soon put us straight.

'It's horrible in the school,' she told us. 'The English teacher can't speak English and everybody hates the headmaster, including the teachers.'

Meg and I went to speak with the baker in the village. His family had taken a shine to Jess, so I thought they might be able to help in some way.

'There are big problems in the school, and most of them are because of the Principal,' the baker's wife told us. She spoke so slowly I wondered if she was on tranquilisers.

Meg and I agreed it would be better to teach Jess at home, so we took her out of school. Some weeks later we got a letter from the head of the local Education authority, enquiring why Jess wasn't attending school and asking for a meeting. Expecting trouble, I was pleasantly surprised at the arrival of a youngish woman who seemed friendly.

'We took her out of school,' I said, in answer to her question,'because she wasn't happy and she didn't seem to be learning much.'

'Would you like to see the things Jess has done at home?' Meg asked. She showed the lady the recipes Jess had written for the meals she'd made, the scores for the music they'd played together, the clothes she'd repaired, the paintings she'd done.

I showed her the work Jess and I had been doing on English, Maths, History and Geography. 'It's not the lessons so much,' I told her. 'It's the bad atmosphere in the school.'

She was sympathetic. 'I'm happy with the education Jess is getting at home. But wouldn't it be a pity if she were isolated from the other children? Would you let her go to school in the afternoons when the children play games and do creative arts?'

'An excellent idea,' Meg replied. 'We'll do it.'

Three other houses were within hailing distance of our dwelling. The neighbours, won over by our winsome red-haired daughter, couldn't have been kinder. They taught us how to garden in a hot, dry climate, when to plant broad beans and garlic, how to dry and store almonds, pumpkins, melons and tomatoes so that they kept for months.

Our nearest neighbours were short and stocky: they were a delightful old couple, both approaching eighty. Joan (the Catalan version of John, pronounced Juan) and Palmyra were teenagers during the Spanish Civil War and had vivid memories of the cold and hungry winters of their youth. Their children worked in offices and had flats in Vilafranca, but Joan and his wife still lived much as they'd always done.

Peasant farmers, they'd worked their own land all their lives. Their livestock consisted of rabbits and doves. The doves flew freely in the day and came home to their cots in the evening for a handful of grain.

Palmyra picked basketfuls of green leaves from the lanes for the rabbits. After rain, she'd go out and collect bucketfuls of large edible snails. She gathered wild asparagus in the spring, herbs in summer and foraged for mushrooms in the autumn.

Like most of the farmers on the fringes of the

156

Pénedès valley, they had vineyards in their lower fields and terraces of almonds and olives above. Around the house were figs, cherries and extensive vegetable gardens. Here Joan pottered for most of the day, when he wasn't tinkering with some agricultural tool in his workshop.

Joan and Palmyra had little to do with money, but they lived a life rich in time. They certainly had time for us and were always ready to stop what they were doing and help with a problem.

One Saturday, when Meg and Jess were in town, I ran over to Joan's house in a panic. 'Joan!'

He emerged from his workshop with his beret on his head and a sickle in his hand. 'What's the matter,' he asked.

'There's a snake,' I paused, not knowing the word for adder. 'It's in our kitchen! What do I do?'

He put down the sickle and picked up a hoe. Smiling merrily at me – the tall, hopeless foreigner – he set off toward our house, beckoning me to follow.

I trailed along in his wake. Snakes really unsettle me. That muscular thrashing on the ground when you tread near a dozing snake in summer…

The adder had disappeared. We searched everywhere but it was nowhere to be found.

'It's gone,' Joan pronounced. 'It won't come back. Snakes don't like people.'

We'd parachuted into their lives from another world. No doubt they found us strangely ignorant of the very basics of life, but they made us welcome and did all they could to help us settle in. When their cat had a litter, we took two of the kittens. Jess named them Timmy and Mottle. Timmy was ginger and white, large and timid. Mottle looked after him. She was a tortoiseshell, small and adventurous.

Driving home on a chill February night after late classes, I swung off the track, rounded the U-turn into our drive and screeched to a halt. 'Jesus!'

Standing in my path, lit by my headlights, was a wild boar, spherical in late pregnancy. She gaped at me, before lumbering off, into the woods.

A few days later, writing a lesson plan late into the night, I paused. A skiffle band seemed to be playing on the hillside above the house.

Picking up the torch, I slipped through the front door and went soft-footed into the dark. Heavy bodies were moving through the broom bushes, grunting, snuffling and whistling. I flicked on the light. A few yards away, half-a-dozen hump-backed boar turned their massive heads towards me. My eyes were level with their tusks. I quickly doused the light and retreated to the house. They retired to the woods. After half an hour they were back.

I woke Meg. 'Come and look at this!'

'What?' She said sleepily.

'Wild boar in the garden! Put some clothes on and follow me.'

We crept out in the dark, huddled under an umbrella. From behind the car I switched on the torch. Ten yards away, through the slanting rain, four adults were rootling in the bank beside the path. Ignoring us, they kept on digging. From their long, mean-looking snouts issued odd grunts and moans. Their jaws snapped together with a fearsome noise. One of them had a dozen striped babies flowing round her feet like water round a pier. They squeaked and squealed while their mother dug up the bulbs we'd planted.

Water poured out of the hills along the valley's spring-line. A two-mile walk on a dusty footpath took us to a pool where a sun-warmed stream tumbled over a small waterfall and mingled with the icy waters of a spring. In the summer holidays we'd go to swim in the pool and sunbathe on the rocks.

I could walk all day with Savage, our old dog, and not see anyone. The dry hills were covered in rocks and pine, scrubby evergreen oak, rosemary, gorse, thyme and lavender. I'd catch sight of a few hawks, kestrels and occasionally an eagle. We'd hear the drill of woodpeckers, the three note song of the orioles and the shrill of cicadas. The air was full of the smell of herbs we'd bruised with our feet.

In our Catalan home, I'd found the closeness to nature that I'd long been looking for. Without my earlier experiences I could have happily lived the life of a Catalan peasant farmer. But I couldn't simply erase whole sections of my existence. My horizons now stretched over four continents, and I wanted to broaden them still further.

Perhaps the secret of a happy life is to find a way to accommodate all that we are, all we've been, and all we hope to be.

17. WORLD CHAMPIONS Nov. 1998

In addition to their passion for football, the Catalans love building human castles: *castells*. They're a symbol of independence and national pride. I'd seen quite a few castels being built in the years I'd spent in Vilafranca. Their team of *castellers* were recognised as one of the strongest in the Province of Barcelona.

Meg and Jess were in the UK and so they missed Vilafranca's attempt to break the world record. I was there in the square on the great day, along with the thousands of people who'd packed the town centre in the hope of seeing history being made.

The *Castellers* formed a solid platform with dozens of the strongest people in town tightly linking arms in a circle. A smaller number clambered onto the shoulders of those forming the base, then ever lighter people climbed up to form the bases for subsequent layers. The upper layers were made by light, but strong, young men or women. I held my breath when the children started clambering up the outside of the human tower; they looked so tiny and vulnerable. Small boys and girls formed the top two or three rows. 'Hang on tight,' I silently urged them. My fingers were crossed, my heart had leapt from its housing into my mouth. 'Hold on,' I urged the tiny climbing figures. 'Hold on.'

The atmosphere was electric. The Vilafranca *Castellers* were attempting to become the first team ever to build a *très de deu*, a tapering human column, ten people high with three youngsters making the top layer. When the topmost lad raised his hand, the column was completed and the entire square roared.

They went berserk. I did too. I knew many of the people in the crowd and several of those who formed the human tower. There was a huge lump in my throat; it was one of the most emotional moments of my life: the first world record I'd seen in the flesh. Hugged and kissed by dozens of people, I embraced and kissed everyone around me.

The wild celebrations destabilised the base and the tower collapsed. Nobody was badly hurt. Cuts and bruises are common when a castle goes, broken limbs are not unusual, but deaths are very rare: the falling *castellers* usually land on those below. I'd watched many *castells* being built over the years, but none of them matched this extraordinary achievement. The partying went on for most of the night. Wine and *Cava* were flowing freely. The upstairs windows around the square sported Catalan flags. Everybody was delirious with joy. What a privilege to have been present on the day when little Vilafranca, a town of 30,000 people, became the world record holders of this extraordinary sport.

A castell being built

18. GOD TALKS TO BARRY

An English couple turned up at our house one summer's day at lunchtime. They looked to be some ten years younger than us. He was large and relaxed and had the jovial confidence common to many big men. His huge forearms were covered in red hair and freckles. She was small and intense, with piercing blue eyes and cropped greying hair.

'Hi. I'm Barry and this is Lesley,' the guy said, instantly giving himself away as a Brummie. 'We're doing our best to speak Spanish to our neighbours, but it's hard work. The people next door told us there was another English family over this way, so we've come to say hello. It's a relief to be able to talk without always having to struggle to find the right words.'

He held his hand out. I took it and felt all the bones in my hand squeezed together as if in a vice. Wincing, I extracted my bruised fingers and rubbed them with my good hand to restore circulation.

'Barry!' Lesley scolded.

'It's all right,' I told her. 'Once crushed... I'll keep my hands behind my back next time.'

'We're about to eat,' said Meg. 'Please join us.'

We laid the garden table with plates of salad, cheese, bread, almonds and fruit. I brought out bottles of wine, olive oil and water and we all sat down to eat in the shade of the plane tree.

'Are you living here or on holiday?' I asked.

'We've bought a house in La Granada.' Lesley replied. 'I'm a sculptor and Barry's a cabinetmaker. We're trying to get ourselves established here but it's not easy. We haven't sold any work yet but we haven't given up.'

'Right.' Barry added emphatically. 'We haven't given up. But we'll have to sell something before too long or we're going to run out of money.'

In spite of the bone-crushing start, I warmed to Barry as the afternoon progressed. He had an irreverent approach to life that I could identify with. We spent an enjoyable afternoon drinking, talking, laughing and joking. As they left they invited us to dinner at their place. We accepted gladly.

Apart from teachers and a few translators, I didn't know any English people in the area. Though the College House teachers were likeable and good fun to be with, it was reassuring to know that our conversations wouldn't inevitably turn to talk of classes, students and Godfrey, the small bad boss. Soon we were hanging out with Barry and Lesley most weekends.

Barry constructed extraordinary furniture; it was unlike anything I'd ever seen. He showed us a couple of perfectly functioning wardrobes that happened to be a pair of huge monkeys, nigh on seven feet tall. One was clearly male, the other obviously female.

'There can be no metal in my work. None. Everything has to work perfectly, and it does!' Barry was a perfectionist.

'I only use metal in my pieces,' Lesley countered.

The difference spoke volumes about their relationship. Temperamentally and physically they were worlds apart, but were united in their passion for their art.

Lesley managed to get a venue for an exhibition

and sold some of her work. It was a huge psychological boost for them. The first piece of hers that I saw was a little metal man sitting in one corner of a big metal cage.

I could see that it was some kind of statement about freedom, life and art, but it struck at my soft underbelly. I'd been there: I didn't need to see any more men in cages. From then on I couldn't look at Lesley's constructions with any enthusiasm.

While she was finding some success, Barry was struggling. He hardly made any money from his work – his furniture took a long of time to construct and it was expensive.

'The Catalans are a conservative lot,' he grumbled. 'Outside of Barcelona they don't seem to be interested in anything new or avant garde.'

He sold a few small pieces, but not enough to keep him busy so he concentrated on rebuilding their house and did occasional odd jobs for other people.

'If you give me a hand with the plumbing at Cal Xaiu,' I suggested, 'I'll help you re-tile your roof.'

'Done,' he said quickly. 'Roof work is a very hot and sweaty business in the summer'.

When one of the staff quit unexpectedly in the summer term, I got Barry taken on as a part-time teacher at the academy. He needed the money and we had to have someone to cover the Saturday morning children's class. It seemed a good arrangement for both of us.

Untrained but enthusiastic, Barry made a good start, but then he went through a low patch and lost confidence in his ability to teach. His behaviour became increasingly erratic. It got to the point where

I couldn't be sure if he'd turn up for his lesson. If he did, there was no guarantee that he'd stay to the end.

A few weeks later, Lesley drove over to see us on her own. She was obviously in a state, so Meg sat her down in the shade. She talked to Lesley while I went to the kitchen and made a pot of coffee.

'I wouldn't mind a shot of brandy with the coffee.' Lesley's long sigh was an emptying out of her troubles; they flowed over the table and pooled on the ground.

'Thanks, Leaf.' She took the coffee and added a large measure of *Soberano*. 'Barry's going nuts.' She always spoke softly, but now she was whispering, as if afraid her partner would overhear. 'He's talking to God.'

Meg was one of humanity's peacemakers. 'A lot of people talk to God,' she volunteered, 'it's not unusual'.

'I know – but Barry thinks God's talking back!'

A few days later the four of us had an evening together in Vilafranca. Barry was in good form all through dinner: amusing, volatile, incandescent at times. We laughed all evening. Suddenly I realised it was one o'clock and the bar staff wanted to close up and go home.

We stood between our two cars, agreeing what a great evening it had been. Then Barry grabbed me by the shirt, stared at me intensely with a demented look on his face and whispered, 'We must go to Calafell beach, Leaf.' He paused and added, 'A sign will be revealed.'

'Another time, mate,' I replied. 'It's late, we're tired and I'm working in the morning.'

'No. We have to go now!'

'Not now, Barry,' Lesley said quietly, as if she were speaking to a fractious child. 'We've eaten, we've drunk, *you're* drunk. Now we need to sleep.'

Barry grew more agitated. 'You don't understand.' He appealed to us with arms outstretched, like a preacher, speaking to the flock. He was dripping with sweat, wreathed in his own pungent odour.

'I don't know why – out of all the people in the world – but somehow I've been chosen. Me. Little me!' He laughed hysterically. 'I know it's ridiculous, but God is working through me. He's shown me several signs already. We must walk by the sea at Calafell, Leaf. There's no time to waste. Our whole friendship depends on it!'

We all go through difficult periods when we need our friends' help and support. Agreeing to go along with them to the beach, we got into our cars and drove over the low range of hills that lay between us and the Mediterranean.

'I hope this won't take long,' I said to Meg. 'I'm not staying here all night.' We parked behind Lesley at Calafell, crunched onto the sand and waited to see what Barry was going to do next.

'I can't stand much more of this,' Lesley whispered to Meg.

'I know you think I'm nuts…' Barry said exuberantly to the three of us, 'but you'll see. You'll see the truth. Come on then!' He strode off down the beach. We straggled along behind him.

'What are we looking for?' Meg called to Barry.

'I haven't a clue,' he replied, laughing. 'But we'll know when we see it. Oh ye of little faith… Listen, what's that?'

There was a distant rumble, just audible in the lull between the breaking of the small waves. A light appeared in the sky to the west. It grew brighter as it headed straight towards us. We stood transfixed on the sand.

'There!' Barry exclaimed triumphantly. He clapped his hands together and performed a little dance of his own invention. 'Now perhaps you'll believe me.'

The light grew nearer, it resolved into several pinpoints that had the form of a perfect sine wave. I was gobsmacked, quite unable to speak.

'Thank you, Lord, thank you.' Barry sank to his knees on the sand.

Meg, Lesley and I shared a confused look. None of us knew what to say. The lights were getting closer. The sound was clearly the roar of jet engines. Six planes flew low over our heads. The din of their passage slowly receded and silence lapped over it.

'Come on, Barry. Let's go home,' Lesley broke the spell.

Barry was humble now. 'I'm sorry to drag you out in the middle of the night, but now you've seen the glory of God, I'm sure you understand.'

The next day the news spoke of waves of American planes crossing Spanish airspace en route to the first Gulf War. Soon afterwards Lesley threw Barry out. She'd had enough of living with the new Messiah.

He left with nothing and came to stay at Cal Xaiu, sleeping in Richard and Jane's half of the house and eating with us. There were still odd flashes of his visions but God had stopped talking to him.

'I couldn't live up to my role,' he whispered in a husky voice. 'I'm too flaky.'

167

He was a chastened man. Weeks turned into months before he came out of the shell he'd squeezed himself into. He started talking to people again, began to do a little building work and slowly got himself back on his feet.

In the evenings we frequently turned to the backgammon board. Barry played with total commitment and took great risks; our games were full of unlikely advances and reverses. Life around Barry was never dull. After five months with us, he finally found himself a place to live and moved out.

I missed him when he'd gone.

Towards the end of the summer term, I began to think about the future. Time had been galloping by, ever faster. The challenge of getting the school back on its feet had been stimulating, but I'd done the job for four years. Did I want to carry on forever? The strains between the owner and the staff had been mounting.

Godfrey's economies were all at the expense of his teachers. Last year he'd lopped a week off the paid Christmas holiday. His latest stroke had been to cut the school year from nine months to eight. The curriculum remained the same but we had a month less in which to teach it. This measure would save Godfrey thousands of pounds, It would also put pressure on the staff to rush through the syllabus, and leave them with four unpaid summer months. I was sure many of the teachers wouldn't be coming back in the autumn.

I decided I wouldn't either and handed in my notice. I'd had enough of being the lubricant between the staff and an owner who thought little of his teachers. He was sickly, peevish and he could be stunningly rude. He was the kind of guy who could make a thousand pound suit look like a sack of potatoes – and he had thousand pound suits: I'd seen the price tags.

When Godfrey wasn't around, the academy ran smoothly, but his rare appearances scraped a knife across the slate of the school and left everyone on edge.

I'd done a good job for him – the number of pupils had doubled from three to six hundred in the time I ran the Vilafranca academy.

At the end of the school year he said to me, 'I'd like to give you a farewell dinner at the best restaurant in town, a thankyou for all the hard work you've done in making a success of the school.'

At the start of the next academic year, I dropped by the school to see if the new head teacher needed a hand. Malcolm looked extremely embarrassed. 'I'm very sorry to have to say this-' he was whispering so that Ana couldn't hear, 'but I've had strict instructions from his majesty: you're not allowed on the premises.'

'What?'

'And he's ordered the teachers not to talk to you. I have to ask you to go, but I'll see you for a coffee downstairs if you're around in an hour.'

'What's his problem?' I asked Malcolm when he joined me in the bar.

'He thinks you've been stealing his students.'

'That's rubbish!'

'That's what he said.'

'He's lying, Malcolm. He must be talking about Yolanda's advanced group. He said he wouldn't run their class because, with only three students, it would cost him money. They asked me if I'd teach them and I said I would.'

I didn't go back to the school after that, but the bar was my local – I knew the staff and many of the customers. I carried on going to the bar and continued to socialise with my friends among the teachers and students.

Happily Godfrey avoided me from then on. I was pleased about that. I didn't need arseholes like him in my life.

I resolved never to have a boss again. I would work as an independent teacher from now on. I had a good reputation in and around Vilafranca. I knew I'd be able to feed my family. I wouldn't lack for students.

Our wonderful old dog, Savage, died of old age. I dug his grave and buried him on our land. I was blubbering helplessly; my eyes were so full of tears I could hardly see what I was doing. With his passing, our family suddenly seemed diminished.

19. CRASH

It was a relief to be self-employed again. I soon picked up quite a few students.

'Will you teach me privately?' a friend, Jaume, asked me one day. I'd taught all three of his children in the academy. When his classes went well, he asked if his wife and sister could do a course for beginners.

My dentist wanted to study English. We worked out a deal where he would replace all the mercury fillings I'd had and fix up my remaining teeth.

'Agustí, you've done so much work in my mouth, I should move my bed into your practise and save travelling time and petrol money!'

The notary in Vilafranca asked me to teach him. He was mostly interested in talking football. As he was a Real Madrid supporter and I was a fan of Johan Cruyff's Barcelona, our classes were fiery, disputatious, but always in English and always good-humoured.

One day he couldn't wipe a huge grin from his face.

'Something must have happened to put you in such a good mood, Jordi? What is it?'

'I just handled the sale of a hotel, for a hundred and fifty million pesetas! I get one per cent.'

A quick calculation told me that, for half a morning's work, he'd received seven thousand five hundred pounds. At my initial school salary, I'd have had to work for over a year to earn as much.

In the early days of being my own boss I had plenty of time for toiling in the garden and wandering in the hills. I continued work on the extension, adding a kitchen, a roof terrace and new flight of stairs. In the school holidays Jess often helped me with the work.

After taking Jess out of school, we continued to teach her at home.

'Mum,' she said one day. 'I don't want to go back to the local school, even though the afternoons are fun. I'm not learning anything much. I'd rather be at school in Somerset, with my best friend Flora.'

We would have preferred to have her with us, but we didn't want to keep her in Spain if she wasn't going to be happy. On a family trip to the UK, we met up with Meg's Dad, John.

'She needs an English education.' He wasn't shy about giving an opinion. 'I don't know why you went off to the Third World in the first place.'

'Spain isn't exactly the Third World,' Meg replied.

'Don't contradict me, young lady!' John made no attempt to hide his displeasure. He was something of a tyrant to his only daughter. I was fairly sure he'd bullied her as a child. I wondered how much his controlling hand had played a part in Meg's somewhat pessimistic stance on life.

Grandad got his way, as usual. Jesse came home in the holidays, but she was in Somerset for most of the year. Without the leavening effect of our girl our lives felt more than a little flat.

Each time she left, Meg and I rattled around the house, achingly aware of the empty spaces where Jess had just been. Every time she arrived, we were aware of changes and growth, sometimes subtle, sometimes evident.

We saw her journey through adolescence in a series of time capsules: three or four weeks at Christmas, and Easter and around seven weeks in the summer holidays. Each capsule was separated by a gap of three months.

At the end of every holiday I said to Jess, 'You don't have to go to boarding school. You can stay here if you like.'

'I know. But it's all right. I'll go.'

In order to pay for Jess's schooling, Meg's work as a peripatetic English teacher went from occasional to almost full time.

Sometimes our timetables coincided and we could travel together. More often they didn't. The preparation, the teaching and the travelling used up all her energy and left her exhausted and often depressed. Life was starting to feel like something of a grind.

March 1st, 1992, marked the tenth anniversary of my release. Although prison seemed very distant, it was never entirely absent from my mind. The years as an outlaw and a convict were burnt into my being. I still had two or three prison dreams a month. Would I ever be free of these nocturnal regressions, I wondered, or was I doomed to spend the rest of my life dealing with the after-effects of incarceration?

The anniversary jerked me into an awareness of the passage of time... I'd walked out of Leyhill a decade ago. That meant it was fifteen years since the bust... twenty without meat... a quarter of a century separated me from my first trip. My god, I'd gone to boarding school thirty-six years ago! To a seven-year-old a school term seems an eternity. But the seasons roll remorselessly by, each one a little faster than its predecessor.

~

Diary: March 1ˢᵗ St David's Day, 2015.
I was released from prison thirty-three years ago today. I was thirty-three at the time. This divides my life neatly into two equal parts: From birth to release from prison, and from release onwards.

I've done a fair bit of travelling in both halves of my life – and I'm not talking about the snail trails of my wanderings over parts of planet Earth: I'm looking at the bigger picture,

We are, on average, at a distance of 93,000,000 miles from our life-giving sun. In one year we complete one circuit, 580 million miles.

We're travelling at a speed of some 60,000 mph – and Lewis Hamilton thinks he's fast…

In my lifetime I've clocked up over thirty six billion miles, and that's not taking into account the rotation of the Earth (over 1,000mph at the equator) or the sun's movement around our galaxy. No wonder I'm a bit knackered.

~

Over the years in Spain I'd got to know several translators. One of them, overstressed by the deadlines she had to meet, put some work my way. On the back of that, her agency offered me the job of translating – into English – the action surrounding the opening of the imminent Barcelona Olympics.

The games were going to be inaugurated by an archer firing a flaming arrow through the hole in the *Pebetero* and lighting the Olympic flame. The translation wasn't a difficult job – except for finding an English equivalent of the untranslatable word

Pebetero.

'Esteban, how would you define the word *Pebetero*?'

Like the other Spanish friends I'd asked, he suggested the best phrase would be 'The little man.'

But I had a picture of the *Pebetero* and it didn't look anything like a little man. Eventually I settled on 'the censer'. Nobody made any adverse comments on my work, and I was paid well for the work, but I'd already decided against becoming a translator.

It wasn't a sudden decision. I'd been thinking for a while about the pros and cons. The huge advantage was that I'd no longer have to do the grinding round of classes, but the downside seemed enormous. You don't earn much money unless you're at the top end of the profession – doing legal work, simultaneous translating at multinational conferences, or putting foreign best sellers into English.

My translating friends almost always worked all weekend, they never rejected a job for fear that their agency would turn to someone else. Nobody gave them a translation saying 'There's no rush, just give it to me when you're ready.'

Translators were always on a tight deadline and never knew when the next job would materialise. I knew that wasn't for me.

Meg and Jess went to a couple of the horsy events at the Barcelona Olympics, then we drove up to my brother's place in Normandy to have a break with Roger and his family. I was glad to be avoiding the tightly-packed streets during the sportsfest, but I loved Barcelona and often took the train and spent the day exploring this fascinating city.

Sometimes I'd meet up with my old friend, Dave. Years before, he'd met and married a wonderful Catalan woman named Pilar. They lived in the heart of Barcelona. He was teaching English, she was a dancer. We'd see a film, visit museums and galleries, go out for a meal or just walk and talk.

He never joined me when I went to the Camp Nou to watch Barça play. Dave wasn't interested in sport, but he would come along to a good concert. With him I finally got to see my old hero, Bob Dylan, long years after he, Orwell and Kerouac had sounded the reveille on my life.

Some old sage said 'Be careful what you wish for, because you might get it.' I'd achieved the life I'd left England to find. I was contented and yet I was aware of a growing groundswell of unease. My relationship with Meg had settled into a fairly dull routine. We got on OK but the spark was long gone.

Thinking about how that had happened led me to the conclusion that much of the light and life in our family had been provided by Jess. When the holidays came we all bucked up, but when she wasn't there, I had to spend a fair amount of time trying to cheer Meg up and find things for her to be enthusiastic about. At home I was under-stimulated.

Did I really want to be in semi-retirement? 'Is this it?' I'd be asking myself, at the end of another lovely day. 'Is this as far as I go? After all I've done, am I really just going to potter about on this hillside for the rest of my time?'

Surely I had more adventures left in me, different roads to travel, new people to meet.

We can run along calmly, following our routines for months or years on end without anything much happening. It's easy to forget that changes can be sudden rather than gradual.

We were travelling at a hundred kilometres an hour, driving down the N340 on the way to have dinner with Richard and Jane.

Meg and Jess were singing Beatles harmonies, as they often did on car rides. At the start of the long empty stretch, south of the town of Arboç, we were overtaken by a white van. It took a while to get past us before gradually inching away. Four cars emerged from the hamlet ahead and sped towards us. Without warning the third car in the line abruptly flipped sideways into our lane, right in front of the van. The Transit smashed into the side of the car and sent it spinning into the ditch. The van juddered to a halt.

I slammed my foot on the brake and managed to stop a couple of yards short of the Transit. Its rear doors opened and blood-spattered painters began staggering out and falling over our bonnet. I looked sideways at the ditch where the car had ended up. The doors were open. There was nobody inside... I was pouring with sweat and felt sick to my soul.

Improbably, the man in the car survived. He couldn't have been wearing his seat belt and was lucky enough to have been thrown clear.

The Transit crash was a slap-in-the-face reminder that things can go completely to pieces in a moment.

Catalunya burst into flames in the searing summer of '94. The temperature was in the mid-forties and wildfires broke out all over the place. A firework factory near Vilafranca caught light and launched rockets in every direction to start new blazes. High winds spread more fires. Three days later Catalunya had over forty fires burning out of control. Seaplanes and helicopters dumped their loads of water on the conflagrations to little effect. The emergency services were overwhelmed.

You have to see a forest fire close to hand to understand how scary they are.

I arrived at my factory class one afternoon. Montserrat came in late as usual. 'Nigel, a new fire has started. It looks like it's over your way.'

I went outside to have a look. 'OK, everyone, That's it for today. I'll see you next week.'

Jess was alone in the house and I was seriously worried. One wildfire outbreak had already come to the crest of the hill behind Cal Xaiu. The wind had changed direction and we'd been spared.

I set off home, driving much too fast. When I was nearly there, I saw the fire was in another valley and we were in no immediate danger.

Shaken to the core, I asked myself if it was a good idea to live in such a hot, dry region. Once I'd remembered how much I loved rivers, meadows and tall trees, I began to think of myself as stranded, high and dry in a parched landscape.

By the end of the teaching year, it felt like Meg and I had been on top of each other for too long. We agreed we needed some outside stimuli and arranged to have separate holidays, partly because it removed the problem of finding animal sitters, but mostly because we needed a break from each other.

I drove Meg to El Prat airport in Barcelona. We travelled through air that was thick with smuts and smouldering fragments of vegetable matter. The temperature was in the mid-forties: air much hotter than blood.

Strong winds whipped the flames. Fires were still burning unchecked. Unable to open the windows, we sweltered in the car and sipped water. I've never been so hot. It seemed our old Renault 4 could spontaneously combust at any moment. Wherever we looked columns of smoke were ascending into the scorched air.

The fires had burnt out by the time Meg flew back to Spain.

I jetted off to England to spend a few days in London with my pal, Dave Tomory.

We were at the somnolent end of a fine dinner when the bell rang.

'Ah, that's probably Rosie,' Dave said, 'She told me she might drop by tonight.'

Rosie had shoulder-length chestnut hair. A fringe hung above her large brown eyes. Under her coat she was wearing a trim two-piece that showed her figure to good advantage. She was smiling as she walked towards me. Suddenly I was wide-awake, on my feet before I knew it, my senses singing five-part harmonies.

'Leaf, this is my old friend Rosie. Rosie – Leaf.'

'Less of the old,' she said to Dave in a pleasant contralto. We shook hands. She had a firm grip. She gave me a quizzical look and I realised we were still holding hands.

'You have a strong handshake,' I commented, 'Un like most women.'

She shrugged, 'I have strong arms too. Massage is my metier. I'm an aromatherapist.'

Rosie smiled at me again and the years fell away. I felt like a young man once more, capable of anything. The conversation moved on through work, travel, interests and mutual friends, of which we had a few. All the while our chemicals were dancing through the room and I was feeling more truly awake than I had done for years. This lovely woman seemed interested in me.

When she left, I sat on Dave's sofa, too charged up to be able to sleep. I couldn't remember much of what we'd talked about, but I could see her face in front of me, hear her voice in my ear. Her perfume lingered in the air. In the morning I pestered Dave for her address. I went to see her in the evening. I wasn't able to stop myself.

Rosie and I were drawn to each other, it was plain, but she made it clear she wasn't interested in getting involved with someone already in a relationship.

'You learn a few things as you go along,' she said, 'usually through previous mistakes. I can tell you from bitter experience: two-timers are nothing but trouble.'

My head on fire, burning with unfulfilled desire, I returned to Spain. Meg was there to meet me at the airport. She knew something was up immediately, probably from the way I greeted her. Women have senses that have atrophied in most men.

I wasn't capable of pretence and told her I'd fallen in love.

How could I do it? We'd spent eleven years together, a quarter of our lives. How could I possibly do it? I felt awful and yet part of me was shining. What sort of man was I? Clearly there was much more to me than met my eye. I was not simply the nice guy I'd always assumed myself to be. I went down in my own estimation: I was just another of those selfish bastards who were happy as long as they got what they wanted.

Meg couldn't bear to be near me. 'Just go away, will you!' she stormed, and threw a textbook at me. 'And don't you dare come back until I've packed up and gone.'

I went to stay with my friends Paddy and Mandy. A few days later Meg flew to England. I returned to an empty Cal Xaiu, to sift through the debris of our life together and to put the house on the market.

20. ICARUS

Rosie was a widow who had been on her own for some time and had come to enjoy her independence. She hadn't fallen for me the way I had for her, but we'd sparked and I'd sparkled. Raised up on wings of inspiration, my ad-libs kept her in fits of laughter. We were enjoying each other's company. She was definitely interested and so was I.

I was sure we were made for one another. We'd grown up in the same hippy ethos and had similar ideas about life, love, food and humour. Having so many common reference points made it seem natural for us to be together. With echoes of her laughter ringing in my ears, I called her.

'Rosie, it's Leaf. Yes, I'm fine. How are you? Good. Listen, I told Meg about meeting you and, as a result, I'm suddenly a single man.'

There was silence from the other end of the line before Rosie said, 'You did what?'

'I told her about you. I couldn't possibly pretend nothing had happened?'

'You don't waste time. So how do you feel, now that you're single?'

Her question threw me. 'How do I feel? I feel very light. I don't know, I feel fully alive, more than I have for some while. Rosie, you wouldn't like to come and visit me in Spain, would you?'

'I don't know. I'll think about it.'

'Hey, that's fantastic! Sorry, I interrupted. What were you saying?'

'I was about to say you mustn't take anything for granted, Leaf. We hardly know each other. Tell you what, I'll come for a three-day visit, see how we get on.'

We got on wonderfully well. Every day together was a celebration of the bond that was growing between us. She fell for Catalunya in a big way. With her olive skin, Rosie looked like a Mediterranean woman and was taken for a local more than once.

'God, this is a world away from Kensal Rise. I love it,' she kept saying, as we walked in the mountains, on beaches and around Barcelona. In the rich warmth of autumn, we sat outside for hours, eating tapas in seaside bars, talking idly and daring to make tentative plans for the future.

She had spirit, strength and wit. I loved her more each day and my feelings were beginning to be reciprocated. We were glowing, getting higher and higher on each other. Then she had to return to London and go back to her life as an aromatherapist.

We wrote to each other and talked on the phone, planning our next moves. Every day I strode the hills with Harry, the whippet-lurcher I'd inherited from Richard and Jane when their marriage broke down. Harry stayed at my heel, as if he were hanging on my words. I had quite a lot to say, giving him the latest news on the major upheavals that had occurred in my life and in Meg's.

The late autumn colours were more beautiful than I'd ever known, the vines a glory of red and gold. Never had I felt so wonderful. Never had I known myself to be such a worthless arsehole. I could sense the waves of misery, confusion and anger emanating from Meg. A thorn was plucking at a taut string in my soul and inside my head Lennon's *'Instant Karma'* was promising to get me. My mind was jumping around all over the place. I was a flea on speed. One minute I'd feel terrible, a moment later I might say out loud, 'I'm the luckiest man alive.'

I knew that to be true at the end of the year in London. Rosie and I moved in a sphere of light. Our world sparkled in the frosty air. We went up to East Anglia to spend Christmas Day with her family.

In the early afternoon we all sat down at the dinner table.

'Would you like a little wine?' Rosie's sister Lettie asked me.

'No,' I replied, 'I'd rather have a full glass.'

After a second's pause, everyone laughed. The mood relaxed considerably. They liked me. I liked them too. Christmas Dinner relaxed into an enjoyable affair. I think they were expecting the worst and were relieved to find I was half-civilised. I was enjoying myself. England was much better when you were in it, I remembered. From afar it appears rather cold, small and damp.

After seven years away, I was all set to return.

'I'm thinking of moving to London,' I said at the end of our Christmas break. 'Maybe in the summer...'

'Are you crazy?' Rosie cut me short with an impatient chop of her hand. 'I'm going to come to Spain! It won't be easy and it might take some time, but I'm going to do it.'

Every chance we got, one of us travelled to be with the other. We poured our hearts into those short meetings; they always ended too soon. She came to me at Easter. I drove to the UK for the summer holidays and spent six glorious weeks at her place. England is beautiful in the warm weather. Again I talked about returning to the UK. A year had passed and we didn't seem any nearer to her move to Spain.

Rosie, a feisty Taurean, wouldn't hear of it.

'What could you do in London?' she asked dismissively.

I didn't know the answer to that. But after being a teacher for eight years, I needed a change. 'And what can I do in Spain?' I replied, saddened by her offhand response. 'I don't think I can go on teaching for much longer. I'm reaching the end of my chalk.'

Teaching puts strange demands on its practitioners. At the beginning you try to make up for your lack of experience by preparing well and putting all your energy into the work. Each class is an exhausting but rewarding performance. As lessons merge to become terms and terms combine into academic years, you slowly come to master the art of mastering.

After three or four years, you can do it well and you're still getting better. This is the peak. Knowing the whole damn syllabus, you don't really need to prepare for the class. It's enough to glance at the course book and check your notes from previous years. For a term or two you're surfing with your students, on the crest of a big wave.

But every wave loses power as it rolls along and eventually you recycle yourself so many times you're in danger of becoming a teaching machine. Lesson inexorably follows lesson, five times a day, week after week, year after year. However good your intentions are, it's impossible to put heart and humour into every class of every group you teach.

I returned home after a visit to Rosie in London, and made reluctant preparations for starting another academic year. The house had been on the market for ten months. I'd almost given up hope of selling it, when the small ad I'd put in the local free paper attracted a buyer. He turned up at the house with an offer just below the asking price – contingent on a quick sale. Richard wanted to sell up too, but was being unreasonable over the division of the sale price.

I'd renovated and extended our half of the house, Richard had done virtually nothing to this side. I was feeling generous, because without their initial input we wouldn't have been able to buy the farmhouse, so I proposed a two-thirds/one third split.

Richard demurred. 'I want forty percent.'

'What? You're kidding!'

'No, I'm not,' he said flatly. 'Forty percent.'

'Richard, be reasonable. In your half of Cal Xaiu you've got two bare rooms and a garage, with no services. We have two bedrooms, a large living room, a kitchen, a bathroom and a roof terrace. We've got wiring, plumbing and a septic tank. Our vegetable garden is productive and the fruit and nut trees we planted are growing. I don't suppose your side is worth a quarter of ours, but as a friend I'm offering you a third.'

'No, I want forty percent.' Richard was playing monopoly, like he'd done in the City. It's a game – the last one to blink comes out on top.

On several occasions I tried to reason with him, but he wasn't listening. I had a final attempt to talk him round then, nettled by his stubbornness, I quit and gave him an ultimatum.

'I'm getting a surveyor to legally divide the property in two. I won't have any trouble selling our side – it's a fully functioning house. I don't think you'll get much for your bit, that's if you can find anyone who's interested in it.'

186

'OK,' he said without further argument. I'll accept a third,' He gave me his winning smile. 'But you can't blame me for trying to get the best deal I can.'

'You've been fucked up by your life in the city, Richard.' I was angry. It's rare for me to be so openly rude, and when I am it's usually because I've lost it. Then I'm quite capable of saying things I regret later.

'Richard, I thought we were friends, but you've been screwing me around for days and days. Does money mean more to you than friendship? What's the matter with you? I hope you're not going try to put one over on Jane the way you attempted to rip me off.'

'Of course I won't,' he said icily. 'She's bringing up my children.'

That was the end of our friendship. I was sad that it terminated in the messy way it did, but friends don't always last a lifetime.

Because of my animals, I couldn't rent a flat in town. The only place I could find was a big house in the village of Pontons, way up in the hills. I took it and started moving my stuff into my new home.

Mottle didn't like being torn away from her territory. She disappeared the day after I moved in. I went looking for her. Harry trotted at my heels every step of the way. With nobody else to talk to, I chatted to the dog and replied on his behalf. We walked miles every day.

'Mottle!' I called for her every couple of minutes. After weeks of searching I sadly came to accept that I wouldn't see my dear Mottle again.

Living in Pontons was OK, but getting anywhere else was a pain. I was spending thirteen hours a week driving the sinuous road between the village and my classes in Vilafranca.

Half of our share of the money for the sale of the house had gone to Meg. Now that I had rent to pay, I needed to earn more money. Providence stepped in.

My Spanish friends and students all called me by my given name. A doctor friend, Josep Maria, rang me.

'Nigel, we've been awarded an allowance on top of our salaries to be used for whatever form of education we choose. We've decided to spend it on English classes and we'd like you to be our teacher.'

'I'd be delighted to teach you, Josep. When would you like to start and how many hours a week do you want to do?'

The following week I began a couple of English groups for doctors and nurses at the hospital in Vilafranca. They were a great bunch and soon we were all friends. Our classes were full of humour and learning in roughly equal proportions.

Reckoning my Spanish was good enough to teach beginners, I started doing one-to-one classes in Castilian. My students were English and Japanese businessmen and women working in the auto industry. I continued teaching English to the company's assembly-line workers.

Though I habitually swore, dreamt and talked to myself in Spanish, teaching it as a subject meant I needed to take my command of the language up to another level. The challenge improved my Spanish no end and revitalised my job.

Yajiri was short and fat. He was the incompetent son of an important man in one of the Japanese automobile giants. He'd screwed up in his own country and then again in Australia. Rather than firing him, the company sent him to a small factory unit in the outskirts of Vilafranca, where he wouldn't be able to do any more damage.

The workers assembled air-conditioning units for cars. Yajiri's job was to make sure that they never ran out of any of the hundred and fifty components, sourced from Britain, Holland and a couple of other countries. As his English teacher, I soon realised that he pretended to understand much more than he did, which is why the assembly line twice ground to a halt.

'Another fuck up and you're out!' roared the angry manager.

'Sorry, sorry.' Yajiri was abject in his apologies. 'No more fuck up, sure.'

Amazingly, he was as good as his word. From then on the assembly lines ran without any more problems.

Shortly before he was due to return to Japan, Yajiri invited me and Sarah, a new Englishwoman working at the factory, to dine at the top Japanese restaurant in Barcelona. Yajiri was trying to get off with Sarah. He wanted me to do the sweet talking that would get her into his bed.

No sooner had we sat down than a stunningly beautiful blonde, in a full length sable coat, swept into the restaurant. Sarah was forgotten as Yajiri leapt to his feet.

'I Japanese,' he said, his tongue hanging out. 'Me help you good food.'

I'd heard, from my old friend, Dave Dukes, that a Russian oligarch had moored his yacht in the harbour. This vision had to be his woman. She ignored Yajiri completely.

'Bring me everything,' she said imperiously to the waiters. They scurried to do her bidding. Two tables were put together and piled with food.

She tasted a bit of this, a morsel of that. 'Champagne!' she demanded. She knocked back a couple of flutes, nibbled a bit more food, then rose to her feet, scattered a load of high denomination notes on the tables and swept out.

Yajiri was a punctured ballon.

He pulled himself together for his farewell party. There were small presents for everyone and plenty of booze. Sozzled, Yajiri put his underpants on his head and tried to kiss all the girls. He left on a high note.

Soon after his departure, the boss discovered the secret of Yajiri's sudden efficiency: he had a confederate in Japan. Every weekend his friend air-freighted the components Yajiri had ordered. The duplicitous schemer got up early, picked up the parts from Barcelona airport and delivered them to the factory before the workers arrived.

Yajiri's name was poison when it was discovered that the weekly air freight bills had wiped out the entire annual profits of the factory.

In spite of the extra money from my medical friends, I was uneasily aware that my share of the money from the sale of Cal Xaiu was continually shrinking. Another chunk went each time I flew to England or Rosie came to see me. Her move to Spain never seemed to get any closer.

When Rosie and I met up, one of us was always on holiday. We'd buy each other presents, eat out, go to the seaside or drive up to the Pyrenees. Being together was sufficient cause for celebration.

Experience had taught her to be wary of men. Her marriage had been a slow-motion disaster. I'd already put her in the picture about my meandering course through life, so she knew I wasn't a model of steadiness. I saw she needed time to develop the confidence to make that big scary leap into another culture, but I'd felt certain she'd come to join me in Spain. The more time passed, the less sure I became.

'Really, your life is in London,' I said in frustration, one out-of-sorts evening in Pontons. I'd had several opportunities when I could have brought the subject up and I'd let them slip by, unaware that bottling up my thoughts had caused them to ferment inside me. I found myself blurting out, 'Catalunya is just a place you visit for fun. We don't have a genuine relationship, it's more like a serial holiday romance.'

'What?' Rosie was furious. She clenched her jaw and glared at me, her eyes shining with the light of battle.

'It's just that nothing ever seems to come of our plans,' I said. 'Time rolls by, but nothing ever happens.'

'Oh, thanks a bunch! How dare you belittle all my efforts to find a way to earn money here? It's not easy you know.'

'The thing is, you can't sort out things from London. You have to be on the spot to make things happen. Come and live here with me. I'll help you get started.'

She stared at me stonily. 'Oh yeah, brilliant idea. Give up my livelihood, my flat, my family and friends. Give up all that, and my independence too, for a man who thinks this is just a holiday romance?'

'I didn't mean that. I'm sorry, I'm just frustrated that we have so little time together.'

We were both shocked by the sudden baring of teeth and quickly made up, but echoes of our first clash hung in the air for some while. Angry words cannot be unsaid. Cutting remarks had weakened our connecting fabric. Rosie flew back across the water; our honeymoon period was over.

It proved to be the start of a slow deterioration. We'd broken the ice of contention. Occasionally at first, then more frequently, our reunions became disfigured by smouldering or blazing rows, poorly patched up with tearful reconciliations. Then we'd be in our different countries again, the basic problem between us unresolved, and fundamentally insoluble, while we remained abroad to each other.

I grew ever more convinced she'd never come to live in Spain. She liked to get out and about – dancing, partying, socialising. She was lively and beautiful. It was only a question of time.

Jess brought her boyfriend Carl out to Pontons to meet me. We'd kept in touch since Meg and I split up. Now she was at Derby University, uncertain if she was doing the right degree course. She brought me up to date on her news while I prepared dinner. At the end of the meal, I said what had been on my mind since we'd arranged the visit. 'Jess, it means a lot to me that our relationship has survived the er… the break-up with your mum…'

'Leaf…' she said in the tone she uses when I'm

being particularly obtuse or embarrassing. 'Come on. You're not the only person ever to have left their partner. Most of my friends' parents are separated.'

'Even so-'

'No, stop it. Look, it didn't work out between you and Mum. OK, I'm sad about that, but the fact is that you both brought me up.' She gave me a hug. 'Of course we've got a relationship, you idiot.'

Meg had been universally liked amongst our friends. Many of them took her part when we separated. My social life dwindled. I didn't like it, but I had to accept it as a consequence of my falling for Rosie. Lonely, I hung out with the friends in Vilafranca who weren't boycotting me. I spent a lot of time with my animals, chatting away to the dog as we took long walks in the hills. At home I philosophised with the cat in my den.

To keep my mind active, I dug out the account of the acid years that I'd written in Goa and was labouring at the second draft. This became another bone of contention with Rosie. Not wanting her family to learn about my past, she gnawed away at my will to continue writing my memoirs.

Two years after leaving Cal Xaiu, my share of the house money was all but gone. In September '97, I left Pontons and rented a cheaper house in the old part of the village of Sant Martí Sarroca.

Immersed in William Boyd's latest novel, *Armadillo,* I let the phone ring and leapt up at the last moment, grabbing the receiver just before the ansaphone cut in. 'Hello.'

'Leaf, hi. It's Rosie.' Her voice was muted, deep. 'How are you? Good. Me too. Listen, I'm truly sorry

193

to tell you this but I'm not coming back to Catalunya... Leaf, Can you hear me?'

'Yes. What are you saying Rosie?'

'It hasn't been going well for a while, has it? Be honest.'

'Tell me, is there someone else?' I winced at my inept phrasing, then realised that my words were neither here nor there. She was dumping me.

'Yes, there is. Look, I'm really sorry. We had some great times, didn't we? But in the long run it didn't work out.'

I listened numbly for a few moments while she tried to make me feel better by pointing out the positive aspects of the situation for both of us. Then I put down the phone, stared out of the window and watched the rain lash the bare countryside.

How could I have got it all so wrong? How could I have screwed up so comprehensively? Forty-nine and broke, I was sick of my job and had just been dumped, face down in the mud.

The stupid thing was that I'd seen it coming. After the first flush of infatuation, I'd realised we had to live in the same country if our affair was to ripen into something more. I'd seen the likelihood of that shrinking, but I hadn't wanted to believe it. I'd thought we'd overcome the obstacles. I had just been proved wrong. The heights, the giddy highpoints in my existence had all vanished in the mist. Were they ever real? All I could see were the swampy places in the valley of my life. Karma had got me, not instantly, but surely. I'd cut my moorings and taken to the air. I had flown.

Now I'd been ditched.

21. COVERED IN BRUISES

Writing and teaching were the only strings that held me together that winter. Almost anything else could make me unravel: I was emotionally incontinent. Books and films made me cry uncontrollably. I kept seeing fresh meanings in songs I thought I knew – fundamental insights that could tear me apart without warning. I felt wretched.

We go through life thinking we're standing on solid ground, but we're just perched on a thin crust which can give way when under stress. It's molten below: we can disappear without trace.

Spring did its thing, but the exuberant fresh growth and the new life had nothing to do with me. I plodded on, trying not to think too much about what a mess I'd made of my life.

What might I have done better?

I'd won Rosie's heart but hadn't been able to keep it. I could see that ringing her the day after returning to Spain and telling her I was now a single man must have raised flags of alarm in her mind. If a woman had done the same to me so early in our relationship I'd have been concerned about her stability. That alone might have been enough to make Rosie have major doubts about me, but it hadn't impeded the growth of our love. To my mind the insurmountable problem had been that we were a thousand miles away from each other.

I was better off without her; that's what I told myself, but I missed her terribly. The practical man within said it could never have worked out, but I grieved for my lost love.

Mechanically I forced my way through the joyless days. I felt beaten up, a mass of bruises. I taught my classes, I shopped, cooked and ate without tasting the food on my plate. When the phone rang, I answered it with a little blip of hope in my heart.
It wasn't Rosie, saying what a terrible mistake she'd made. It was my old mate Lewe, in Reading.

'Hi, Leaf. Been talking to Adam in Tanzania,' Lewe said, getting straight to the point, as usual. 'He doesn't think his contract is going to be renewed. He says if we're going to visit, it'll have to be very soon. I'm up for it. What about you?'

We had a standing invitation to visit Adam, Lewe's ex-brother-in-law, a civil engineer who'd been working in Africa since the early eighties. 'Good idea, we must do that,' we'd agreed, year after year. 'Are you serious?' I asked.

'Yeah.'

'OK, let's do it.' For the first time since I'd been in Spain I was making decent money. Some months before I'd begun giving one-to-one classes with the top three people in Cristalerias Españolas, a huge glass factory that daily turned five hundred tons of sand and trace elements into rear windows for small European cars. 'What are your rates?' They'd asked at the job interview.

Fed up with working for a pittance, I'd replied 'I charge thirty-two euros an hour.' I was hoping they wouldn't kick me out. It seemed like an awful lot of money to me, but it was nothing to them.

I was screwed up, but not so damaged I didn't recognise some travelling would give me something fresh to think about. I'd been driving myself nuts, running round and round the same small circles, like a mad hamster in a wheel. I needed a change of scene. I reckoned a couple of weeks in Africa would be just the ticket.

Lewe grew up in Whitley Wood, the toughest part of Reading. When I went to the University in '66, I was warned that the Whitley kids would beat up any students who strayed into their territory.

All that changed the following year, in the Summer of Love, when townies and students started turning-on together. Lewe came to score at Upper Reds one night towards the end of the sixties. We'd got stoned together and had been pals from then on.

'When the school holidays started,' he once told me. 'My mum would give me a sandwich and tell me not to come back until supper and not to bring the police with me.'

Lewe was intelligent and ill-educated: a jewel in a rough setting. Like many people whose hearing is poor, he spoke loudly. When he was low he wrote extraordinary poems.

His fingernails, bitten past the quick, suggested a nervous disposition, but he was totally down to earth and quite prepared to criticise anyone to his or her face. I liked his fierce honesty, his rough humour and his readiness to puncture anything pretentious or inflated. Lewe had been to most of the countries I'd visited and several more besides.

We'd found we were compatible travelling companions on a trip to Morocco in '85, but neither of us had visited Sub-Saharan Africa before. Liaising by phone, we worked out what we'd need to take and then got visas, jabs, plane tickets, malaria pills, mosquito nets and maps. We sorted out torches, a First-Aid box, binoculars, a few music cassettes hooks, string, clothes pegs, sewing kit, wash bag... It seemed like an awful lot for a fortnight's holiday, but they were all small items. I was suddenly excited and fearful. I was getting on for fifty and I hadn't been anywhere new for ten years.

In June I had a barbeque with friends before leaving. They all shook my hand and told me to have a great time – all except Juan who said 'Goodbye Nigel, I won't see you again.' His words echoed in my mind as I flew to England. What did he mean?

Was he leaving Catalunya or was he suggesting I would die in Africa?

Lewe and I took the coach to Heathrow. He went to check out the duty free shops. Alone, I wobbled and collapsed onto a seat, undone by a great spasm of terror. Lions, crocodiles, snakes, hyenas, malaria, sleeping sickness, voodoo... I was going to my death! I had a quick look around. Nobody was paying any attention to the balding man, panicking on a row of red plastic seats. Lewe returned, his hands full of wine gums. 'OK?' he asked, giving me an odd look.

'Er, fine.' The calling of our flight spared me any further questions. I hoisted my rucksack on my back and spoke firmly to the coward within. 'You can't back out now. If you do, you'll never go anywhere again.' In the duty free shop I bought vodka for Adam and Joyce, and a box of liquorice allsorts for their kids. 'Here we go then,' Lewe muttered, as we shuffled forwards in the queue. 'Into the unknown.'

22. THIRD WORLD MAN

Adam and his brother-in-law, Charles Nyirenda, met us at the airport and drove us into Dar es Salaam. The city was spread-eagled in the heat. Lewe, leaning forward, was chatting with the others. I listened and looked out of the window, drinking in our new surroundings.

It looked like everyone had tumbled out of the shabby, crumbling buildings and into the crowded streets. Under huge acacia trees, lines of vendors were selling a bewildering variety of goods, from beds to tyres, candles, clothes and kittens. There were vendors everywhere, some with tiny stalls, many with their wares spread out on the ground around them. Laughing children played in and around the puddles. Straight-backed Masai warriors strode purposefully through the crowds.

'Know what happened when we landed in Zanzibar, Adam?' Lewe was excited, gesticulating wildly. 'The plane stopped on the landing strip and everyone's luggage was emptied onto the tarmac. It was just a strip in the jungle. Then a crowd of people came out of the trees, on both sides, and went through our gear. We were stuck inside the fucking plane, man! Couldn't do anything but watch. They nicked all the stuff from the side pockets of my rucksack – torch, clothesline, knife... they even took my wine gums!'

Charles's laugh was was deep and wide. The 'Eeeeeee!' that followed was surprisingly high-pitched. Then he added 'Aaaa, Zanzibar,' as if that explained everything. Perhaps it did.

We passed large black and white crows flying among the palm trees and stalking over mounds of rubbish. I opened the window and breathed in the rich earthy smell of tropical air. A lot of time had passed since I'd been in the Third World. Now I was back, I remembered how much I liked it, how much I'd missed it.

Adam and Joyce lavished their stored hospitality on us. We were the first visitors from Europe they'd ever had, in all their years in Africa.

I'd met Adam at Reading Uni. He was a kid then, the son of the Sociology professor. Lewe knew him much better than I. Back in the hippy days Adam's elder sister had been Lewe's girlfriend.

On the first evening of our stay, our hosts threw a party so we could meet their friends. It was a kind gesture, but neither Lewe nor I had much in common with the well-to-do expat set. I was ill at ease being waited on by servants and I knew Lewe felt the same.

In the morning we were introduced to the house servants who lived in a hut in the compound. We said hello to the dogs and held out our hands to be sniffed, so they'd know not to bite the next time they smelt us. Then we jumped into Adam's jeep and drove to a steeply shelving beach, where the breakers of the Indian Ocean queued up to rush the shore. I picked up a couple of shells and looked out across the water, visualising the beaches of Goa on the other side of the ocean, round the curve of the planet.

That evening Adam and Joyce took Charles, Lewe and I to an Italian restaurant and then on to a nightspot, featuring the sexiest dancers I've ever seen in my life. We gaped spellbound until they ran offstage. The next act came on. The men opened a huge trunk and tipped out an enormous python. The handlers poked the sluggish snake to get it moving.

'I'm not watching this!' Lewe was highly agitated. He leapt to his feet and shot off towards the exit.

We looked at each other, got up and followed.

'What's the matter?' Joyce asked when we caught him up outside. 'Scared of snakes?'

'No, I like snakes' he replied. 'Their skin is delicate. They get damaged with that kind of treatment. One thing I hate is cruelty and that was fucking cruel!'

Adam and Joyce lived in a posh suburb, a guarded island of luxury in a sea of poverty. Their kind of life wasn't for us; we wanted to meet the folk on the other side of the wire. All over the world we'd been welcomed with warmth and open-handed generosity, by people who owned next to nothing.

Our travels on four continents had shown us that people are mostly helpful and friendly – if they haven't got wealth to protect – in which case they are usually mean and suspicious.

Every day of our stay, when Adam was working and Joyce was out playing tennis or shopping, Lewe and I slipped away from the compound and set off to explore Dar es Salaam. On the edge of a clearing, near an open-air market, we found a great place to hang out.

A small huddle of kiosks clustered in the shade of a huge mango tree. Wherever else we wandered, we came here most days and spent an hour or two sitting on worn-out tyres, smoking grass, joking with the cigarette seller and enjoying the breeze that seemed to favour that old tree. I juggled fruit for the crowds of kids who gathered around the white strangers.

'White men always busy,' said the teenager who ran the cigarette stall. 'The kids don' understand why you doing nothing.'

We weren't doing nothing, no, we were hanging out, flirting with the hairdressers, watching the carpenters at work, talking with the cigarette seller's customers or just observing the ebb and flow of the sea of humanity.

Charles Nyirenda, our friend and guide

Charles and I were the only two people in the house who had any interest in football. We watched the opening game of the 1998 World Cup from the deep sofas in front of Adam's huge TV. A thousand-mile bus ride lay ahead, just a short sleep away.

We left the house at four in the morning to catch the video-bus to Malawi. We were going for family reasons: Charles was Adam's brother-in-law and so was Lewe, after a fashion. We were going to meet more members of the large Nyirenda family. Charles, lean, good-looking and very laid back, was to be our guide and mentor.

At the bus station by four-thirty, we squeezed into our places, our knees jammed into the seat in front. Ahead of us lay a thirty-two hour ride with insufficient leg room. The driver spent a full quarter of an hour revving the engine, wreathing the vehicle in black smoke. Finally he let off the brake and pulled out of the bus station.

The sky lightened as we drove out of the city. Then we were clear of the suburbs of Dar and looking at trees and more trees and the odd dusty village. After a few hours, it felt like the bush would go on forever. A video started up - a film about the Angolan Civil War, all guns and blood, explosions, helicopters and sand. Lewe dozed, jacket draped over his head.

'So who's going to win the World Cup, Charles?'

'Aaah, I think it will be Brazil. Yes. Brazil is very good at football. Who do you think is going to win?'

'Well, I'm backing Spain.'

'Spain?' Charles squeaked in disbelief. He slapped his thigh and laughed loud and long. People across the aisle and in the seats in front turned to look at the source of the infectious laugh. They all smiled back.

'Spain never does anything!'

'I know, but the Spanish do play lovely football. They just can't produce an international side. One day they'll click and then you'll see what they're capable of.'

A grainy video came on of a tubby old guitarist playing by a swimming pool. The camera lingered lovingly on images of opulence: big cars, shiny suits, and the pool-babes – a couple of fat girls in tight red dresses, wobbling their bits in time with the wonderful music.

I jotted down a few observations in my notebook. My knees and my bum were aching already and we hadn't been going long. Soon I was aching however I sat. I remembered my long Indian bus journeys with nostalgic affection, for this trip was well over twice the distance of the longest bus ride I'd taken in the subcontinent.

We made a brief stop at a kiosk by the roadside. I stepped down to stretch my legs, have a pee and buy peanuts and bananas. Charles and I munched on the provisions. Lewe slept on. After Morogoro, the road went through the Mikumi National Park.

'Wake up, Lewe. Look!' A troop of monkeys crossed in front of the bus. Soon we saw a herd of antelope, a few zebras and a lone elephant. Then two enormous giraffes, necks swaying, ambled through the forest, one of the loveliest sights I've ever seen in my life.

'Aren't they amazing! So beautiful.'

Lewe's reply was a non-commital grunt. He shut his eyes and pulled his jacket over his face.

The bus wound up the hills towards Iringa. The lunch stop was a mercy; twenty minutes to eat, urinate and walk around. Lewe stayed in his seat. In no time at all we were back on the road. The going was painfully slow as we laboured into the Poroto Mountains. We'd gone from sea level to seven thousand feet in twelve hours.

'I don't feel so good,' Lewe mouthed weakly. He looked awful, his face had turned a mottled grey-green. Just in time, we found a bag for him to throw up in.

The sun abruptly fell out of the sky. We reached the Malawi border just before it closed for the night. Then we were back on the road, driving through the dark. The bus slowed to a crawl and began lurching around alarmingly. We seemed to be travelling along a dry riverbed, all potholes and boulders. The bumping and groaning went on and on.

'What happened to the road, Charles?' Has it been stolen?'

'Aaah, this was the Karonga road. It got washed away in the rains three years ago and hasn't been rebuilt yet.'

Lewe started vomiting again. 'I'll be OK,' he said stoically. He fell into a half-sleep, riding the jolts, surfacing with the bangs. It took us four hours to cover the twenty miles of washed-out road.

We stopped in Rumphi, Mzuzu, Mzimba, Kasungu… At every halt figures rose from the ground like zombies, or materialised out of the shadows. Passengers got off the bus and the night people took their seats. Eventually a hint of light crept into the edge of the sky, gathered its strength and dispelled the night. I hadn't slept and my aches had aches. Ready for the worst I asked, 'How long's it going to take, Charles?'

'Just five hours.'

'Five more hours. Oh fuck.' Lewe pulled his jacket over his head.

Charles wouldn't let us get a room in Blantyre. 'Nearly there' he said. A minibus ride took us to

Limbe.

'Is this it, Charles?'

'No, just one more short ride.'

Lewe groaned. Finally the bus stopped outside a motel in Bangwe Township. By this time we didn't care where we were as long as we could lie down and sleep.

Charles appeared in the morning, looking as dapper as ever. 'I'd like to take you to meet my family,' he said.

'That would be good,' Lewe seemed to have recovered from the marathon bus ride.

Hundreds of bottle-tops were embedded in the soft bitumen of the tarmac road. We followed it for a while then took the dirt track – muddy and strung with puddles – that led to Charles's place.

His wife was young, beautiful and very shy. She showed us her baby, then they disappeared out the back. Charles said something in Chichewa and she returned.

'She's not used to white people,' he said, laughing. 'And you're the first *Mzungus* my baby has seen.'

'*Mzungus*?'

'White people.'

I put out my hand and the baby started crying.

'It's OK, Jonathan,' Charles said laughing. The *Mzungus* aren't going to eat you!'

Charles and Violet lived in a tiny two-roomed house without water or electricity. All around were flowering trees and bushes. Small stands of maize grew here and there among the little shacks, chickens scratched in the dirt. Every woman seemed to have a child on her hip or back. There were kids everywhere. They all stopped to stare as we passed.

Bangwe had a reputation as a tough place. White people rarely ventured into the rundown township.

Bangwe sprawls across across the lower slopes of the hills to the east of Blantyre-Limbe, Malawi's largest city. The township was rough, but friendly. The barman told us we were the first white guys ever to visit the Shake-Shake bar, where scores of drinkers sat at concrete benches downing litres of cheap maize beer.

We stayed in the Bangwe Motel, a pink and blue one-story hotel built around a huge stone sugarloaf. Barefoot, we scrambled up the smooth surface of the rock. At the top there was a good view of the township and the maize-covered hills that rolled to the Mozambique border. The motel was mostly patronised by Mozambiquan businessmen on sugar-buying trips to Malawi. Sometimes girls came to see if they wanted company.

The Bangwe Motel was run by a redoubtable matriarch, Grace Tambala, and staffed by an amiable crew. The courtyard reminded me of Goa, with its pink and blue arched cloisters and its riot of giant flowering plants bursting out of old cracked pots. Big Brendan was in charge of the courtyard rooms.

'Is good, yaar?' he said in a Louis Armstrong growl, crashing through the foliage and handing me a bunch of bananas. He looked fierce, until his face burst into a delighted grin. We slapped palms all round. You only had to look at Brendan with the hint of a smile and he'd start laughing.

'His real name is Kenneth,' one of the motel boys told us, 'but he prefers to be called Brendan.'

'What's your name and what do you do here?' I asked him.

'Sir, my name is Witika and my job is downwash,' he replied.

'Well, good for you,' laughed Lewe.

'Please don't call me sir. My name's Leaf.'

'Leeeaf,' Brendan growled. 'Yaar.'

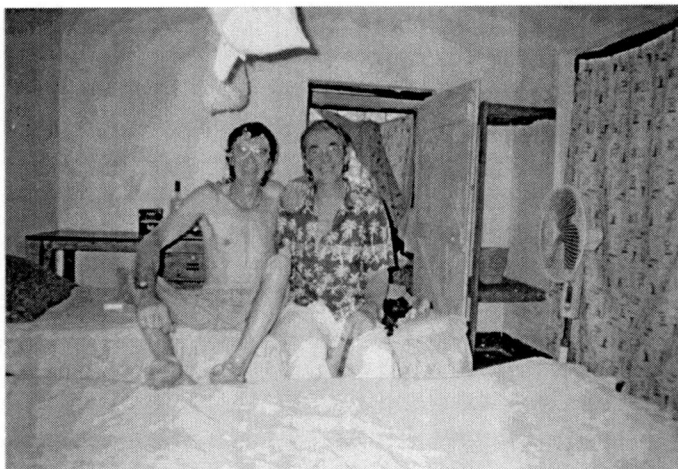

with Lewe, in the Bangwe Motel

23. MALAWI

On a map of Africa, Malawi has the appearance of a long, crooked penis, lying between the spread thighs of Mozambique.

Landlocked, mountainous and with few valuable resources, Malawi is a backwater, a land of subsistence farmers. It's one of the poorest countries in the world.

There were only three or four TV sets in the entire township. The Bangwe Motel had one of them. The staff sold tickets for the World Cup matches. They carried out the tables and chairs and packed the dining room with up-ended beer crates, to fit in as many people as possible.

Soccer is a passion among Malawians. The room was full for most games, but when there was an African interest, the place was so jam-packed it was impossible to leave until the match was over.

At the back, beside Charles, I perched on my crate for the Spain–Nigeria game. I was the only Spanish supporter among scores of fervent Super-Eagles fans.

'Goal!' I leapt to my feet when Spain equalised. A hundred faces turned to look at me in disbelief. Charles pushed his golf cap onto the back of his head and made a comment in Chichewa. The room filled with laughter and the people all around me shook my hand. What a roar went up when Nigeria scored again. Everyone turned to laugh at me – friendly laughter, no edge to it at all.

Malawians are welcoming people. Living at the southern end of the Great Rift Valley, the ancestral source of the human race, they never left home.

They're still at home – with themselves and their environment – in a way we exiles find almost impossible to understand.

In Tanzania, Charles had been a foreigner like us: a guest, unsure of his surroundings. On his home territory he was a social phenomenon. He had the rare gift of being able to make perfect strangers smile within moments of meeting them – not that there were many strangers in Charles' world. He seemed to be on speaking terms with everyone.

Wherever we went people would call out a greeting that sounded like the old English phrase 'I say.' The tone always suggested they were delighted to see him. Then they'd be off on a long animated talk punctuated by bouts of palm slapping and laughter.'

'Who was that?' Lewe or I would ask when the encounter was over.

'Aaah, that was the Limbe chief of police,' Charles said once. Every time it was different: 'He's from our village... I met her up north... I went to school with him... She's my cousin… We worked in South Africa together...' Charles knew everyone. We ran into his pals Ronald and Roland in a bar.

'So, what do you do, Leaf?' asked the nattily dressed Ronald.

'I'm a language teacher,' I replied. 'And you guys? What's your work?'

'Aaah, we don't work,' Roland confided, laying a gentle hand on my arm. 'We're businessmen.'

I laughed and we slapped palms, Malawi style.

We met more of Charles' family, made friends, went dancing, wandered the markets... Suddenly we were galloping through our last few days in Malawi and it was time to take the dreaded bus-ride back to the coast.

After the return trip to Dar es Salaam, we were too knackered to do much more than hang out with our friends under the big mango tree. In the final hours, projecting forward along my imminent flight path to Europe, I realised that I'd been so bound up in the raw dramas of Africa that I'd gone for days at a time without thinking about my uncertain future or what my lost love was doing. There was life after Rosie after all.

A fortnight in Tanzania and Malawi was just what I'd needed to take my mind off my troubles.

Our holiday had been wonderful, Lewe and I agreed. I figured it was a one-off. I had no idea what an important a role Malawi would come to play in our lives.

24. THIS TOO SHALL PASS

On the plane back to Europe, I started to feel the effects of some kind of bug: My mouth was dry, I was sweaty and giddy.

London, through my feverish eyes, was full of ugly white males with shaven heads, clenched fists, hard looks and fuck-you vibes. I looked at Lewe and knew what was in his mind: we'd returned from poor, smiling Malawi to the rich miserable West. I wished I could get on a plane back to Africa.

By the time I returned to Spain, my chest was hurting. I put it down to the black smoke that poured out of most of the vehicles in Malawi – that and the weak bush I'd been smoking. Figuring the ache would soon go away, I bravely carried on rolling up. But instead of receding, the pain grew worse. After a week every breath hurt.

Lung cancer? Once I had the thought, I couldn't put it out of my mind. I've been a smoker since I was seventeen. Needing to know, one way or the other, I went to see my doctor.

'Hello Nigel. I haven't seen you for some time. How are you?'

'Hi, Josep. I'm not so good. I've been in Southern Africa. The traffic fumes are terrible and my chest hurts. Can you give me a check up?'

The wait for the results was interminable; why hadn't I brought a book to read? At last Josep breezed in, a sheaf of plates in his hand.

'Your lungs are clear. You're lucky. You should stop smoking now'.

'I'm going to. Seriously, I'm going to stop.' I meant it; I felt like I'd just been reprieved and my relief was enormous. I still had pains in my chest though. I knew I had to quit smoking if I wasn't to spend my life wheezing and worrying.

'This time you'll do it,' I spoke sternly to my image in the mirror, trying to psyche myself into a positive frame of mind. 'No more cigarettes for you.' I stopped. Just like that. No gradual cutting back, no nicotine patches, nothing. Wanting to get the drug out of my system as soon as possible, I went cold turkey. I exerted willpower.

The exhilaration that came from finally confronting my addiction got me through the first five days of physical withdrawal. I fought each imp of craving and won every time. It hadn't seemed so difficult. Why hadn't I done it before? Then I remembered that I had – twice.

~

The first time I'd cracked it, going ten months without any tobacco. Then, on honeymoon in Kashmir, I started having the odd *bidi*, emptying the bits of tobacco out of the leaf in which they were rolled and replacing them with a crumbling of Kashmiri hash. I was smoking again, but it wasn't tobacco. I'd told myself I'd stop once I was back in Europe.

I bought a few packets of Ganesh bidis to take home. When they ran out, I went straight to the tobacconist, bought a packet of fags and carried on smoking for another ten years.

My second attempt at giving up ciggies ended ignominiously. I suffered for five or six weeks before coming to an abrupt decision. 'I can't stand any more of this.' I yelled and lit up. My decision to quit quitting led to a further decade as a stinking smoker.

~

I put thoughts of past failure aside. This time it would be different.

My optimism wore off as my suffering mounted. My body had become absolutely used to having a smoke at frequent intervals. Aside from the honeymoon break of ten months in 1976, I'd been having a fag some ten to fifteen times a day for the past thirty-odd years. I calculated I must have lit up well over a hundred thousand times. That gave me something to chew over. At first I tried keeping my oral cravings at bay with a joint of neat grass, but getting stoned only made me feel shaky and anxious. I had to stop smoking everything. I gritted my teeth and determined to see it out.

After a month, the chest pains grew more muted then went away altogether. I was holding on, keeping the tobacco devil at bay, but I was struggling. Time and again, I was desperate for a puff. I could grow seriously angry about not being able to finish my dinner with a joint. I wanted a smoke, dammit!

Knowing the craving would pass, I clung on, but at the back of my mind, in an ill-lit, cobwebbed corner of failure, festered the demoralising knowledge that I had to win every battle after every single fucking meal! Lose just one and I'd be smoking again. There was no halfway.

'You know you're going to fail again,' sneered the weasel-voice within. 'Why suffer unnecessarily? Go on mate, do yourself a favour, have a fag. Face the facts, man: you're a smoker.'

The internal battle raged on. My personality seemed to have fragmented. I spent a lot of time arguing with myself. The desire for tobacco was almost overwhelming. I knew that, if I gave in, I would never even attempt to quit again. Countering the host of defeatist whisperers, with all their compelling reasons why I should have a smoke, one lone voice was chanting the mantra Smiles had given me some years ago in prison, a small set of words to help us get through hard times. 'This too shall pass.'

'Hang on.' I encouraged myself. 'You've got this far. You will get through it.' I hung on. After four months everything I ate and drank tasted of tar. I knew it was in my power to bring an end to this agony of absence. That awareness made every day an ordeal. Joylessly I struggled on, doggedly holding on to the advice of an ex-smoker: 'It gets easier after six months.'

The anniversary of the day Rosie had dumped me came round. I wasn't entirely over the pain, but I could handle it. It was just another of the dull aches I seemed to be collecting.

Dining with friends on Christmas Day, awash with alcohol, I ate a hash brownie and rediscovered my appetite. After the pudding I steadily carried on eating – walnuts, dates, chocolate, tangerines... anything to postpone that crisis moment after the meal when the tobacco tang was greatest. Once I'd started eating, I couldn't stop until I was stuffed. I got a potbelly for the first time in my life. Between New Year's Day and Saint David's Day, I went from sixty to seventy kilos. I knew I was behaving obsessively and was repelled by the sight of my bloated body in the bath, but I was prepared to grant

215

myself almost anything if it helped me beat the killer drug.

In the depths of winter, I went quite insane. I held my act together in the classroom, but raved to myself at home, unable to settle on anything. It was supposed to get better after six months, the ex-smoker had said. It was seven now and I felt worse than ever.

'It's not fair!' I wanted to wail. I'd only been misinformed, but it felt like I'd been betrayed.

April is a beautiful month in Catalunya. The swifts and bee-eaters return from Africa, thyme flowers on the hillsides and the nightingales begin to sing again. I love the Catalan spring, but that April, undergoing my worst tobacco crisis, I scarcely noticed it.

One sad Sunday, at a summit meeting round the kitchen table, all the various factions warring in my mind agreed that I'd had enough. A body can only stand so much flaying. I would go and get a packet of *Ducados* from the tobacconist in the village. It was unconditional surrender.

Shattered by my defeat, I sat at the table, head in hands, congealed in misery. It was dark when I came back to my senses; the shop had closed and the overpowering need had passed. It had passed! It never returned with such force.

I still had cravings, especially at the end of dinner, but for the first time I felt confident about beating nicotine. I knew that all I had to do was hold firm through each mini-crisis, recite the mantra and the tobacco itch would diminish and eventually disappear.

As a new challenge for my flagging teaching career, I set up a ten-week language course for the wine trade. I was going to teach the Pénedès winemakers how to sell their products to the English. Teaching and talking to the growers and wine-masters, I grew interested in their world and found out at least as much about wine as they learnt about marketing to the Brits. Filled with enthusiasm for my new subject, I went to the forge of the last working cooper in Vilafranca.

'Could you make a small oak barrel for me?' I asked.

'How small? Twenty litres?'

'That sounds about right. Do you mind if I watch.'

'Of course not. There's a seat over there if you want to see how I work.'

I sat down on the stool. The cooper was a short, broad-shouldered man dressed in leathers. His workshop was warm and ill-lit. Great showers of sparks sprayed through the air and bounced off the floor when he welded the first pair of metal hoops. I felt as though I'd stepped back into the Iron Age. A singed smell filled the room as wooden staves met hot metal bands. Water hissed and spat; clouds of steam drifted through thin shafts of light.

The cooper took his wooden hammer and gave a few light taps until he was satisfied that the wooden end discs were as they should be. Four more times sprays of sparks filled the room while he fitted metal bands around the barrel. Again the workshop filled with steam as he doused the rings. He drilled the holes for the bung and the tap and fitted them. My barrel was ready.

It took him just five minutes to knock up a stand

for the barrel to sit on. He'd made it look easy, but the keg had materialised like magic in front of my eyes. In the space of an hour, he'd made a finished barrel out of eighteen curved oak staves of differing width, a couple of wooden end rings, six strips of metal, a tap and a bung.

'There you are,' he said, as he gave me the keg in exchange for a small wad of notes. 'Don't let it dry out and it'll still be good for your grandchildren.'

'Thank you. I really enjoyed watching you make the barrel. It was extraordinary, fascinating. Don't worry. I won't let the barrel dry out.'

Back at home, I carried out his final suggestion and poured a bottle of brandy into the barrel. I swilled it around daily and after a fortnight it had all been absorbed. Then I filled it with my neighbour's young Pénedès wine. I was pleased to have found another interest. I needed stuff to occupy my mind.

I was still on my own and not happy about it, but I recognised I was in no fit state to be good company for anyone. I realised I'd better get used to facing life as a single person.

25. A STONE OF POWER

Not long after burying Harry, my lovely old dog, a starving whelp turned up at my door.

Tens of thousands of bewildered strays wander around Spain at the start of the summer holidays – going away for a month, unwilling to pay for kennels, pissed off anyway because the little bugger has chewed everything in sight, Dad takes the overgrown Christmas puppy for a drive in the country. He stops by the roadside, kicks the dog out of the car and comes back alone, hoping the kids will have forgotten about the mutt by the time they return home after a month at the seaside.

Worried that the stray would freak out Timmy and the little kitten I'd adopted, I went onto the verandah and shouted *'Fuera, Fuera!'* Go away! He fell over in fright.

I relented when I saw the ribs protruding from his thin body. I gave him some milk in a bowl and then some cat biscuits. That made him my dog.

'I'll call you Sirius, after the Dog Star. What do you think of that?' He wagged his tail and licked my hand. Sirius grew into a handsome wolfish beast. The two of us walked for an hour or two every day.

In the middle of a field of bare vines one winter's afternoon, on the lookout for the lovely red pebbles I sometimes found in the area, I heard a voice say, 'I am a stone of power. Pick me up.' So I did.

I held the small stone in my hand and inspected it: a rough elongated cube, dark brown with white veins. More than anything, it resembled a quid deal of Afghani, back in the days when you could buy quid deals. It didn't look as though it was going to change my life.

I pick up quite a few things on my walks. Most of them go back where they came from, but if something catches my fancy, I take it home. I put the stone in my pocket and carried on walking. I'd never heard of a talking stone, but I wasn't too bothered. After a lifetime of getting high, I'd learnt to tolerate the fluctuations in reality.

The next day, before my doctors and nurses class in Vilafranca, I went to the lottery shop to do the pools. It was something I did every week during the football season. I followed the Spanish league but, though I knew a lot about the teams and players, I was no good at predicting the outcome of matches.

I made my selections and stood in the queue to place my bet. Glancing in the window whilst waiting my turn, I saw the array of five-figure numbers the shop had for sale in the Lottery. Each week the kiosk carried four or five different numbers and sold them in fractions. One of the numbers was 19999.

I handed the pools coupon to the sad blonde at the hatch. On the spur of the moment, in an attempt to make her smile, I said: 'Give me a fraction of this year's ticket, too.'

'We don't do a year ticket, it's just for one day.' She frowned and looked past me to the next customer.

'No. What I meant was, the number on the ticket is the same as this year... only with an extra nine,' I added lamely, wishing I'd kept my mouth shut.

Muttering, she went over to the window display to retrieve the ticket. The people in the queue behind me shuffled unhappily at the delay. They were waiting to place their bets before going on to the afternoon's work.

It was the first time I'd ever bought a National Lottery ticket. It cost me a thousand pesetas – four quid. That was eight times the price of my pools coupon. I had no idea the lottery was so expensive and regretted my stupid impulse.

On Sunday evening, as usual, I watched *Gol a gol*, the football round up. Once again I hadn't won the pools. Days later, hurrying past the kiosk on the way to a class, I saw a sandwich-board in the street, saying that 19999 had won second prize in last Thursday's draw.

'That could be worth a few quid,' I thought. 'I hope I've still got the ticket.'

Back at home I found it on my desk. A few days later I went to claim my small fraction of second prize in a mid-week draw.

The faded blonde with the pink lipstick went all dithery when I handed her my winning ticket.

'We can't pay out that kind of money,' she said, flustered. Visibly pulling herself together, she continued. 'You have to take the ticket to the bank. They'll check it and authorise the payment. What else? Oh yes. I'll take a photocopy, if you don't mind. Back in a moment.' She disappeared into the street.

I waited and waited, beginning to wonder if she'd run off with my winnings. When she finally returned it was with a volley of apologies. A line of people followed her inside, talking animatedly about the big win.

For a moment I wondered what was going on, then I realised: she'd been showing my ticket around the market square.

'Can you tell me how much I've won?'

'You've won two million pesetas,' she replied, breathlessly.

That was eight thousand quid.

I walked around with a big smile on my face for weeks after the lottery win. What a windfall! Maybe my luck was turning. I didn't spend any of my winnings for a while. Then I replaced my expiring old car, and bought myself a computer. That was almost half the money gone. While I was still feeling rich, I thought I'd treat myself to a bottle of the best wine in Spain.

~

'Did I ever tell you that I once drank a bottle of *Vega Sicilia Unico*?' Dave, my old pal in Barcelona, had asked me one day.

We were sitting at a table in the shade of a plane tree in a square just off Paseo de Gracia, having a coffee and watching the girls go by.

'I don't think so. What is it?'

'It's only the most expensive wine in the country – about five times the price of the best Rioja!' Dave leaned forward with his shining honest eyes and whispered, 'and you know what? It's worth it!'

~

My friend's words had made an impression on me. Remembering them, I headed towards the top *bodega* in Vilafranca. I looked around a bit, to get an idea of prices. There was a lot of good *Rioja* and a fair selection of *Ribera del Duero* but none of Spain's most celebrated wine.

'Do you have any *Vega Sicilia Unico*?'

'Oh, Señor!' she wailed. 'I'm so sorry, but we're

out of stock. Normally we'd have some, but last month the King bought six hundred cases as a gift for your Queen. That created a shortage, so naturally there was a race to get hold of what remained. Everyone grabbed as much as they could. It's all gone.'

Not everyone, I thought. Not at a hundred quid a bottle.

In the autumn, Lewe rang from England and asked what I was doing for the millennium. I hadn't planned anything, nor had he. We agreed to travel somewhere unusual. Following the Lottery win, I could afford to go over the hills and far away.

'What about the South Pacific? Tahiti and Bora Bora, I loved those names when I was a kid. They rang bells in my imagination.'

'Samarkand and Bokhara for me,' Lewe said wistfully. 'The golden cities on the old silk route...' We talked the world, thinking long and hard about New Zealand, then swung through a score more possibilities before agreeing that it would be brilliant to visit our old pal John Newson, in Hong Kong.

Lewe rang his friend Lisa at the Travel agency to make the booking. He was too late. Every ticket to Hong Kong for the month of December had been sold. He rang me and we agreed to go with our fall-back plan – New Zealand – but all planes to the Antipodes were fully booked too.

'Lisa said there'd been a massive rush to buy tickets to the Far East,' Lewe moaned. 'Those sad fucks want to be the first to see in the third millennium.'

'Let's change our approach, Lewe. Ask Lisa if there are any flights that still have seats available.'

He rang back a few minutes later.

'We can get a flight to Lilongwe. What about it? We had a good time on our last visit to Malawi, didn't we? Only we've got to decide right now, on the phone, or those seats will be gone too...'

'Let's go for it,' I said. 'Malawi it is.'

26. LAKE MALAWI

We flew out of Heathrow like a stone from a slingshot. Reloaded at Addis Ababa, we were flung to Malawi and dropped into timelessness. Charles wasn't there to meet us at Lilongwe Airport as we'd arranged.

When the post-flight bustle calmed down, we realised the terminal was emptying fast. A look at the board showed we'd arrived on the last flight of the day.

'Is there an Airport bus?' I asked the Avis lady.

'There's no airport bus any more,' she replied. 'They cancelled it because there were too many passengers.'

Going outside was like stepping in front of an industrial blow-heater. The sun was frying an egg on my bald patch. There were no taxis. There was nothing outside except large palm trees and a double line of huge flowering jacarandas disappearing into the heat-haze.

'No go.' I told Lewe, back in the cool cafeteria. 'And no more flights today, so probably no more cabs. Charles could arrive at any moment with a taxi, but what if he doesn't?'

Our driving licences were in Europe, so we couldn't hire a car. We weren't going to walk it – Lilongwe was fifteen miles away. It looked like we were stuck. I was tired and hungry. I needed some proper food – something that didn't come wrapped in cellophane. I rationed myself to occasional small sips of my cold drink. My hopes of seeing Charles sank with the level in the bottle.

A taxi pulled up outside the main door of the

terminal. Lewe and I looked at each other, grabbed our bags and ran outside, into the heat. Covered in a film of sweat, we haggled with the driver and paid over the odds for a ride to the capital.

Early the next morning, we heard Charles's voice outside our flophouse room. I leapt out of bed, struggled into my trousers and opened the door. There he was, looking cool in his golf cap, a massive grin on his handsome face: Charles the Great. Somehow, in a city of half a million people, he'd tracked us down.

'Sorry,' he said. 'The bus broke down at Dedza.'

'Charles! How did you find us? Hey, good to see you! *Muli Bwanji.*'

'Ndili Bwino.'

'Kay I ino.'

'Zicomo.'

After the ritual Chichewa greeting, we did the Malawi triple handshake, slapped palms all round and had a great big hug.

'Come on,' said Lewe, buttoning his shirt. 'Let's get some breakfast. I'm starving.'

'The bus broke down at Dedza last time, remember? We had to stay the night.' Lewe mopped up the rest of his egg yoke with a piece of bread. 'Hey, maybe the hotel owner pays the driver to stage a breakdown and gives him a cut from the rooms he rents.' He laughed aloud, pleased with his idea.

'I'll never forget Dedza,' I said. 'Crappy hotel, the best sunset ever and the most beautiful woman in the world, gliding gracefully along in the middle of a great flow of people.' I paused, seeing her again on the screen of my memory: she stopped, turned her head and we stared at each other longingly until the

226

river of flesh carried her away.

Dawn is the best time in the tropics. I got up and took an early morning walk. The nascent day was full of promise, on the verge of greatness.

I wandered over to the market in the clearing. It wasn't noisy and colourful as markets usually are – this was a private affair. It clicked: I'd gatecrashed a witchdoctors' surgery. Healers and sufferers squatted on the ground, having earnest whispered consultations, exchanging money for magic cures wrapped in a banana leaf.

An ancient, stone-faced medicine man gave me a hard look. I got the same shivery feeling I'd had when I met the giant in prison, five years after dreaming about him. Bad magic was in the air. I shot off, before the witchdoctor put a curse on me.

After breakfast we headed straight to the lake. Three bus rides got us to Monkey Bay, then we jumped into a pick-up that was leaving for Cape Maclear. After bouncing along a rutted track for half an hour, we arrived at the lake.

'Here we are,' Charles said. 'We'll put up at Steven's. It's the best place to stay.'

Lake Malawi, the southernmost of the African great lakes, is four hundred miles long. It has more varieties of freshwater fish than any other body of water in the world, and everyone is after them. Men in dugout canoes use line and net, day and night. Pied kingfishers patrol the shallows, hovering over the water like kestrels. Above them kites and buzzards cruise and, higher still, fish eagles describe great dinner circles.

Cape Maclear consisted of a handful of tourist beach shacks tacked onto a traditional fishing village. It was a relaxed and beautiful place. People who'd made the effort to get there usually stayed a week or two. When we arrived there were around twenty young backpackers from half a dozen different countries.

Local carvers were trying to make a living from the few tourists, but they were struggling. Travellers don't want to lug heavy wooden souvenirs around. Life was hard for these artists and craftsmen and if they hadn't caught any fish, they were usually desperate for a sale just to get something for dinner. Their hassling was positively gentle by Moroccan standards, but it was normal to be accosted a dozen times a day.

I walked up the beach, well away from the village, and sat by the water's edge, watching the kingfishers and letting the wavelets nibble my toes. All too soon I became aware of the scrunch of feet on sand.

'How are you?' The voice came from behind me. Following the exchange of *Muli bwanjis* the man continued,

'Maybe you'd like to have a look at …'

'Thanks, but no thanks,' I replied, staring out across across the water. 'I don't want to look at anything today except the lake.'

'It doesn't cost anything just to look.' He squatted beside me, waving a card on the fringe of my vision.

'Please,' I wailed. 'I'm not buying anything today, I just want to sit quietly on the beach.'

'Sorry,' he said, retreating. 'Have a good day.'

'Wait!' I called. My brain had belatedly registered the image on the card. 'Let me have a look at that.'

He passed it over. It was postcard size, a painting on heavily textured paper. Three women, each with a baby on her back, were pounding maize with long poles in giant mortars. There was life, movement and colour. It was wonderful. On the back was written, *Skinny Women*, by Jefferson Gulo.

Jefferson was an odd looking man, tall and thin with a tubular head. As an artist, he had something special. I looked through his wad of cards, sorted out half-a-dozen and bought them. That evening I scrawled lotus-eating messages on the back to send the postcard paintings off to people I thought would appreciate them.

After a few lovely, lazy days by the lake, the three of us caught a series of buses down to the deep south of the country. We were going to visit Charles's mother and sisters.

Almost all of Malawi is mountainous, over three thousand feet, but the lower Shire valley isn't much above sea level and it's sweltering.

Stuffed into a bulging minibus, we zigzagged down the huge Thyolo escarpment towards the lowlands where the Shire River joins the Zambezi. The heat rose up to meet us. We staggered off the bus in Nchalo with sweat coursing off our bodies. The thermometer stood at thirty-seven – air as hot as blood. Charles's mother greeted us in the little flowered courtyard in front of their house.

'Isn't it a nice cool day,' she said.

Lewe spluttered as he shook her hand. 'Well if this is nice and cool,' he asked earnestly, 'What's it like when it's hot?'

Charles led us inside and introduced us to two of

his sisters: Susan and Mary.

'Would you like to go to the Elephant Marsh?' Susan asked.

'That doesn't sound too good.' Lewe laughed. 'What is it?'

'It's a wildlife reserve. My husband works for the sugar company. If you like he can borrow a jeep for the afternoon and take you to look at the wildlife.'

'Great,' Lewe and I said in unison.

with Lewe and Susan at the Elephant Marsh

We stood in the back of the open pick-up, holding on to the metal rail, on the lookout for sunbirds. The passing air was hair-dryer hot. At the river, a group of twenty hippos basked in the muddy water. We stayed high on the viewing platform. well clear of them. Hippos are easily irritated and have a habit of killing the curious. It's said they do for more people than any other African animal. Surely the mosquito...

Crocodiles, not hobbits, swim in the Shire River. One of these prehistoric reptiles heaved itself out of the opaque water and slapped onto the bank. It seemed large to me, but was revealed as only a youngster when a truly enormous beast, five or six metres long, appeared on a sandbar upstream. One moment the sandbank was clear. The next instant there was a croc. It had materialised, as if by magic.

Back at his mother's house, Charles said 'Take a look at this.' He handed me a copy of the local paper. I read out the headline: 'Crocodiles are killing fifteen people a week on the Nchalo stretch of the river. The Government must take action!'

'Parliament has been discussing the problem,' Susan said, 'but so far they've done nothing. That's why the sugar company hired a hunter: He shot seventy crocs in three days, but it's made no difference. People are still getting eaten.'

'Who gets caught, Charles?' I asked.

'Fishermen, goatherds, lovers, children... anyone by the river.'

Lewe made disbelieving noises. He wasn't having it. 'Fishermen, sure, but on land you can run away. I've seen Aussies do it on TV.'

'I don't know about Australia, but African crocodiles have magic powers,' Charles said, in a voice that grew deeper and more sombre as the sentence progressed.

We laughed.

'I'm not joking!' When indignant, Charles's voice became high-pitched. 'Crocodiles put spells on people – make them sleepwalk to their death. Believe me,' his voice quivered. 'Never go anywhere near the river.'

I went to sleep with my head full of Charles's words. In the morning we got up and returned to the

Elephant Marsh. I parked the jeep on the hard standing. We walked the duckboards to the viewing platform. Some nagging thought was troubling me. I clicked my fingers as I got it. I didn't have my license – I shouldn't have been driving the jeep. The others had turned at the click.

'Nothing,' I said. 'Carry on, I'll be right with you.' I watched to make sure they were leaving, then headed back to the car to get my cigarettes. Wait a minute, I didn't smoke any more, or was I a secret smoker? What was going on? My confusion grew when the fallen tree trunk beside the duckboards morphed into a crocodile. I stood paralysed.

'I called for you,' it said, chuckling. With a lightning lunge, it fastened its jaws on my leg and dragged me towards the water; I knew my dismal fate. I'd been reading about these beasts the day before: they terrified me. I'd be taken to the croc's pantry, a sunken tree trunk, under which I'd be wedged until required.

I grabbed a tree stump on my way into the water and held on for my life. The crocodile clamped its jaws tighter. I screamed. It pulled and shook its head. The muscles in my leg were tearing and Lewe was shouting in my ear, 'Wake up! Bad dream.'

The following morning – the real morning – we slung our hook. Our abrupt departure had nothing to do with fear of the croc, (tick tock). The Shire valley was just too hot for us.

27. THE BANGWE MOTEL

Our reception at the Bangwe Motel was moving. We shook everyone's hands again and again and got a huge hug from big Brendan. Witaka came running up to say hello.

'Welcome. You are most welcome!'

'Witaka! Good to see you. How are you?'

'I am very well, sir. Yes.' With shy pride he added, 'I am up-wash now, Mister Leaf.'

Everyone was pleased to see us, including Grace Tambala, the matriarch, with whom we'd been a little uneasy on our first visit. Our wariness had been because she was the boss and a very large lady, in every sense; hers because we were *mzungus* and everyone knows that white people are powerfully crazy.

Even Grace thawed to us on our second visit, dissolving into an ocean of giggles the night we toasted the discovery that she, Lewe and I had all been born in nineteen forty-eight and were all fifty-one.

I produced the Frisbee I'd brought with me. 'Grace, will you join us in a game?'

She laughed and said, 'I'll watch you play first.'

We gave the employees a demonstration of Frisbee throwing and the entire Bangwe Motel staff, including Montfort, the manager, joined in the game.

They'd never seen a Frisbee before and they loved it. We had a session every day of our stay. The cooks, cleaners, barmen and waiters leapt wholeheartedly around the large compound, oohing and aahing at elegant throws and catches, hooting derisively at failures. Grace enjoyed watching, but her size and sense of dignity prevented her from taking part. The boss had her status to maintain.

On Christmas Eve, we went to a concert in Blantyre, danced until dawn and slept through most of Christmas Day. We went to three gigs in that final week of the old century. Malawi is big on music and dancing can break out anywhere, anytime. It's in the blood and the hearts of the people.

'Let's go to Zomba for the millennium,' Charles said. 'It's a friendly place with a relaxed atmosphere. The botanical gardens are among the best in Africa.' Lewe and I looked at each other doubtfully.

Zomba: the name was reminiscent of the living dead. Charles's description of the town made it sound interesting though...

'There's Zomba Mountain,' Charles continued innocently. 'With lots of birds in the treetops and sweet fruit in the forest, if you know where to look for it.' He knew he'd got us with the birds. 'We can have a picnic lunch on a big rock in the middle of the beautiful Mandela Waterfalls.'

'OK. We get the message'

'And you can get some of the stones you were hoping to find.' Charles was relentless.

'Stop there, Charles,' I said. 'We surrendered a while ago.'

At the end of the rather boring journey to Zomba we got off the bus and hoisted our backpacks. Lewe strode on ahead of us. We hadn't gone twenty yards before he slung off his pack, reached into his back pocket and came out with a fistful of small notes.

'Oh man. Passion fruit!' His crackly voice was

full of excitement. 'I've never seen so much at once!' He bought a big bagful for a few pennies from a street vendor.

'Anything else before we check into the hotel?' Charles asked.

Lewe's mouth was full of fruit. Yellow-green juice ran down his chin.

'No thanks, Charles,' I replied. 'Let's get these bags off our backs first.'

We wrote our names in the book of the small hotel and were given a room with three beds, two chairs and a shower. After quenching our thirst with passion fruit, we took it in turns to shower.

When we were all dried off, we set off on a long leisurely walk, to get the blood circulating after the bus ride and to check out the town.

Back at the hotel, there was an attractive young lady sitting in reception.

'Would you like some passion fruit?' Lewe asked, holding a fistful of the fruit out to her.

She looked alarmed and shook her head. 'Don't worry,' Lewe assured her, 'they don't work.'

After dinner, I read Charles and Lewe the poem I'd been struggling with for months, swapping and changing until I was finally happy with ....

THE TWENTIETH CENTURY KISSOFF

Picasso, Profumo, Sarajevo twice,
Lasers, Lindberg, Biafra, Spice.
Blackshirts, the greens, Orangemen, reds,
Auschwitz, Apollo, all-weather treads.

Khomeini, Kon-tiki, Mata Hari, Spock,

Dylan, Disney, Mao, Mau-Mau, rock.
Tenzing, Pele, Chernobyl, AIDS,
Haile Selassie, wrap-around shades.

The Boxer rebellion, Tienanmen Square,
Garbo, Houdini, Quisling and Blair.
Vichy, Gandhi, LSD, slacks,
Sharpeville, the Beatles, PCs and Macs.

Charles Atlas, Nkrumah, Jung, Marley, gay,
Flappers, pulsars, Sartre, DNA.
V bombers, U boats, nuclear fuel
X files, Y fronts, Muffin the Mule.

Moonies, the Sun, Mars bars, Pol Pot
'Finnegan's Wake', 'Some like it hot'.
Einstein, Chaplin, Tokyo Rose,
The Clash, the Somme...what's next?
Who knows?

On the first morning of the new millennium,
Charles, Lewe and I got up at dawn and set off
towards Zomba Mountain. We'd had a quiet evening
at the bedside of the expiring twentieth century and
were clear-headed for the climb.

It was cool on our walk through the long-
shadowed town but the temperature rose with the
sun. After an hour we paused to drink water and get
our breath back. We stood in the shade of a huge
tree, looking at the town below, hypnotised by the
twists of smoke from scores of breakfast fires
ascending towards us and dissolving into the air.

'Come on,' I said, breaking the spell, hoisting our
lunch bag onto my shoulder. 'Let's get moving.
We've got a mountain to climb.'

Further up the path we halted again, to watch two men at work. One was on the edge of the track, the other in a hole in the ground. Using a six-foot, two-man saw, they were hand-cutting a hardwood tree into long thick planks.

They paused at our arrival and the older man spoke to Charles in Chichewa. The only words I recognised were *chamba* – marijuana, and *mzungu* – white man. The sawyer guffawed at our friend's reply. Everyone we'd met cracked up at his comments. Tall, lean and laid-back, Charles the Great always found the right words to say.

Lewe unrolled his dirty laugh and nudged me in the back. Pointing at the guy in the hole, covered in sweat and sawdust, he said, 'Look, Leaf. It's the pits!'

The sawyer with the upper hand got out a bag of grass and made a fat little joint. He offered us a toke but we declined and moved on. It was too early to get stoned. It wasn't a difficult climb, but we still had a long way to go.

We stopped around midday and ate our picnic lunch on a flat rock in the middle of the Mandala cascades. Water bubbled and gurgled all around us, bouncing spray off rounded stones and rushing down the mountain. It was a magical spot. Lewe and I sat silently on our slab in the river, on the lookout for wildlife.

The longer I live, the more I've come to love birds. Lewe's the same. Malawi was an avian paradise for us: it was full of new species. There were big bold tropical types, bright and raucous, and slim, quick birds that you only saw out of the corner of your eye, flitting and darting in the forest canopy.

237

I'm not a bird nerd. I don't want to categorise or name them, stuff or cage them. I just love everything about birds – their songs, their colours, their freedom of flight...

Charles went for a wander and came back with a bag full of freshly-picked passion fruit. His other hand held golden berries.

'They're like the raspberries I used to nick from next door's garden,' Lewe said, 'only they're yellow and unbelievably sweet.'

We climbed the last stretch of the mountain and splashed out on a fruit juice at the four-star hotel, perched incongruously on the plateau. We spent a few minutes relaxing, letting the life come back into our tired legs, then we knocked back our drinks and went to check out the crystal sellers who hung around below the hotel.

The stone hawkers scratched a living by scraping the mountain for tourmaline and quartz and selling the semi-precious stones to the handful of four-star tourists in Malawi. None were in evidence on the first day of 2000. They were probably in bed, nursing massive hangovers.

A dozen of the hawkers pressed round us, jostling each other, thrusting their finds in our faces.

'How much,' I pointed at a fine quartz crystal on a grubby scrap of cloth.

'Only forty kwacha, boss.'

He was elbowed out of the way by a larger, man. 'Boss, boss! My piece bigger. Thirty kwacha.'

'Sir,' another wailed, 'buy mine, twen'five.'

I stood, silent and horrified, while the crowd of hawkers grew around me. They beat each other down until they were offering me their stones for pennies. Lewe was besieged by a similar crowd of hungry men. I spotted the owner of the first crystal and gave him forty Kwacha. Forty pence wasn't much for such a beautiful stone. I bought half a dozen pieces of tourmaline off some of the other guys.   Lewe was trying to make his way towards me, waving his arms to clear a path. Our imminent departure increased the frenzy of the men who'd sold nothing. Thin hands plucked at our clothing. Were we going to have to fight our way out?

'Come on. Come on! Let's go NOW!' Charles yelled. He was standing by a taxi, waving furiously for us to join him. We pushed our way through the crowd and clambered into the back seat. The car shot off down the road.

'Sorry,' Charles said. 'Sorry. I didn't realise that things were so bad here.' We sat in silence, stunned by the sheer desperation of the men we'd just encountered.

A couple of days later we were on the streets of Limbe, on our way back to Bangwe township.

Lazing by the lake, picnicking in the middle of a waterfall or strolling in Zomba's fine botanical gardens... it had been easy to enjoy the beauty and charm of Malawi. Now once more in the city, we saw the desperate side of Malawian life.

Limbe was a disintegrating mess. The air was foul, the roads were falling apart and the drainage system was collapsing.

There'd been beggars in Limbe on our first trip to Malawi – the old, widowed, maimed or blind. Now there were children too, dressed in rags, looking for food. The bigger ones hung around the bus stops, waiting for the opportunity to earn a little money by carrying someone's bags. Groups of tiny waifs clustered at the doors of the supermarkets and begged food from the departing shoppers.

When we went out, we frequently saw funeral processions moving downhill towards the river. At the cemetery, the pall-bearers waited in line to get their coffins into the ground.

'This is unbelievable,' I hissed in Lewe's good ear. 'It must have been like this during the plagues of the Middle Ages!'

'Oh, man!' he wailed. 'It's fucking awful: breaks your heart.'

Giant billboards proclaimed the news beside the highway that joined the twin towns of Blantyre and Limbe. The country's huge AIDS problem was finally out in the open, after years of denial. Official figures were that fifteen per cent of the population were infected. That amounted to a million people.

'It's worse up in the north around Karonga.' Charles's voice was sombre. 'My uncle said whole villages have been abandoned; the adults die, the children go off to beg in the nearest town. In the early days, orphaned youngsters were taken in and looked after by aunties and grandparents. But, as more adults died, orphans started appearing on the streets of the cities.'

To lose your Mummy is the worst thing that can happen to any small child. I felt so sorry for these little mites. I'd known their desolation, the huge hole in the heart of their life. But I hadn't had to struggle on my own, in a desperately poor country of subsistence farmers. I was crying for them, the way I'd once cried for myself and prayed for sleep.

We gave our coins to the tots hanging around outside the supermarket when we went to into town.

'What can you do?' we'd say sadly to each other, back at the Bangwe motel. 'What can you do?'

I was much more affected than I was letting on. I didn't want to go out any more. But lying on my bed in Bangwe, waiting for the days to pass so we could fly back to England, only depressed me more. It reminded me of my year of living on a bed, banged up on remand in Horfield prison. Whatever I did I couldn't stop my thoughts returning to the plight of those kids on the streets.

Orphans' temporary shelter, Blantyre

28. THE WARM HEART

I'm still not sure how, but our despairing lament, 'What can you do?' was somehow transformed into a genuine question. 'What can we do?' Changing that one little word changed everything.

'This is fucking shit, Leaf,' Lewe sat up. In the echoing silence he stared at me, anguish pouring from his seamed face. 'These are good people. They don't deserve all this!'

'I know,' I replied. 'We can't just sit here, doing nothing. And it's no good pretending it isn't happening. We've got to do something.'

'Sure, but what the fuck can we do?'

'These kids need a home,' I said. 'They need food and a safe place to sleep.'

'I know that. But we're not rich, we can't give them a home.'

Desperation somehow became inspiration. 'We could ask our friends and families.' I said. 'We've both got lots of friends, haven't we? We could try raising money from the people we know.'

Attempting to find a solution felt much better than being smothered by a feeling of hopelessness. I looked up and saw Lewe was grinning. He's a cheerful guy, but he hadn't smiled much lately.

'We could, you know', he said. 'Build a home for some kids... It's not a bad idea... in fact it's a fucking good one! Are you serious, do you want to have a go at doing something for them?'

'Yes. Yes I do.'

'So do I,' he said decisively and leapt to his feet.

He began laughing but managed to stop long enough to say, 'We don't know anything about orphanages.' I was a half a beat ahead of him as we chorused 'We'll ask Charles.'

'One thing, mate,' I added. 'If we do decide to go ahead, we can't just quit if it gets difficult. We have to see it through. Are we agreed on that?'

'Course. What a turn up, eh?' His chuckle was a dirty swampwater gurgle, a sign he had something funny to say. 'You know what's happened, don't you? We've been captured by the Malawians!'

We roared with laughter. The sound died away and the silence was filled with our growing awareness of the magnitude of what he and I just had agreed to do. For a moment doubt threatened to overwhelm me, but I pushed it away and then, all at once, I felt good, very good.

In my head, I heard the Electric Eel saying 'Nothing much happens if you stay at home. You have to get out there and make your own life.'

'How could we live with ourselves,' I murmured, 'if we just flew back to England and pretended none of this had happened.'

'What?' I'd spoken on Lewe's deaf side.

'Nothing. Listen, we've only got tomorrow.'

'Yeah, I know. So let's find out as much as we can.' He paused before asking, 'Leaf, we are going to do this, aren't we?'

'You bet your life we are!'

'Well, we ain't an organisation. We'll do it as people.' Lewe held his hand out. I took it and shook it. Both of us were trembling with emotion. Then we went to look for Charles.

Lewe had travelled even more extensively than I. We'd both been unimpressed by what we'd seen of charity work in the Third World: aid workers bombing around in air-conditioned top-of-the-range Land-cruisers at forty grand apiece – each one costing enough to provide a home for scores of children.

'Look at those prats,' Lewe said scornfully. 'Their European salaries make them rich in the poor countries. But what are they doing? I ain't noticed much of their wealth going to help the kids on the street.'

In spite of all the money donated by kind, well-meaning people, the charity system wasn't reaching those in need. Millions of pounds given to help the helpless went on paying often inflated salaries, rents and admin costs.

Lewe had wound himself up. 'You know what the trouble is? The bastards who control the reception of the aid keep most of it for themselves!'

'Sadly it's true. Charity is a profitable racket for those on the inside track.'

'Listen. If we really want to help these kids, we'll have to pay our own way.'

'Of course we will,' I replied. 'We'll pay our own expenses and see to it that the home gets set up properly. All the money we raise – all of it – will be for the children.'

There were only thirty hours left before we'd have to leave. Needing to find out as much as possible about Malawian orphanages, we asked Charles for help. He took us to an orphanage that was up the road from the Bangwe motel; we hadn't even known it was there. It was called Chitolera House and was run by a Malawian charity called the Samaritan Trust.

A tall, thin man came out of the building and

greeted us on the steps. Charles spoke to him in a rapid burst of Chichewa. He turned to us. 'This is Mr Joseph Bande, the warden of the home.'

Joseph had a wide mouth and a massive smile.

'Eeee,' he began. 'You are most welcome. Mister Nyirenda tells me you want to help the homeless children. That is very good!'

Lewe was fanning himself with his floppy hat. 'Let's get in the shade,' he croaked. 'This heat's too much!'

We moved and sat down in the shade. A breeze wafted by and set the banana fronds clacking. Joseph did his best to answer the series of rapid-fire questions that Lewe and I flung at him.

Joseph didn't know all the answers about administration and finances, but he told us how the orphanage functioned. His excellent English was peppered with lots of Eeees and Aaaahs.

'The Government provides free education for all the Samaritan Trust children, up to the age of fourteen. Local businesses, mostly run by the Asian community, donate food to the Trust.'

'What about the street kids?' I said. 'How do they survive?'

'Aaah, that is difficult. When we have surplus food, we take it around the camps that the children make in Limbe and Blantyre.'

'How do you get surplus food?' Lewe asked.

'We go around the supermarkets at the end of the day and take the unsold bread and any fruit and vegetables that won't last.'

'How many kids do you look after?' Charles wanted to know.

'Around a hundred and fifty. We have three centres: this one, which feeds over fifty kids and has room to house twenty-five boys. We have a large tent in Blantyre; it's a transit place where the children can stay for a time. The Samaritan Trust's main centre is at Stella Maris,' Joseph continued. 'The government gave us a twenty-acre plot with several buildings. It was one of the centres of the Young Pioneers: the thugs of the old dictator, Hastings Banda.'

'What about the girls?' Lewe asked. 'Where do they stay? There's some of them here now.'

The girls, who had been edging closer to catch our conversation, were all suddenly busy, attending to each other's hair or looking intently at their schoolbooks.

'Aaaah, they stay with aunties and family friends here in the township. We don't have facilities for girls,' Joseph admitted.

'Thanks, Joseph,' I said. 'You've been a big help. I can't think of anything else to ask at the moment, but I'm sure we'll have a lot more questions. We'll see you on our next visit'.

We had just enough time to check out another orphanage in Blantyre. Surrounded by large trees, it was a dark and dismal place. The kids appeared cowed, subdued. I asked the principal if they had a religious agenda

'We only take Christians,' he said.

Forgetting diplomacy, I replied, 'That's not a very Christian attitude. Come on, Lewe, we're out of here.'

14.1.2000

Hi Lewe,

This is a test to see if I can send stuff direct from my computer to your fax. If it works, brilliant – if

not I'll fax you photocopies.

These are early drafts of things I've been working on. At the moment I'm just throwing up ideas, thinking aloud – making a start.

What do you reckon on the following?

THE WARM HEART PROJECT

On our first visit to Malawi, in 1998, we were struck by the grace and friendliness of the people as well as the beauty of the landscape. Malawi is a very attractive place. Only on our return did we begin to see beneath the surface and start to appreciate the problems of this wonderful country.

Government statistics admit that one in twelve adults is HIV-positive; Newsweek magazine puts the figure at between 10 and 15%. Either way the country faces disaster. In the coming years, even if the spread of AIDS were to stop now, the working population will be decimated and the number of orphans will soar.

We aim to do all we can to help these children and have resolved to set up a home (to be known as The Future) where orphans will be able to live and grow in a loving environment.

To that end we are asking everyone we know for help: we need money and later we will need volunteer workers, second-hand clothes, toys and other surplus goods.

100%, or as close as is humanly possible, of what we receive we pledge to use directly for the benefit of the children. We will publish a list of all donations and donors (unless you specify anonymity) and will detail how the money has been spent and how it will be used for future projects.

247

Accompanying this letter is an outline of the way we intend to go about setting up The Future and the principles on which it will be based.

HELP BUILD THE FUTURE FOR THE CHILDREN OF MALAWI

What needs to be added, deleted or changed? Or would you go for a totally different approach?
I'll give you a ring over the weekend.
leaf

Lewe rang. He agreed with the broad outline but didn't like my name for our project, thinking it sounded much too grand.

'It's just you and me, Leaf,' he said. 'Face it, we're not going to build the future for the children of Malawi, we're just going to help a few kids have a home.'

He was right. I'd been carried away by my rhetoric.

'Got any suggestions then?' I asked.

'I've been thinking about *The Warm Heart*.'

Once he'd said it, it was obvious: Malawi promoted itself to the outside world as 'The Warm Heart of Africa'.

'Yeah, great.' I said, 'It's the right name.'

'And what about adding a sentence of encouragement at the end? Something like 'You don't know what you can achieve until you try.''

By phone and fax we worked on refining our message, then started sending out our appeal. Good friends of ours in France, John and Ghyslaine Cloke, immediately sent two hundred quid. Loads of people

248

in Reading chipped in. Cheques began arriving from my family and my old pals in England. Mates in Spain made contributions, as did many of my students.

My doctors and nurses group in Vilafranca clubbed together and came up with three hundred pounds. I knew they were warm-hearted. Many of them spent their holidays working for nothing in clinics in Central America.

In stark contrast, I didn't get a single peseta from any of the well-to-do businessmen I taught.

Sometimes money came in from unexpected sources. My barber chipped in the equivalent of fifty pounds. The garage where I had my car serviced gave seventy quid. It was a good start, but still too early to say how much we could achieve.

Our families and friends may not have been wealthy but they were generous. There was no flood of money but it kept coming in. By the Spring we'd received three thousand, five hundred pounds and had another fifteen hundred pledged. We were definitely going to be able to do something.

In the summer of 2000, I finally made the step I'd been turning over in my mind for the past year.

I'd found an English agent for my Spanish Civil War story. She was excited about its prospects; convinced we were going to break the mould of the conventional thriller with a work that brimmed with wit and humour.

I had a project in Africa that had come to be very important to me. It also seemed as though I had a new career as an author. It was time to move on. I packed my things.

After thirteen years – a quarter of my life – I waved goodbye to Spain, to my students and friends. I said *adéu,* to Catalunya and drove to the UK to meet up with Lewe.

Needing to know how best to use the money entrusted to us, Lewe and I flew to Malawi in September. We paid our own way, of course. The day before leaving, we'd gone to a megastore in Reading to buy a giant box of a hundred crayons.

Surrounded by mountains of shiny plastic toys, Lewe said 'I feel sorry for kids today. They've had their childhood stolen from them in the shops.'

Lewe's an original thinker and comes out with some amazing stuff. He was on good form that day.

'My life is like a child's picture,' he said, looking at his daughter's drawing pinned on his notice board: 'a complete mess, but full of colour.'

'My life canvas isn't so different,' I said. 'There are some dark areas, as you know, but there are plenty of highlights too.'

29. BILHARZIA

Diary: Malawi, September 2000.

Twenty-two of us in a minibus: Lilongwe to Blantyre. It's a journey of five to six hours. Facing my row of four are four others, knees jammed against ours. The guy on my right has an overripe smell of sweat and poultry. It's very tight in the bus, but just about OK until the conductor gets in. He leans into us and, with a strong flick of his wrist, slides the door shut behind him. The conductor is the final piece that locks all the other components of the puzzle into place. We are immobilised.

The bus judders out of its cloud of black fumes. Slowly, inexorably, the pressure of the conductor's body forces the whole leg-jam to the right. As our torsos are wedged in place, each and every body gets skewed. After an hour the aches begin. After another it seems as if the weight of the whole continent is pressing on one twisted knee and one groaning buttock.

Bangwe. The dirt path to the market is strewn with wads of chewed sugar-cane, banana skins and chunky fragments of an unknown shell. Baobab, Charles tells us. Hey! We don't have many new fruit days in our lives. This is special. A man sitting with a dozen of the nuts neatly whacks the tip off a shell with a machete. The pink-white pieces look like chunks of coconut-ice. The taste is someberries, edged with rhubarb. A crowd is gathering around us – white people are a rare sight in the township. We

*amble on, eating our baobab fruit. On the other side
of the market, I spit a seed into a ditch. In a
thousand years it could be a huge wrinkled old tree*

At the Bangwe motel, Witika was now a waiter.

'Another promotion!' Lewe exclaimed. 'Witika,
That's incredible! At this rate it won't be long before
you're running the whole country. We'll have to
bow and call you Your Excellency.'

Witika's eyes bulged and his hand flew to his
mouth. He giggled convulsively then, pulling
himself together, said: 'You are most welcome,
sirs... Aaaah, Lewe and Leaf.'

With Witika as a waiter, the formerly haphazard
provision of dinner was transformed. In pre-Witika
times, guests had gone to the dining room, ordered
and waited for up to a couple of hours before their
food arrived.

Witika now took it upon himself to go to the
rooms and see what the guests wanted from the
limited menu: beef, chicken, fish or beans, served
with rice, Irish potatoes or *nsima*: maize porridge.
He would pass the information on to the kitchen and
call by your room a few minutes before the meal was
ready. You could arrive at your table with enough
time to wash your hands in the water bowl provided
before eating your food.

Witika was a delightful, intelligent young man
with initiative. Whatever he was doing, he thought
about how it might be better done.

At the Chitolera orphanage, up the road from the
Bangwe Motel, we gave the crayons and the paper
we'd brought to the warden. The kids looked excited
and started whispering among themselves.

When Joseph started handing the crayons out, the

whispering turned into laughter. A couple of the older boys showed off their whistling ability. There were two crayons each. Under Joseph's instruction, the kids gathered in groups of four or five to share their colours. They settled down on the polished concrete floor and began to draw their pictures.

There was no squabbling, no talking at all, just purse-lipped concentration and total silence for a full hour. 'Isn't it a joy to see the pleasure the children get out of a few crayons?' I said.

They don't need much to be happy,' Lewe replied. 'And you know what? Their happiness gives me such a lift. I'm glad we're doing this, Leaf. It makes our lives seem like they're worth something.'

The only toys the children had to play with were discarded bottle tops and a knotted bundle of rags that served as a ball. They'd had a drum, but it had been beaten so much the skin had broken. We got it re-skinned, so there was a background rhythm for their introduction to a new sport: Jess had given me five frisbees.

Lewe and I showed them the way to throw the frisbees and they were off, running and laughing excitedly. They played until called in to dinner.

We began to look at properties that might serve as the kids' home. Dumbo Lemani, government minister and MP for Zomba, heard about The Warm Heart and offered us the Zomba training camp of the Young Pioneers, the now-disbanded youth wing of the former dictator. Dumbo was charming, bright and very, very sharp. Charles told us he always carried a revolver, even in parliament.

'That guy makes me feel extremely uneasy,' I muttered to Lewe.

'Yeah, I know what you mean.'

Happily, Dumbo soon realised our initiative was personal. There was no way we could take on the huge camp he was offering us.

We visited several orphanages and talked to the children, the staff and the organisers. What we learnt was discouraging. Aside from the expense of setting the operation up, the running costs of a home for twenty kids worked out to six thousand pounds a year. We'd raised sufficient money to build a home, but nothing like enough to run it.

We went to Cape Maclear for our last few days in Malawi and soon ran into Jefferson Gulo.

'Mistah Leaf! Aaah, it's good to see you again.'

'And it's good to see you, Jefferson. Listen, we're raising money to make a home for some of the Bangwe orphans. I'd like to buy ten of your cards. I think I'll be able to sell your paintings for several times your price. People in England love your cards.'

At the end of our visit, penniless because I'd spent the last of my cash on carvings to sell for the Warm Heart, I only had the money for eight cards. I hustled Lewe into getting another two.

'If I can sell them, Jefferson,' I said, 'I'll send Charles some money and the next time he's over this way, he'll buy a load more.'

Diary. Lake Malawi, October 6, 2000.
Fifty-two today – I'm supposedly playing with a full deck, but half my cards are jokers. Fifty-two! Time to do some adding up: no money, pension or insurance policy - just like most people in the world. No clubs or societies, no job, no debts, no house, no relationship, few possessions.

How do I feel about my life? Good, at the moment. Sky and water are complementary shades of blue. The only sounds are distant conversation and the lake-water lapping at the sand. Life is sweet.. There's just time for a last swim before flying home.

Two days later, Lewe was back in Reading and I was in Somerset with my friends Andy and Sally. They'd invited me to stay at their cottage near Glastonbury.

For a while we reminisced about our wonderful winter in India, then talk turned to Malawi.

I told them about our Africa trip and mentioned Jefferson Gulo's cards. Andy grew enthusiastic when I laid the cards out on the kitchen table.

'They're great! Hey, can I show them to a friend? I'm just back from fitting out the art gallery he runs in London. They've set up a new exhibition. I think they could be interested in Jefferson's art, it's just their sort of thing.'

A few days later, we went to a pub in Bath where Andy introduced me to the gallery manager. Joe was young, sparky and enthusiastic. He loved the paintings and took eight to show to the gallery's principal backer. The following week, Joe rang.

'We're prepared to offer you two thousand pounds for the eight miniatures.'

'I...I'll have to talk to Lewe,' I stammered. 'But I'm sure it will be OK.' Two thousand quid! The eight cards had cost two pounds forty. This huge boost to The Warm Heart funds brought our total to nearly seven thousand pounds.

The gallery printed double-sided postcards from Jefferson's originals, promising half the sales money to The Warm Heart.

255

Jefferson's paintings made their London debut at the Stuckist exhibition. Lewe and I were there, selling the reproductions along with our small Malawian carvings.

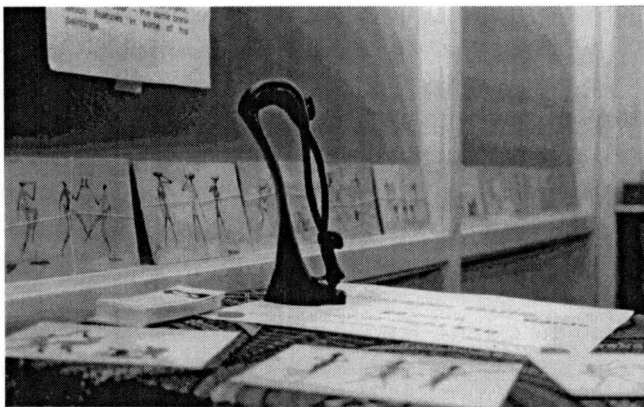

Jefferson Gulo's paintings + Malawian carving, Mother and child.

Me, Lewe and Artist at the Stuckist Exhibition

At the exhibition I got talking to a guy who clearly had high opinion of himself. I didn't get his name. He was quick to tell me he was Tracy Emin's ex.

'Leaf', he said musingly, when I told him my name. 'Let me think... Hmm... leaf mould... loose leaf... Aha! Tea leaf!' He looked at me roguishly, 'Perhaps I'd better watch my wallet.'

Pissed off with this poseur, I shoved my face up against his and, reverting for a moment to prison manners, growled 'It's your tongue you need to watch, shitface!'

His mouth dropped comically. He gave a little backwards jump, moved away rapidly and kept out of my sight.

Autumn blazed defiantly, until the rain put it out and the wind blew it to tatters. In spite of the massive lift from the sale of Jefferson's paintings, I felt terrible. Each morning I wanted to throw up. I went to the doctor to be checked out for tropical diseases. All the tests were negative. My nausea would pass after an hour or so and I usually felt well enough to do some writing in the afternoons. I was putting the finishing touches to the seventh draft of my Spanish novel. Before the end of the year, I sent the book off to my agent, Caroline.

The first publisher she approached had nice things to say about the work but there were no offers. My idea of writing a novel that turns into a thriller hadn't been so clever after all. A book has to be displayed somewhere in the shop. Not slam-bang, cliff-hang enough for the modern thriller, nor a true novel, my book had fallen between two shelves.

Confident that I'd get an advance on the book, I'd ignored the advice of those pessimists who'd said 'Don't give up the day job'.

I felt like a complete idiot. I was flat broke, ill, and entirely without energy, I had to sign on for the first time since leaving University. This meant that I couldn't stay with Andy, as it would have caused him complications with the taxman. My brain wasn't working properly and I had no idea what to do next. Lewe came to the rescue.

'Think I told you,' he said, 'when my mother died, we sold her house in Reading. With my share of the money I bought a small place in Telford – really cheap. There's no-one living there. You can stay, if you like.'

'Thanks mate, that'd be great. Telford's not far from my sister's home.'

Shropshire is a beautiful part of the country, but a massive outbreak of foot and mouth disease meant that I couldn't go walking; the countryside around Telford was closed to the public. I stayed indoors. Following my agent's advice, I worked on shortening and tightening the novel. I cut the opening drastically to make it start with much more oomph. When I sent it to Caroline, she returned the manuscript, saying it needed more work; the book had to be right when we offered it again. I didn't know if I had the energy for yet another rewrite.

I was supposed to be going back to Malawi with Lewe to complete our research, but I had no money. I had to tell him I wouldn't be able to make it. Though hard up himself, Lewe said he'd pay my fare.

Daffodils trumpeted spring then withered into ochre. On March 26, the anniversary of Operation Julie, I remembered – as I did every year – waking in Wales and being pinned to the bed by a knot of undercover police. That was twenty-three years ago. I thought

I'd left the Operation Julie shackles behind me, but it wasn't that simple. Would I ever be free of these anniversaries?

Where does the time go, and what happens to it when you've spent it?

I began to dread going to the toilet; peeing had become painful. One day I noticed my urine was pink. The last few drops were red. I was pissing blood.

'Nothing to worry about,' the doctor said. 'It's just a urinary infection. These antibiotics will clear it up.'

They didn't. They made peeing hurt more. The bleeding continued. The doc prescribed me stronger antibiotics, but they only gave me more acute pain. Bits of tissue were coming out in my urine. I was pissing away my organs.

On the point of telling Lewe that I wasn't up to the rigours of African travel, I said to myself 'Sod it. I may as well go. This could be my last trip. I don't expect I'll be around for long.' I should have been seriously depressed, but I didn't have the energy. I felt a bit sad about my life petering out with a whimper, but strangely resigned to it.

Once again in magical Africa, we called by the Chitolera orphanage in Bangwe, to see the warden, Joseph Bande. All the kids were at school, all except for Norbert.

'What's his problem?' Lewe was curious, always wanting to find things out.

'He's had bilharzia,' Joseph said, rubbing Norbert's head. Norbert smiled ruefully. 'He's recovering now. He'll be back at school... aaaah, in a day or two.' Joseph grinned broadly and clasped my hand. 'Aaaah, Mistah Lewe and Mistah Leaf, it's good to see you both again!'

'It's great to see you too, Joseph. It's so good to be back.'

Bilharzia: the word echoed in my head. That could explain my lack of energy and direction. Despite the negative results of the tests from Taunton hospital, I felt sure that this must be my problem and went straight to the clinic in Blantyre to be checked out.

'Yes, Mr Fielding, you have bilharzia.' The white-coated doctor looked up from his clipboard.

'That's not what the tests in Britain said.'

'It can take three months before the disease shows up in tests,' he replied. 'When were you last in the tropics?'

'Six months ago.' It was sinking in that the microscopic worms had been swimming in my body for half a year. I shuddered at the thought. They'd been living off me since my birthday dip in the lake.

'How can I get rid of them?' I asked.

'It's simple.' The doctor handed me a clear plastic bag containing six pills. 'Take three pills at lunchtime and stay in your hotel room. Take the rest in the early evening and don't go out after you've taken them.'

He leant forward and spoke quietly. 'Be warned. Have a bucket handy. It's not at all pleasant, but it is over in one treatment.'

'So what's in the pills?' I asked.

'It's a vermifuge, much like you'd give your pet, if it got worms. Just follow the instructions and tomorrow you'll be fine.'

I swallowed the first three pills at lunchtime and lay on my bed, reading, waiting to see what the effects would be. Nothing happened, nothing at all. In the evening, Lewe and Charles went out to a gig in Blantyre. I took the rest of the pills.

I started to read again, but had to put the book down when the pain, which had started as a low growl in my stomach, grew louder. It rose in volume and heat as it slowly passed up through my chest. By the time it reached my neck it was a deafening blaze.

On fire, I catapulted to the toilet and threw up mightily. Feeling weak, but much better, I collapsed on the bed. The low growling pain began again in my stomach and, as before, burned and deafened me.

I had to endure three cycles of this before falling into an exhausted sleep. When I woke, I felt hungry – an excellent sign. I hadn't experienced genuine hunger for a good while. In the succeeding days I felt much better. I was no longer fading away. The pills had expelled the intruders and my life was my own again.

Once more I had energy to put into our project. We could see we weren't going to raise enough money to set up our own home. We'd already asked all the obvious candidates and donations had slowed to a trickle. Lewe and I agreed that we needed to work with an existing organisation. There was no doubt in our minds about our choice: the Samaritan Trust, the Blantyre-based group that ran the Chitolera orphanage and two other centres.

The other charitable organisations we'd visited had a religious agenda, the SamT didn't care what religion the children had been born into, they'd look after them all just the same.

The British Council had built Chitolera House for the Samaritan Trust. It stood on land donated by Blantyre City Council. Twenty-five boys slept there, in two dormitories. Another seven boys and twenty-one girls ate and played there and slept with relatives in the township.

The place had a happy atmosphere. Joseph Bande and James Lipenga, the head boy, were clearly loved by the smaller kids.

James had lived in a village close to the Mozambique border. He was eleven when his parents died. Hungry and desperate, he walked the forty miles to Blantyre. In the city he found he was just about able to scavenge enough to stay alive.

After two years of living like this, he was approached by one of the Samaritan Trust's social workers and offered a place to stay and regular food to eat. In return he had to agree to stop begging and go to school.

'I suppose you jumped at the opportunity, James.' I said.

'Aaaah, no,' he replied. 'It wasn't easy. They wanted me to give up my independence!'

James had lived rough for long enough to know where to find shelter, handouts and leftovers. He knew he could survive on his wits, and he couldn't help wondering about these people. They pretended to be nice and offered to give him things for nothing. He was suspicious, but tempted at the same time. It would be nice to sleep in a bed and go to school. Why not give it a try then? And if he didn't like it, he could always leave. It only took him a few days to realise he loved it.

James was bright, but his school career had come to a halt at fourteen. We paid his school fees of seventy pounds a year. It was the first money The Warm Heart had spent. We agreed to look for individual sponsors for more smart kids. The ravages

262

of AIDS meant that Malawi will soon be a nation of children.

with Lewe under the baobab at Cape Maclear

30. A STRONG ATTRACTION

Faced with all the depressing and fear-inducing news that the media routinely vomits over us, we can easily become demoralised defeatists, consuming frantically in a desperate attempt to blot out our feelings of helplessness. But we don't have to react negatively, we can be useful, even if only in a small way. And usefulness may bring unexpected rewards.

When driving between England and Spain with Rosie, we'd stayed a couple of times with an old school-friend of hers. Miranda lived in Lot et Garonne, in South West France. On leaving Spain, I'd stored my possessions in a corner of her huge barn. In the early summer I got a call from her.

'Hello, is that Leaf?'

'Speaking.'

'Leaf, it's Miranda in France...'

'Miranda! How nice to hear from you.' Her voice sounded a little weak. 'Are you well?'

'No, as a matter of fact I'm not. I've just had a hysterectomy. Leaf, I've got a favour to ask you. If you're free for a few weeks would you consider coming down here to look after the garden and do my shopping?'

I liked Miranda. She was good fun to hang out with and I had a couple of months free before the next trip to Malawi.

'I'd be happy to, but I'm pretty broke so I'd need to find some paid work.'

'What sort of things do you do?'

'Painting, gardening, building...'

'Don't worry,' she said. 'I'll find work for you.'

'OK. Give me a couple of days to sort out things here, then I'll be on my way.'

Her call was a lifeline. I was fed up with Telford and longed for a change of air, a change of country. I packed a suitcase and drove to Lot et Garonne.

I stayed in a little stone cottage in Miranda's garden. I weeded the flowerbeds, pruned her laurel hedge, carried her shopping and mowed the lawn, being careful not to decapitate her wild orchids.

Doing building work got me into shape and provided the money I'd need to keep me during the coming winter in Malawi, when Lewe and I hoped to complete The Warm Heart project. In the evenings I worked on the final rewrite of my Spanish novel. When it was finished, I sent it off to my agent.

By this time, I'd been single for nearly four years and was well used to being on my own. I'd come to prefer the total independence that comes with solitary living. Well, that's what I thought until I went shopping with Miranda at the Saturday market in the nearby town of Monbartier. Carrying arm-lengthening bags crammed with fruit and veg, I followed her towards the Bar Midi.

'We can have a drink with my friends,' Miranda said, pointing to a group of ten middle-aged ladies, sitting under parasols at an outside table. We went to sit with them and Miranda did the introductions. Then my eyes met those of a long-legged blonde, with bobbed hair who also joined us.

'And this is Sue,' Miranda continued…

I shake her hand and feel an exchange of energy that I can only describe as a psychic electric shock –

a jolt of recognition. I don't hear the rest of the introductions. I'm in another space altogether, wondering who on earth this stranger is with whom I share an immediate affinity.'

Sue

We were driving back to Miranda's house after the market and I was thinking about the magnetic attraction of this woman I'd just met. Had I been younger, less love-battered, I'd have thrown myself at her. But I'd done that before, convinced I'd found the love of my life – and I'd been wrong.

'Sue's the most intelligent woman I've ever met.' Miranda broke the silence. 'She has an extraordinary energy. It's tragic, really. She was a successful casting director, who was moving into production. She had a big hit with her first venture: *Blott on the landscape.* But soon afterwards her husband had a bad car accident that left him severely damaged, physically and mentally. This happened over a decade ago. She's still looking after him.'

I met her husband that evening, for a dinner the two women had fixed up at Trevor's restaurant in Corroque. Terry was cheerful and talkative, though difficult to understand. His mouth seemed full of pebbles and there wasn't much continuity in his conversation.

'This steak – fucking tough,' he mumbled. Turning to Miranda, he leered and asked 'Are you wearing knickers? What colour are they?'

I could hardly believe what I'd heard. Nor could Miranda. She spluttered and went bright red.

Terry smiled beatifically and hobbled off to the toilet. Sue apologised to Miranda and explained that the brain damage he'd suffered meant that he'd lost all social inhibitions. 'We were having lunch with friends of mine, John and Irene, when Terry, who hadn't uttered a word all through the meal, suddenly turned to Irene and asked, "Why did you marry him? Is he a good fuck?" Irene, to her credit, had replied, 'Yes, he is actually.'

Sue's chuckle was infectious; we all started laughing and when the mirth was dying away, one of us only had to say 'Is he a good fuck?' for the laughter to break out again.

We all took off, that hilarious night in the

restaurant. Flying, we laughed more than we ate and at the end of the meal, we sailed out into the night on wings of angels. Right from the first moment of meeting there was a strong attraction between Sue and I. It was a fact we both recognised immediately.

Two days later, she called by to talk to Miranda about a local flower fair. She had an entry in the home-made hat competition. I joined them for a drink.

'Silly me,' Miranda was saying. 'I'm such a scatterbrain. I've double booked myself. Leaf, would you be an angel and step in for me at the fair?'

'I'm no angel,' I said with a smile, 'but I'll help if I can.' Hearing Sue was going to be there was enough. I was also invited to have supper afterwards with her and Terry in their house near Montour in the Lot.

The sun shone on the flower fair. I was really enjoying myself. I was pretty sure that Sue was too. Conversation came easily, I felt relaxed and stimulated by her company. She was as delighted as a child to win a prize with her Worzel Gummidge hat. After the fair, we went back to her house. 'Terry's resting,' she said 'Shall we take the dogs for a walk?'

'That would be good. I need a walk: been spending too much time in front of the screen.'

Sue put on the dogs' collars and leads. 'You can take Tommy,' she said, 'I'll look after Mac. We can let them off once we're across the road.'

'It must have been really tough for you,' I ventured, 'having to look after Terry for all this time.

She gave me a very direct look. 'It was.' The silence stretched out to breaking point before she came back to the present and continued... 'At first all our friends rallied round – that was a big help. To begin with he was a vegetable, then he moved, began to make noises, tried to speak. Little by little, he improved and I dared to hope for a full recovery, but the progress tailed off. For a long time he was on a plateau, then he slowly got worse. Most of his former buddies fell away, once it was clear that the old Terry wasn't ever going to return.'

'Look, I'm sorry if this is distressing you...' I paused, unsure how to continue.

'It's OK. I've been living with it long enough. You can let Tommy off the lead now.'

The dogs bounded away up the track. A couple of minutes later they returned, closely followed by a red-faced man with a gun, striding towards us and shouting at the top of his voice.

'I'll shoot those bloody dogs of yours,' he screamed. 'If I see them anywhere near my sheep I'll kill them!'

Sue called the dogs back and we put them on their leads.

'They're not sheep-killers,' she told the man, but he wasn't listening.

'That farmer's a lunatic,' she said as we retraced our steps. 'Bloody men! I've had enough of them for a lifetime. You know, I'd made a firm decision that I wouldn't take any more of Terry's constant criticism and lack of affection. For him affection was just a prelude to sex. I was right on the point of leaving him when he had his accident. Afterwards he was a helpless invalid and I couldn't just abandon him.'

'God, It must have been hard! How long ago was his accident?'

She thought for a moment before replying. 'It

269

must be fourteen years now.'

'Fourteen years! How could you stand it?'

'I don't know, really. You do what you have to do. At first I was busy dealing with all the consequences of the crash: contacting his brother and the other people who'd need to know, trying to keep his hairdressing salon going, sorting out the insurance, keeping my job going.'

'What a nightmare that must have been!'

'Yes. After the initial rush of things that had to be done, my focus was on his recovery and that was a long slow process. We moved to France to start a new life. A couple of years back I took a lover. What a disaster! We started an antiques business with my money. Any cash he took went straight into his pocket or was spent buying rounds for his friends. In two years he got through my money and left me deeply in debt.' She paused and took a deep breath. 'He was manipulative, jealous and violent. It was horrendous. At least I learned something from that ordeal: not to get mixed up with a man again.'

'Well, you never know. You might change your mind one day.' I was hoping she would.

The more I saw of this woman, the more I was attracted to her. The situation could hardly have been less promising, yet I knew with absolute certainty I was going to try to overcome the obstacles that stood between us getting together. She was a lovely lady, trapped in a situation that wasn't of her making. I wanted to rescue her. I wanted to make her happy. Sue was such a joy to be with. Magnets to each other, we were soon spending more and more time together. I knew I had to tell her about my past before she found out from someone else. I'd   hardly begun my explanation when she interrupted.

'Operation Julie, what an extraordinary coincidence! I did the casting for the TV film of Operation Julie!'

'What a load of crap that was,' I growled... 'Er, I didn't mean the casting!'

We saw a lot of each other that July: at a local fête, an art exhibition, an Indian festival, an open day in the Chateau de Bonaguil, where we shared our first kiss, and at an fashion parade where Sue was one of the models. The clothes were all designed and made by her friend, Hassanah.

I was sitting on a bench in the town square watching the show with Miranda. As Sue swished past in a flowing yellow creation, she threw me the sunflower she'd been holding. I leapt to my feet and caught it. That evening we stole away from the parade and began kissing in a stone alcove.

'I've been listening to Pharoah's music. I really love it too,' she whispered in my ear. 'Thank you.'

I'd given her a copy of my favourite CD by sublime saxophonist, Pharoah Sanders. I was sure she'd love it: we had so much in common.

Our affair was developing apace. Having been in AIDS-soaked Africa and following her ill-fated affair, I thought it would be a good idea if we were tested, to see if we were infected. We were clear and soon made up for lost time.

In August, I took a week off from painting and decorating to travel with Miranda and Sue to Marciac jazz festival. We arrived, put up our little tents in the parking area and sat around the campfire we'd made, laughing and talking. Soon we were

271

joined by our friends, John Cloke and Raymond and Hassanah Burton. The main topic of conversation was Malawi. The others were all fascinated by my story and offered to help.

When Sue and I went for a walk before going down to the town, she was unusually quiet.

'Are you OK?' I asked.

'Yes and no,' she replied. 'Everyone's so excited about Malawi and the prospect of doing something useful and, well ... I was feeling very left out. I don't know how I'll manage it, but I'd like to come too. I wouldn't just be a passenger,' she insisted. 'I could take photos and make a documentary film about the project – help it get off the ground... and I can raise money for you here. There are obstacles in the way, but somehow I'll make it happen. That is if you'll have me.'

'There's nothing I'd like better,' I said. I meant it.

When the wood we'd collected ran out, we went off to check out the bands that were playing all over town.

There was still music in the air when Sue and I tottered back to our camp at two a.m. for our first night together. We heard our friends return moments later. Focussed on each other, we paid them little attention. In our tiny tent, we were having trouble with the blow-up mattress. 'Hey, it must be leaking. My arse is touching the ground.' I got up and rhythmically pumped air into the flaccid sack until my arms were aching. 'Is it hard enough yet?'

'No, pump harder!'

I carried on but before long my arms were aching. I needed a break. 'Is it firm enough now?' I said wearily.

'No, keep pumping! It was hard but it's already going soft again…'

That was when we became aware of the stifled laughter coming from our friends sitting just a couple of yards away, beside the fire.

Once set on a course, I soon discovered, Sue pursues it with enthusiasm and persistence. To raise money for The Warm Heart, she organised a dinner auction at seven quid a head. She first convinced Colin, Shelagh and Angie, three friends who ran a *Chambre d'Hôte*, to provide the venue for nothing and do the catering at cost.

Because of her work as a photographer for a gite agency, she knew dozens of comfortably off ex-pats – she'd been to their houses and photographed their pools and properties.

She persuaded a wealthy couple to pay for sixty litres of excellent local wine from the barrel to help lubricate the bidding. She inveigled everyone who was invited to donate at least one lot to go under the hammer. I accompanied her on a few of her visits to loaded friends. She didn't mess around.

'I happen to know you've got more furniture than you have room for, John. What about all the stuff in the attic, those paintings you no longer display, the mirrors and clocks, the badminton and tennis racquets you don't use any more?'

She talked to scores of people; few could resist her persuasive powers. Virtually everyone that Sue approached came up with something of value.

A dozen friends were dragooned into acting as waiters, washers-up, parking assistants and ushers. Around eighty people turned up on the evening. We allowed them an hour for drinking wine, chatting and looking at the smaller donations and the twenty-five lots that were to go under the hammer.

I gave a brief talk about Malawi and outlined the aim of The Warm Heart, which was to provide a safe home for orphaned children who'd been living on the street.

Then our extrovert auctioneer, Keith Burton, brought down his hammer and began to knock out the lots. At one point, Keith got the wealthiest man in the room so excited he was bidding against himself. A couple of helpless minutes ambled past before the laughter calmed down enough for us to continue. Jake had coughed up six hundred quid for the wonderful handmade carpet I'd bought on my honeymoon in Kashmir.

He got a bargain – the carpet had well over a million knots – and we got more money for the orphanage. On that memorable evening we raised twenty-five thousand francs: two and a half thousand pounds.

That great occasion was a sweet contrast to the news I was getting through the post. I received a rejection slip from a UK publisher. It came with kind words of encouragement, so my hopes weren't entirely dashed, but subsequent replies just contained rejection slips.

31. A ROOK'S WEDDING

I stepped outside of Miranda's cottage to look at the sunset and gasped at its beauty. 'Darling, come and see this!'

As Sue came out onto the terrace, a dozen rooks flapping up the valley met a similar-sized flight coming down. The meeting happened right above our heads. The rooks joined forces and flew off up the valley together. Then they wheeled and came back, as if to have another look at us. They circled us, again and again, then performed an incredible ballet, full of complicated interweaving manoeuvres, directly overhead.

They were silent except for the occasional croak of one bird. They kept up the Red Arrow routine for several magical minutes until, one by one, they peeled off and dive-bombed us before swooping up to land in the tall trees behind the house. We stood entranced. Then they took off again splitting into two groups and flying off in different directions, chuckling amongst themselves.

I wrote describing the event to my old friend Martin.

'I've heard about this kind of thing before,' he replied. 'Here it's known as a rooks' wedding.'

Sue was already married, so we couldn't have a human wedding, but two flights of rooks had married us. Few nicer things have ever happened to me.

At school I'd felt sure my existence would be as grey and boring as my school uniform. I had no idea what an extraordinary ride my time on earth was going to be.

32. BAD MEDICINE

None of our Marciac friends followed through with their offers of help, but some others took their places. Three of us were going to be there for a few months. Lewe's girlfriend Kate, Everton and John only had three weeks.

Lewe and I were carrying the cash we'd collected in our money-belts, strapped round our waists. It came to a little over ten thousand pounds.

'Surely that's dangerous.' Sue was seriously worried. 'You are going to put it in a bank, aren't you?'

'Actually no. We don't trust the Malawian banks.' I told her. 'On our first visit, we had a bad experience with Thomas Cook. They refused to honour three hundred dollars worth of traveller's cheques stolen from Lewe by the Bangwe Motel cleaner.'

'The cleaner cashed them in a bank before I realised the cheques had been nicked,' Lewe grumbled. 'She didn't have the right ID, so she must have bribed the guy at the till.'

We later learnt she'd been an officer in the Young Pioneers, the old dictator's heavies. The advent of democracy in 1994 had brought an end to her privileges, but obviously not to her habit of helping herself to anything she could get.

On the 15th November 2001, we assembled at Heathrow, six strong, ready to fly to Malawi. Between us we'd brought two bicycles and sixty kilos of kids' clothes as well as our own gear.

At the check-in desk we were told that we'd have to pay a hundred pounds if we wanted to take the bicycles with us.

'That's ridiculous!' I said to the uniformed man in charge of the desks. 'They're old bicycles, they're not worth anything. They've been donated to the orphanage we're helping.'

'I'll tell you what,' he replied. 'I'll check it out with my boss and see if we can do something.' He came back ten minutes later, looking pleased. 'As it's for charity,' he said, 'I got the supervisor to agree that you'll only have to pay fifty quid.'

Everton was a Jamaican with a short fuse. 'We've been raising money to help homeless orphans,' he yelled. 'We're not going to hand any cash over to you. It's all for the orphanage!' He grabbed one of the bikes and thrust it at the baggage man, who raised his arms to ward off the assault. 'Go on, take it!' Everton commanded. 'Keep it,' he went on. 'Then you can boast to your friends how you stopped African orphans from having bike rides'.

The scene Everton had created made our group the centre of attention. Red-faced, the man took the bicycle, handed it to one of his staff and stalked off.

The check-in staff had been entertained by the break in their routine and joked with us while they processed our luggage. Twelve hours later, when we disembarked at Lilongwe airport, we discovered that both bikes had been loaded onto the plane, free of charge. 'Wow! Thanks guys'!

We took a minibus from Lilongwe to Blantyre, our cramped five-hour journey softened by the sublime music of Mbilia Bel and the rose petal voice of

Tshala Muana. We booked into the Bangwe Motel and washed and changed before lugging the clothes we'd brought up to the Chitolera orphanage for a grand share-out. Sue took photos of the kids in their new togs so that the donors would be able to see the individuals who had directly benefited from their warm-heartedness.

Going to Africa had been straightforward when it was just Lewe and I. Extra numbers multiplied the complications. Sue was acting strangely and so was Everton. She'd been very much on edge when we left France and arrived in the UK. I put that down to the strain of taking her brain-damaged husband to his brother in the North of England. She was going to be leaving him behind after fourteen years of caring for him. Understandably she was besieged by feelings of anxiety and guilt.

On the day before departure her behaviour had been so odd as to be obsessive – all her energy was focussed on the malfunctioning laptop we were taking. Again I'd made allowances, thinking she was panicking about going to Africa, as I had on my first trip. She had more excuse than I, never having been to the Third World before.

Lewe had been making Sue nervous too. He'd made little attempt to hide his dislike of her. Before they'd even met, he'd confessed to a friend that the whole atmosphere of the trip would be different – we'd be together and he'd be the gooseberry. Having travelled with Smiles and Sally in India I understood his concern, but was more than a little pissed off that he didn't want to give Sue a chance.

'A true friend,' I was thinking, 'would be pleased that I've found a partner who makes me happy.'

The great welcome we'd received at the Bangwe Motel had calmed everyone's nerves. At first I was optimistic that, as they got to know each other better, my pal and my lover would come to be friends, but her 'posh' accent raised all his class-war hackles and he kept having digs. They really depressed her.

'No-one's to blame for the way they speak,' she complained to me. 'Why does he dislike me so?'

'He'll get used to you, come to see your good qualities,' I said soothingly.

The truth was that I was having grave doubts about them myself for, after we'd been in Malawi a week, Sue's behaviour had suddenly switched from anxious to deranged. Insanity blazed out of her eyes. In her home environment, surrounded by friends, she'd appeared confident and capable. Now, it appeared, in the confusion and rawness of Africa, she'd fallen apart. It seemed I'd hooked up with a madwoman. What had happened to the exceptional person I'd brought here? I'd believed that our wonderful courtship was ripening into a loving relationship, but had it all been wishful thinking on my part?

Doubt sawed through my faith in my own judgement. The truth was I didn't know this woman very well. We'd only met four months before.

Unable to bear the look of fear in her eyes – fear of me – I left her to go to bed alone and tried to blot out what was happening by sitting up late reminiscing with Lewe.

The following morning, I slunk out until guilt drove me back. I couldn't just leave her, even though her lunacy had completely unmanned me. She was sitting on the bed, looking at a couple of pages covered in handwriting.

'I've written you a letter. I'm trying to get it down on paper, to work out what's going on,' she said, sounding much calmer. 'Can I read you this, please?

'Sure.' I said and sat down beside her on the bed.

Her letter was full of thoughts of rejection and insecurity, fear and sadness…

…We have no real template for life, no copy of the script, so seldom do others tell us really honestly where we are going, until it's too late.

So the rejection ripples outwards, the stone falling into still water. Out of control, disrupting our equilibrium and creating emotional chaos and paranoia. You looked like Dr. Crippen last night.

Now, out of my fears, I can rationalise. I'm in a totally different culture and am emotionally affected by the conditions here. I'm the new girl with two men who've been here before and this is their project. I'm homesick and worried that everything will be okay both here and at home. I feel guilty about Terry and the animals. I'm exhausted in every way following preparations for a huge and complete upheaval. I'm on Lariam, notorious for paranoia and hallucinations. Plus, having come off HRT (again!) I don't know what effect that's having – aside from the frequent hot flushes, which are hell in this heat…

'Stop! It's the Lariam,' I said. 'God, why didn't I think of it before?'

'Do you really think so?'

'Yes. It all adds up. Look, you started behaving oddly just before leaving France, after taking the first weekly pill. That was a Tuesday. A week later, you went nuts over the laptop – Tuesday again. Yesterday, Tuesday, you were seriously insane. It's got be the Lariam! Look at all the heavy warnings on the packet. People are supposed to have committed suicide under its effects.'

I remembered my first trip to Sub-Saharan Africa. At Heathrow I'd been seized by the dreadful knowledge that I was going to my certain death.

'It's the Lariam, I remember now. I had a bad reaction myself, the first time I took it. Oh, darling, I thought you'd gone bonkers.' I gave her a hug and felt the tension ebb from her body. 'Did you really think I was Doctor Crippen?'

She nodded.

'No wonder you were terrified. You don't think I'm Crippen now?'

She shook her head and laughed. 'Of course not.'

I gave her another hug. 'Let me see what else you wrote.'

Now it's over, I'm counting all the good things. You and all you are becoming to me. Experiencing this extraordinary and rather wonderful place. Knowing Terry is being looked after and everything is okay at home. I'm coming out of a long dark tunnel and all sorts of exciting things could happen in the future. With luck this will fade with time and all will be well.

All was well. At the clinic in Blantyre, the doctor put Sue on the established anti-malaria drugs, chloroquin and paludrin. Her acute paranoia never returned.

Everton was another matter. At the end of the fifties, aged nineteen, he'd left his home in Jamaica and moved to Britain. As a young man he must have experienced all the slights and cruelties of an end-of-

Empire society that was fundamentally racist.

Despite the obstacles in his path, he'd made a success of his life. He was a kind, generous person who was widely liked and respected in Reading, the town that had become his home. He and Lewe had been friends for years.

Shortly before our trip, Everton had taken Lewe to Jamaica and shown him round the island, from the slums of Trenchtown to the camps of the Rastafarians, up in the mountains. They'd had a great holiday together.

This was Everton's first time in Africa. He'd been looking forward to getting back to his roots, but Malawi wasn't what he'd expected. Its life expectancy of thirty-five was one of the lowest on the planet. Compared to Malawi, Jamaica looked sophisticated, almost prosperous.

Everton was finding it difficult to get the two countries into a perspective he could deal with. Jamaica's chronic problems were due to the brutal slave trade. The inhabitants were the descendants of deeply traumatised people who'd been sold into slavery and taken across the ocean in chains. The island had still been a white-dominated British colony in Everton's youth.

How could he account for the fact that Malawi was in a far worse state than his Caribbean birthplace?

'It's colonial exploitation!' That was as much as I got out of Everton because after that he stopped talking to us. He no longer wanted to be associated with *mzungus*.

Friends of Charles told us he'd been up at the bar in the market, buying rounds of drinks and telling everyone that all their problems were due to exploitation by white people. As the only *mzungus* in the township, it made us feel very uncomfortable.

At odd moments Everton was almost his old self, but by this time Lewe was angry that his friend had been treating him like an enemy. The atmosphere at our end of the Bangwe Motel had really soured.

Mercifully, he lightened up in the last few days of his stay. He and Kate laid on a slap-up dinner for all the Chitolera kids.

At the Bangwe Motel: Leaf, Sue, Justice, John, Bishop Mercy, Everton, Charles, Lewe, Paul, George (in background), John (seated) big Brendan.

Everything was ready and we were waiting for the signal from Witika that they were arriving.

'Here they coming!'

The children ran out of the light rain and into the Bangwe motel. Witika showed them where to sit. They fell silent in the unfamiliar surroundings of the ill-lit dining room with its strange paintings, carvings and cotton hangings printed with images of

Princess Diana. They looked around, over-awed. It may have been the first time they'd ever eaten at a table.

For this special meal, Lewe and I were the waiters, ferrying food between the kitchen and dining room. As plate after plate arrived, the kids relaxed, the noise level rose and the meal ended in happy bedlam.

Lewe and Sue made a truce. We'd become aware that what we were doing must transcend personal feelings. It wasn't about us, we were doing this for the kids.

33. FRANK VELTHUIZEN

After the return of Kate, Everton and John to Britain, we were able to focus on our reason for being in Malawi. We didn't have the resources to set up our own home, so what best to do?

'What the Samaritan Trust needs most is accommodation for girls. What do you think, Lewe?'

'Yeah, I agree. The girls are more in danger than the boys, they're the ones who need a safe place to sleep.'

'Sue?'

'As a girl, I'm with you all the way.'

The Samaritan Trust's Chitolera home looked after girls and boys, but only had accommodation for boys. The girls who ate and played at the centre were from the area. They slept with relatives or with neighbours.

The Samaritan Trust wasn't able to help other girls who'd drifted in from remote villages. They lived on the street and spent the nights with the market traders, women from the countryside who had a camp in the city where they stayed for a week or two – as long as it took for them to sell all their produce. Life was very uncertain for the orphaned girls from the villages. They were the ones most in need of a secure home.

The best thing we could do, we agreed, would be to give the Samaritan Trust a girls' wing.

We began by looking for a suitable site for a girls' hostel. Unable to find anything near Chitolera House, we asked the mayor of Blantyre if we could build on an unused strip of land next to the orphanage. It seemed a reasonable request as he'd given the Samaritan Trust the Chitolera plot in the first place. An answer wasn't immediately forthcoming. Then we learnt, via Charles, that it could be a while before we got a reply.

Harvey, a friend of The Warm Heart and an old pal of ours from Reading, flew out to see how we were getting on. On Christmas Day we took him to the Samaritan Trust's headquarters at Stella Maris, a twenty-acre plot with an assembly hall and a number of barrack-like buildings. Another camp for the Young Pioneers, the land had been donated to the Samaritan Trust by Bakili Muluzi, Malawi's first democratically-elected President. Now it was the Skills Training Centre for The Trust's kids and home to the older boys.

Henk Munnich, the Dutch Consul and member of the board of trustees, was giving a party for the hundred and fifty former street-children looked after by the Trust. The previous Christmas the kids had had nothing at all. This year kind-hearted Henk wanted to give them something to remember.

In the morning there were football games and a tug-of-war. Not wanting to take any of their special Christmas feast out of their mouths, we arrived after lunch, in time for the disco.

Knackered after dancing our socks off, we collapsed into the chairs that were being set out facing the stage.

Each of the Trust's three centres put on a show. Paul and Simbi drummed in a line of dancers from

286

Chitolera, led by James Lipenga. The line curved back on itself to become a circle. The raggedness of the dancers evaporated as they got into their rhythm. The audience began cheering. The drums beat faster and faster. James, wearing a broken detergent box as a hat, split off and went into an inspired solo, drawing thunderous applause and whistles from the audience. After the show there were cakes and sweets and more dancing from the other centres.

Some of the orphans in the care of the Samaritan Trust

The Samaritan Trust had been through a rough time, but now they were really getting their act together; Henk had persuaded the Dutch government to pay for an advisor on a three-year contract.

Frank Velthuizen, an aid worker who'd been doing a similar job in Uganda, proved much more than an advisor, he was a human dynamo who made the most of the materials at his disposal. 'My aim is to make the Samaritan Trust as self-sufficient as possible,' he told us. 'We've got spare buildings here – let's put them to use!'

He wasted no time, renting out office space to another charity organisation and leasing a block to a supermarket chain. This made money and brought the neighbours into the centre and into contact with the kids.

Frank's next move was to hustle the Dutch government into paying for a borehole to supply the centre with water. He followed that up by badgering them into buying a flour mill.

From that moment the Samaritan Trust ground their own maize and the maize of the local community. This gave them a small revenue and kept them in close touch with their neighbourhood. Frank was doing everything he could to integrate the kids into the local society at the same time as making the Samaritan Trust a self-financing operation.

'Let's get some chickens,' Frank said. 'We can teach the kids how to look after them.'

'Now who wants to learn how to to plant vegetables, maize and fruit trees?' Frank showed them how. The orphans were learning agriculture and starting to feed themselves.

'What do you want to learn, Gideon - bricklaying or carpentry?' He set up courses for the boys in both.

The girls learnt hairdressing and dressmaking, so they'd have a trade when they left the home.

It wasn't all work for the kids. The centre had a long thick rope which was used for games of tug-of-war. The children loved it. The game used up their energy so they slept well at night.

In the evening, after a full day's work, Frank would go into town with one of the Samaritan Trust's social workers. They'd collect unsold bread and perishables from the supermarkets and distribute it around the makeshift camps of the street children. They talked to the ragged urchins and tried to persuade them to come and stay with the Samaritans. The longer the kids had been on the street, the harder it was to convince them.

'It takes time,' Frank said, undiscouraged. 'Winning their confidence is a slow process, but it's worth the effort.'

Frankie V: a totally extraordinary man. If the world were full of people like him, we'd all be living in peace and harmony.

34. NEW YEAR DANCING

Diary: December 31, 2001.

'That door doesn't open,' the taxi-driver says. 'Get in on the other side.'

It's ten o'clock on the last night of 2001. A light drizzle is falling. We're going to the Roadhouse to dance in the New Year. I get in the back and slither across the torn seat. Lewe, Harvey and Charles squeeze in after me. Sue takes the front seat. The windows steam up immediately.

The windscreen has two large depressions. It looks as though bricks have hit it. Most of the glass has fractured into tiny cubes and is quite opaque, but there is one clear lozenge that's almost free of cracks. The driver wipes the rain from this patch with a rag. Getting in, he lets the car roll back, bump-starts it in reverse and sets off up the road.

'Your door's open,' I say as we slow for the T-junction. Swearing, he struggles to shut it and only just stops in time.

'This car's got no lights,' Sue observes.

'Yes, it has!' The driver is indignant. 'I haven't put them on because the street is lit.'

We pull in to get petrol and to put air in a flat tyre. Sue turns round and whispers 'I think something died under my seat.'

To pay for the gas, the taxi man needs an advance on the fare. We halt again at the next filling station to re-inflate the tyre. The rain stops as we drive out of town. The moon sails out from behind a cloud and silvers the night. Despite the help of the moon, we have to go very slowly. We only have sidelights.

Each time we're overtaken by another vehicle, the cabbie speeds up and follows in the wake of the diminishing rear lights for as long as he can.

The driver's door wanders open again. He pulls it shut and turns off the engine to coast down a long gradient. We pick up speed. Warm night air pours through the open windows. Injured noises come from under the car. We hurtle past thatched huts, banana palms, mango trees and stands of sugar cane, shining in the moonlight.

At the gig, we were the only white people in an audience of four or five hundred. Everyone wanted to dance with us; a succession of beaming partners gyrated and swayed in front of me. We were all glistening from the exertion and kept going outside to cool off and gaze at the bright stars of the Southern hemisphere.

The night throbbed with music. Around the compound, people were barbecuing chunks of meat, lounging around, drinking beer and talking. Sue and I were back on the floor as midnight approached, dancing with our arms around anyone.

'Happy New Year!' I said to my partner when the music stopped.

'You are most welcome!' he replied.

35. SHAKESPEARE

We went up to Cape Maclear to give Jefferson Gulo his share of the money from his cards – several bundles of two hundred kwacha notes. Jefferson went into shock and couldn't stop shaking after we gave him as much money as he would normally make in a year.

Sue and I wandered up to the north end of the beach, past the malodorous fish-drying racks, towards a graceful tree with a huge canopy. It was such a pleasant place to sit. I was a little disappointed to see someone already there, lurking in the shade. A tall muscular man in t-shirt and bathing trunks stepped into the light. 'How are you?' he asked in English.

'I'm fine,' I replied. 'How are you?'

'Aaah, I have a problem.'

Here we go, I thought. 'Everyone has problems,' I said. 'What's yours?'

'This,' he replied. His calf was laid open from the top of the thigh to the back of the knee. Flies were crawling around the deep gash. He waved then off; they came back almost immediately.

'My God!' I cried. 'You must have this seen to, or you'll lose your leg.'

'I know,' he said. 'But I don't have money for a ride into town or medicines.'

'We've got a First Aid kit in our room. I'll go and get it. Put your t-shirt over the wound to keep the flies off.' Shakily, I went off to our room, leaving the man in Sue's charge.

I'm a bit squeamish – I've been known to pass

out at the sight of blood and exposed bone, but I managed to keep myself together and returned with a roll of bandage, disinfectant and some sterile gauze squares. Sue dabbed disinfectant the length of the gash, then covered it with the squares and a strip of bandage. She wound the rest of the roll around the man's leg.

'This is Shakespeare,' she said. 'I've told him we'll give him the money for the fares and the doctor. The nearest doctor is in Monkey Bay.'

'How much do you need?' I asked.

'Maybe a hundred kwacha?'

His face was grey and he was pouring with sweat. I handed him the money. 'We'll help you to the pick-up place.'

'Thank you sir, thank you lady.'

'Sue. My name is Sue and this is Leaf.'

'Come on, we'd better get moving.'

We helped him along the track and aboard the taxi. 'Let us know how you're getting on when you return.

'I will. Thank you.'

I winced for him as the four-by-four bounced up the potholed road.

The next time we saw Shakespeare his calf was neatly bandaged and his grin split his face in two. 'Here,' he said, showing us some scraps of paper. They were the doctor's bills. 'I didn't have enough for the taxi fares to Monkey Bay.'

'I'm glad to see you looking well. I was worried about you bleeding to death. Take this.' I gave him what he needed to pay the taxi.

As for us, we'd miscalculated our expenses and had to borrow some cash from Lewe to get back to Bangwe.

293

There was still no word from Blantyre City Hall. Finally Charles discovered that someone with influence had his eye on the land we were hoping to use. An answer could be indefinitely delayed, we were told, and the reply, when it finally came, would likely be negative. It was apparent that we wouldn't be able to stay long enough to see the project through to completion.

Though we still had all The Warm Heart money, our own dosh was evaporating faster than we'd expected. We couldn't stop giving it away, a few pence here, a quid or two there – so many needy people, so many sad stories.

We were seriously alarmed when Grace Tambala told us that word had got out that we were carrying a large amount of money.

'This makes you very vulnerable,' Grace said. 'You should leave as soon as you can.'

Spooked, we put the bulk of The Warm Heart money in a high interest account under the care of the Dutch Consul and booked our flight home.

We took two thousand quid to Europe in case anyone demanded their money back. After all, we hadn't yet achieved our aim.

Nobody hassled us about it. Everyone who'd donated to the Warm Heart had done so because they trusted us and wanted to help.

Back in Europe, we kept in touch with the Samaritan Trust by e-mail. The news was bad. The rains failed and the maize harvest was poor. Food prices rose steeply. There was hunger in the townships. The interest from the Warm Heart money was helping feed the Samaritan Trust's kids and we were working with the Trust to get round the impasse over the hostel.

Changing tactics, we applied for planning permission to attach the hostel to the already partially built matron's house on Chitolera land.

Permission was granted. A local contractor was engaged and work on The Warm Heart Girls' Hostel began in June. This progress gave us a huge lift. The girls' home was happening!

36. THE OPENING

After auctioning off a load of our own stuff to cover the cost of our flights and our stay, Sue and I returned to Malawi in January 2003, to open the hostel and complete the film of our project. Lewe couldn't come. He'd had to stay in England to look after his brother who'd undergone major surgery.

At the Bangwe motel, the usual warm welcome seemed a rather muted. John was around but Big Brendan had shrunk: he was noticeably thinner than when we'd last seen him.

'Where's Witika?' I asked. From the sad expressions, I immediately knew the answer.

'Sorry', Brendan told us. 'Witika passed away. Sorry.'

I cried for my young friend and I wept for all the other young lives, snuffed out before their promise is fulfilled. When we'd last seen him, Witika had been twenty-one, healthy and full of life, intelligence and good will. God knows how far he might have gone.

It was tragic that such a bright spark could be extinguished so easily. Most Malawians have no money for doctors. If they get sick, they either get better, or they die.

Witika had earned nine pounds a month. He also got lunch on the day shift and dinner and breakfast when he worked nights. The wage was just enough, when we first went to Africa, for a frugal young family to live on. Now, with inflation, it was scarcely sufficient to pay the rent of a small hut. Wages hadn't risen at the same rate as prices and almost everyone in the townships was suffering.

Coming out of our room one morning, We saw Brendan and George, the gardener, wolfing the scraps that we'd left on our breakfast tray. They were embarrassed; we were concerned.

'It hadn't even occurred to me that they'd be hungry,' Sue was incredulous. 'I mean, they've got full-time jobs.' From then on we shared our breakfast with them. When Lewe and I first arrived in Malawi, Brendan had been giving us food...

Only able to afford to stay for three weeks, we were under time pressure from the start. The hostel wasn't quite finished. The contractor had taken his team off to another building and nothing had happened for the past few weeks. We hustled to persuade the workers back on site, but it was a struggle to get anything done. Some days nobody turned up. The contractor had little money owing on the job and it appeared that he preferred to write it off in exchange for not doing the finishing. We kept at him to do the last bits, but whenever our attention was elsewhere, he'd pull his tradesmen off the job and send them to another site

We took advantage of a lull in the finishing to make a quick trip to the lake. Shakespeare was one of the first people we saw.

'How's your leg,' I asked.

'It's fine', he replied, turning to show me the long scar. 'I have a canoe,' he continued. 'Would you and Sue like to go out on the lake with me to the fish eagles island?'

'We certainly would,' I said.

We stood on the beach. waiting for help to launch Shakespeare's heavy boat. When his pal arrived we dragged the dugout canoe into the water. It had an outrigger to stop it rolling in the wavelets of the lake.

We got soaked clambering into the boat, but it didn't matter. It was a warm day and the sun dried us out in a moment. The canoe was the hollowed-out trunk of a tropical hardwood. Stone Age technology in the modern world.

'Who made it, Shakespeare?' I asked.

'It was my grandfather's canoe. He carved it about a hundred years ago.'

While we paddled across the water I thought about how the world had changed since the canoe was made in the late nineteenth century. Then the British Empire straddled a quarter of the world. Remnants of it still existed, but it was fast disintegrating when I went to secondary school. I arrived there a jingoistic boy and left an anti-imperialist...

'Eagles!' Shakespeare's call brought me back to the present.

Two fish eagles were circling above the boat. We tried to capture the birds on film, but they were moving too fast. Shakespeare threw a couple of small fish in the air, for the eagles to catch, but even then we couldn't get a good shot.

It was time to head back to shore, heavy black clouds were gathering.

'That was really great,' I said to Shakespeare.

'Yes. Thank you,' Sue added. 'It was such a wonderful treat.'

'It's nothing,' he replied. 'I thank you for helping me when I was in bad trouble.'

Joseph Bande, the Chitolera warden, laid his long thin hand on the head of a young girl.

'This is Zioni,' he said.

'Yes, I know her. *Muli bwange*, Zioni.'

She was a chunky, determined little girl of six or seven with huge eyes and a grave face. Her rare smile lit up the landscape like the sun coming out from behind a dark cloud.

'After her parents passed away she is staying with her auntie up the hill,' Joseph said, pointing to the top end of Bangwe township. 'But it is not good for her up there. Not good.' Joseph's voice rose in righteous indignation. 'Her auntie is cruel to her. We gave Zioni a blanket. Her auntie cut it in two and gave the big piece to her daughter, who already has a blanket!' Joseph's expressive face writhed against the injustices of life. He turned and spoke to Zioni, who nodded vigorously and added some forceful words of her own. 'It would be good for her to stay in the hostel,' Joseph pleaded.

'She is welcome,' I said.

Sue had been filming in the city, the township and at the orphanage as well as doing interviews and getting footage of the kids on the streets by day and by night. Her first time out she hadn't been able to bring herself to film hungry, homeless children. It seemed too hard-bitten, voyeuristic. But now she had forced herself to overcome her scruples. She had little time to get the material she needed for the story she wanted to tell.

With one week left before we had to leave, the hostel still wasn't quite finished. The soak-away trenches for the septic tank, hadn't been dug, the fascia boards and the final coat of paint still needed doing. I helped fit the boards and did the rest of the painting. The contractor was persuaded to send a couple of men to finish the septic tank's trenches. With Frank and James, we bought furniture and built new bases for the bunk beds. We didn't finish until late in the evening before the opening. After collecting the tables and benches we'd ordered, we raced round in Frank's jeep, buying curtains, mattresses, sheets, blankets, pillows, mosquito nets, towels, mirrors, toothbrushes and soap.

My excitement was building. We were approaching the climax of several years of endeavour. I only wished that Lewe could have been here with us. I squeezed Sue's hand. She smiled and squeezed back. Beside the front door, I fitted the plaque we'd brought.

The Chitolera Girls' Hostel

Donated by

The Friends of The Warm Heart

Open 2003

On the 15th of February 2003, in front of a hundred and fifty kids, all the staff from the Samaritan Trust and most of the neighbourhood, we opened our girls' hostel with a small celebration. Led in by the matron, a choir of the smallest kids sang some songs. These were followed by acrobatics, drumming and dancing from the older children.

Before a big lunchtime feast for all the Samaritan Trust's kids, the Acting-Director made a speech. I then spoke briefly, explaining Lewe's absence and thanking the Friends of the Warm Heart. I was

300

choking up, trying not to cry. It was such an emotional moment. We'd done it. We'd actually done it! I ended with a few words to the girls in Chichewa. Charles had been coaching me, so I was able to say: '*Tikukhulúpilira kuti mukhala osangalala pano.*'

There was a collective intake of breath when the kids realised I was speaking in Chichewa.

I struggled on through the scattered applause for several mouthfuls more. 'I hope you will be very happy in your new home. Be good girls and please be kind to new girls when they arrive. *Zikomo.*'

Then Juliet Mwandire, Grace Mailosi, Zioni Phiri and the other girls, who for the past few nights had been sleeping on the floor of the storeroom, moved into their new home.

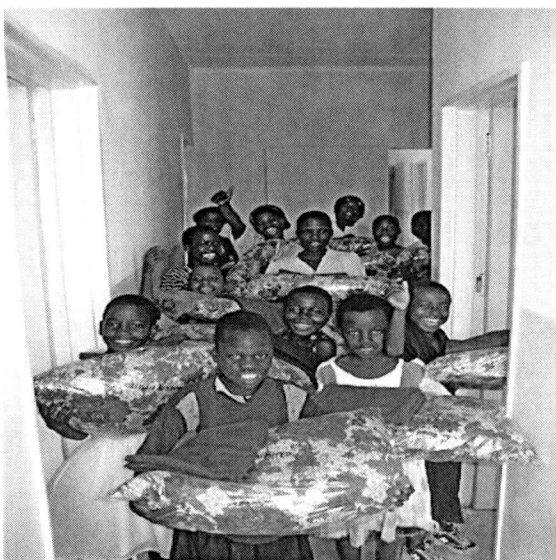

The girls at the Samaritan Trust's Chitolera orphanage go into their new home for the first time

We didn't manage to get back to Malawi again. Totally broke after the last trip, we had to concentrate on earning enough money to keep ourselves alive.

We got frequent updates on the news from Bangwe, mostly from Frank and Henk: Juliet, the eighteen-year-old head girl, ran off with her boyfriend. Grace passed her exams. The first matron had to leave because her husband wanted her at home to cook his dinner... Life went on and the hostel continued to provide a home for twenty-four girls who would otherwise have been living on the street.

THE WARM HEART GIRLS' HOSTEL
AT THE SAMARITAN TRUST'S CHITOLERA ORPHANAGE
IN BANGWE MALAWI
Inaugurated 15th February 2003

The Warm Heart Girls' Hostel, Chitolera, Bangwe

37. OUR FAMILY

Sue sold her place in the Lot and paid off her debts. We drove to the UK to see her husband, Terry, and visited Dad and Katie in the retirement home they'd chosen to live in after they sold their bungalow in Netheravon. We sat down to have tea together in their sitting room, to listen to their news and bring them up to date on ours.

I told them we'd completed The Warm Heart project and twenty-four girls were now sleeping in their new home. We had enough money left over to pay the matron's salary for the next two years and cover the running and replacement costs.

Sue had taken lots of photos and made a short video film of the opening. She had a friend in Leeds, who we'd visited after seeing Terry. Alan Jewhurst had a small recording studio and, with his kind help, she was able to edit the film and add her soundtrack and commentary.

We showed Dad and Katie the film and talked them through the story of the final hectic stages of the construction. They loved the pictures, especially the ones that were unequivocally of the tropics: their best time had been when they lived in Singapore.

Dad picked up the internal phone and said 'Could we have tea for four, and could you get me Philip on the line?' After a while he said, 'Philip, would you be able to come to our apartment for a moment. I'd like to introduce you to my son, Nigel.'

The manager of the home arrived soon after. Dad started showing him some of Sue's photos and telling him about the story of our project. I could see Philip was itching to get away, but Dad wouldn't let him leave. He kept going on about the wonderful work we'd done. Tears sprang into my eyes. My Dad was proud of me – despite all the pain and heartache I'd put him through.

If I could only have the approval of one person in the world, I'd want it to be his.

'You were winding Philip up there, weren't you, Dad?'

'Well, he's rather pompous – he deserves it.' Dad's eyes twinkled. He'd always had a great sense of humour and was well liked by his fellow soldiers. By contrast, Katie wasn't popular with the officers' wives. She bullied those whose husbands were junior in rank and toadied to the wives of the top brass.

Katie, passed away in February 2004. We drove to the funeral service through the bare Salisbury Plain countryside, dusted with snow. I held Dad's frail hand through the journey. He could scarcely believe that she'd gone and seemed at a loss on his own. Roger, Judy, Susi and I were all surprised that she'd been the first to go. We'd thought the tough old bird would easily outlive our Dad.

The passage of time puts a different perspective on life. For years I'd known that Katie wasn't really wicked – just screwed-up by her appalling childhood. Learning early that life was hard and often brutal, she'd developed attack strategies and had never able to set them aside. She'd cast a dark cloud over our youth, but we'd got through it.

You have no choice over the hand you're dealt in childhood, but it's up to you whether you make a good fist of it. Our shared adversity had forged a bond between four very different siblings, born of three mothers.

My brother Roger followed in the path Dad had beaten – making it easier for me to go my own way. Roger went straight from school to Sandhurst and stayed in the army for thirty-seven years, at the end of which he was appointed Diplomatic Attaché to Bulgaria. He then moved to work at NATO until his retirement.

Holding very different social and political ideas, we've argued all our lives, but we've always been able to make each other laugh. As we've grown older we've become closer. I think we're more attuned to each other now than at any time since we lived with our grandmother in Suffolk and Ipswich were champions of the First Division.

Once I'd given up on my long wait for my mother to return, Roger got me playing games again. It was probably the best way of rousing me from deep depression. We played a lot at Nanna Fielding's and always competed furiously.

We spent our pocket money on toy Union and Confederate soldiers and fought military campaigns, with dice and rules of our own making, to decide who would win the Civil War. Roger was the Union General. I led the rebels. Even in childhood we were adopting the roles we would later play in life.

On dry days in the summer holidays we'd play backyard cricket, holding complete Test series whose results depended on how many times we could bounce an old tennis ball against Nanna's back wall without hitting the downpipe, the gutter or anything else that could throw the ball off course. Roger had finely calculated the permissible play area so that the scores of our teams were often not far away from the totals of the Test matches.

When it was cold or wet we played indoors: cards or on our Daddy's old bagatelle board – the precursor of the pinball machine. Roger won the majority of our games. His age gave him an advantage and, when it looked like I might turn the tables, he would turn to psychology.

Being my big brother he knew all the ways to wind me up. He can still do it to this day in his pursuit of a victory at the card table, at petanque or in winning an argument. Roger was, and still is, intensely competitive. It doesn't matter whether we're playing cribbage, backgammon, table tennis or taking sides in University Challenge, my big brother is always in single-minded pursuit of victory.

In spite of our games rivalries and the vast differences in lifestyles and values, we're friends. Roger is an honourable, decent man. He's now the only person who has been a constant throughout my life.

I hardly knew my little sister Judy when we were children. After our mother's death, three-year-old Judy went to live with Auntie Con in Netherstowey on the other side of the country. Two boys were as much as our Nanna could manage in her terraced house. We might see our little sister for a few days, once or twice a year in the holidays and that was it – until Daddy came back from his posting in Hong Kong with Katie, his Manx fiancée.

Roger and I were away at boarding school for most of the year. Judy was the one who suffered the worst of Katie's harsh regime. Her plight got worse, or so it seemed to us, after Katie gave birth to a girl, Susi. At first Roger and I resented the pampered infant who got all the affection and attention that our Cinderella sister lacked.

In spite of everything, Judy became a warm, loving mother to three children who've grown into impressive adults. A teacher for many years, she's now a magistrate, a dedicated gardener and was a marathon runner until her knees made her stop.

Susi was the other rebel in the family, much more fiery than I. It wasn't until she began walking and answering back that she started getting the same treatment as her elder sister. She was the only person I've known who was able to give as good as she got from Katie. Their rows were explosive.

For years a self-centred lover exploited Susi's generous and giving nature. Now she's found herself a kind man, an ex-policeman who makes her happy. She seems more contented than at any time since I read her to sleep with Rupert Bear stories in Singapore.

John Stanley Fielding passed away near the end of 2004. At first I shied away when I came to write about our Daddy. What could I possibly say that would remotely do justice to the man? At the end he went downhill very quickly and died before I could get over to England. I went to say goodbye to him in the funeral parlour. The body in the coffin had undoubtedly been my father, but equally clearly he'd gone from it. That didn't stop me saying what I needed to say: that I loved him and was sorry I hadn't been there to say goodbye.

I'd always loved him, even through the most difficult years when he and I couldn't agree on anything. We all loved him and we knew that he loved us. He was a man of his time, unable to express emotions, but his love shone through without words.

My Dad's father, Stanley, one of the feckless Fielding brothers from Sheffield, disappeared suddenly from his life, never to be seen again. One day our grandmother, Doris, returned home early to find her husband in bed with another woman. In her bed! She threw them and the mattress into the street.

Not wanting to be the talk of the gossips who thrive in every city, our Nanna moved south to Ipswich to be near Hilda, her elder sister. She had to find a job – and quickly. There was no state help for single parents in those days and she had two boys to bring up. Doris was a good pastry-cook and soon got work in a bakery.

John Fielding studied engineering, intent on getting to University. He was eighteen when he realised war was coming. Abandoning his hopes of higher education, he joined the army.

After completing officer training, he was commissioned and posted to Egypt as an artillery officer. Almost immediately he was seriously wounded in a German bombardment. He spent a year in hospital with head injuries. Luckily his brain was unaffected, but his sense of smell was gone for good. He recovered in time to fight at El Alamein. The enormous artillery barrage that preceded the battle left him hard of hearing for the rest of his life.

He fought up through Italy with the Eighth Army. On the first day of the assault on Monte Cassino he was wounded again. He was hospitalised once more and was still convalescing when peace was declared.

Dad left the army after the war, still hoping to pursue an engineering career. He married Joyce Davies from Rhyl in August 1945. The following May she presented him with a son, Roger, and died a few weeks later from an irregular heart. Our Nanna, Doris, nursed my brother-to-be in Sheffield, until he was taken to Rhyl where his aunts looked after him.

Broken by the tragic death of his wife, Dad was bereft. He returned to the life he knew best and rejoined the army in 1946. The following year he met Joyce's sister in Egypt; Thelma was in the WAAF. Their shared loss – her sister, his wife – brought them together. A year and a half later, at the beginning of 1948, John and Thelma were married. I turned up in October, my sister Judy followed three years later.

In June 1955, my parents and a couple of friends were on their way to a party when the driver lost control and hit a telegraph pole. Our mother was killed instantly. Dad had head injuries again, but survived the crash. The driver and his wife were unhurt.

By the age of thirty-four, my father had suffered more than any man should have to bear. He'd lost the best six years of his life to the war. Many of his friends had been killed, some of them blown to pieces in front of his eyes. His sense of smell was obliterated and he was partially deaf. He'd had every single toe broken, several of them more than once. Peace only brought him more tragedy with the death of his first wife, then her sister.

I added to his burden when I disappeared into the

hippy sub-culture in the sixties. It little mattered to me then what he thought of me, but ten years later, when I was sent to prison, I fully understood how deeply I'd wounded and shamed him. Although he'd retired from the army by the time of my bust, he was still working for the Ministry of Defence.

Amid the great blaze of publicity that surrounded Operation Julie, my Dad had to face his colleagues, day after day, in the full knowledge that they knew all about his disgraced son.

I didn't need to be told how hard it was for him to make the long journey to see me in prison and was grateful for his visit. It meant a lot. As ever, he kept his feelings in check. He told me I'd been a damned fool and then we talked in practical terms, mostly about what I should do when I got out. At the end of the short visit, when I tried to express how sorry I felt for embarrassing him, he stopped me short and said 'Enough of that. Whatever you've done, you'll always be my son.'

We embraced. With a knuckle, he wiped a trace of moisture from his eye, straightened his back and strode out of the visiting room.

I have so many good memories of my Dad. It's hard to believe that he's really gone. In a way he hasn't, because for as long as any of his children are alive, his voice will echo in our heads. And we'll follow the advice he invariably barked at us whenever we were stuck, unhappy or paralysed by the complications and contradictions of life:

'Just bloody well get on with it!'

38. THE HIGH PYRENEES

On the last day of 2004, Sue bought a derelict farmhouse in the foothills of the Pyrenees. It had been empty for thirty-two years. The outside toilet had collapsed into ruin. There was no water in the house, no plumbing, drainage or power points, just one working light in a bedroom.

We packed our hightop van with basic house gear, put Tommy and our new overgrown puppy, Mitch, in their beds in the back and drove down to the Hautes Pyrenees. En route to the farmhouse, we stopped at a stove store, attracted by the huge February discounts. We bought a half-price double combustion wood-burning stove and installed it immediately. At least we now had one room where we could keep warm.

The crumbling outbuildings on two sides of the courtyard had been cow barns and were stuffed with broken farm equipment and splattered with cow shit dating back to the nineteenth century – or even earlier. The house was two hundred and forty years old. It had been built before the French Revolution. The construction date, 1764, and a heart were carved in stone over the door. The heart meant a great deal to Sue.

'A lot of love went into making this house,' she said. 'A lot more love will go into the rebuilding.'

We unloaded the stuff we'd brought and took away vanloads of junk to the local recycling centre.

Each weekend we brought the dogs and more of our gear down from the Lot. If it rained we worked indoors, clearing and cleaning the house. In fine

311

weather I'd scrape shit off the cowshed walls and make piles of broken tiles and rotting chunks of wood to be barrowed away across the road and put in our field.

I replaced the twenty-one broken windowpanes in the house and planted a little orchard in our field across the road. The trees would be growing all the time we were working on the buildings.

Once we'd cleared and cleaned enough space, we set up a temporary kitchen and finally moved into the house in March.

Diary: March 8, 2005.
Warming my feet by the stove. It's bitterly cold. This old Pyrenean farmhouse has the deep chill of a place that's been empty for years. We're back to basics. All the electricity comes through a single power point in the outbuildings. the only tap is in the stables. I have to go out there to fetch water, before the pipe freezes.

Crossing the courtyard, I flick off the torch and look up. The stars are ice-diamonds flung across the sky. It's a soul-tingling night and unbelievably cold.

The bucket stirs a deep cell memory: slop out, the morning queue to empty your piss-pot. I realise that today is March the eighth, the twenty-seventh anniversary of my being sentenced to eight years in prison. Again, for a moment out of time, I look right into the eyes of my judge, the poor old judge, gone now in his turn to be judged. Swirled in the bucket of my memories, I fail to turn off the tap in time. Icy water pours over my shoes, yanking me clear of Bristol Crown Court, back into freezing wet feet – feet that have been cold all day. What am I doing out here in the dark, chewing over decades-old memories?

I've done this restoring an abandoned farmhouse business before. But that was nearly twenty years ago, when Meg, Jess and I were setting up home in Spain. Do I really want to be going through this all over again? Perhaps I have no choice. I now recognise that certain themes run through my life: I'm writing away like there's no tomorrow – and maybe there isn't. I bathe in hot springs whenever I can. I'm still hanging around mountains like a groupie.

From Trencrom hill via the Andes and the Himalayas to the High Pyrenees, I've always been drawn to the heights. Up there the air is clearer and so is my thinking. Altitude gives us a different perspective. Above the clouds, it's not full-on humanity, rolling news, atrocities and traffic jams: it's the night sky, the crescent moon, a shooting star and worlds beyond.

Stepping stones towards the stars, mountains show us how tiny we are – and offer us glimpses of greatness.

Diary: March 19, 2005.
We've just gone through the most abrupt seasonal switch ever. For weeks on end the temperature didn't climb above zero. The move from bitter winter to summer, a rise of 30°C, took just three days. Every year we're setting records for the hottest, wettest, windiest or driest year ever recorded.

As a species, though facing the moment of truth, we find ourselves endlessly distracted by a rotating diet of celebs, soaps, scandals, scares, sports and scapegoats... In my mind's ear I just heard Ronnie,

my backgammon partner in Horfield prison,
screaming 'Man, we are SO sophisticated!'

I was trying to get one room habitable before we
moved in, but here we are and the room isn't
finished. Everything takes longer than I thought: no-
one can halt the acceleration of time. We were
sleeping in a room with holes in the ceiling, holes
that could easily grow in the night.

Part of the stable wall collapsed in the worst of
the February frosts. A freak storm that whipped up a
small tornado ripped out a section of the stable roof
and flung it twenty yards across the courtyard to
smash the roof tiles on another of the decaying
outbuildings.

For a few weeks I had the dismal feeling we'd
taken on too much and wondered glumly whether the
place was going to fall down around our ears before
I'd had time to stabilise it. But winter passed and
with it went the blues.

By late spring I'd made us a bedroom/office, put
in a septic tank and the first sets of wiring circuits.
With the considerable help of a new friend, Neil, I
patched the holes in the roof, repaired the
disintegrating walls and worked until I was happy
that further collapses weren't imminent. Our pal
Derek, my old work partner in the Lot, came down
to sort out the plumbing for us, then I put in a
bathroom and life seemed almost civilised.

Young Mitch was turning out to be an amazing dog:
super cool and extremely bright. Tommy returned to
his former status of being the underdog, he seemed
happy that way. Mitch was more like a person than a
dog. As he grew he turned into an unkempt

Rastafarian. Dog Marley we called him. Normally his eyes were hidden but if you saw them you knew there was an intelligent being under all the hair. I've had some lovely dogs in my life, but Mitch was in a league of his own.

All the time that I was working on stabilising the structure of our buildings, Sue was busy turning a long-neglected house into our home: dressing the set, as she puts it. Little by little, our house came to look less like a building site and more like a dwelling. She has a real flair with décor and placement and an eye for combinations that work and those that don't. With very little expenditure she transformed our shabby ancient building into a lovely home.

Once the basics of the house were done we began exploring our beautiful surroundings. We made new friends and began to feel more and more at home. I've travelled quite a bit in my time and visited some amazing parts of the world, but this is the place to live.

When I first arrived in the French Pyrenees in the early nineties, I had the eeriest sensation that I was coming home – a feeling I'd never had before. I knew instantly that this was where I should be living, but it took some time to get here.

38. VOLCANO

The work at the house had been going well. It wasn't far from finished when I lost my footing on the ice, fell badly and buggered up my shoulder. Then Sue, leaning out of the bedroom window, slipped and cracked a couple of ribs. She hadn't recovered when her son's marriage exploded. As her daughter-in-law was also her best friend, Sue found herself in the middle, trying to help both sides come to terms with a situation that held out no hope for recovery. As if that weren't enough, she came back from her annual UK visit to see Terry in a very depressed state and soon developed a terrible case of eczema. It raged all over her body: an outward manifestation of the agony inside. Desperate to do something to help, I said I'd take her away for a holiday, give her a complete change of scene. We chose Guatemala.

If I haven't said much about Sue and our relationship, it's because we started off wonderfully well and just kept going that way. Living with Sue is so easy, so rewarding. That shorthaired blonde who threw me a sunflower in the fashion parade has lit up my life. I thank the Universe for allowing us to meet.

Guatemala is a country of dramatic extremes. It has a Pacific and a Caribbean coast. Between ocean and sea there are lakes and forests, mountains and volcanoes that rise to nearly fourteen thousand feet.

The people were still trying to come to terms with the civil war that had cost tens of thousands of lives.

GUATEMALA

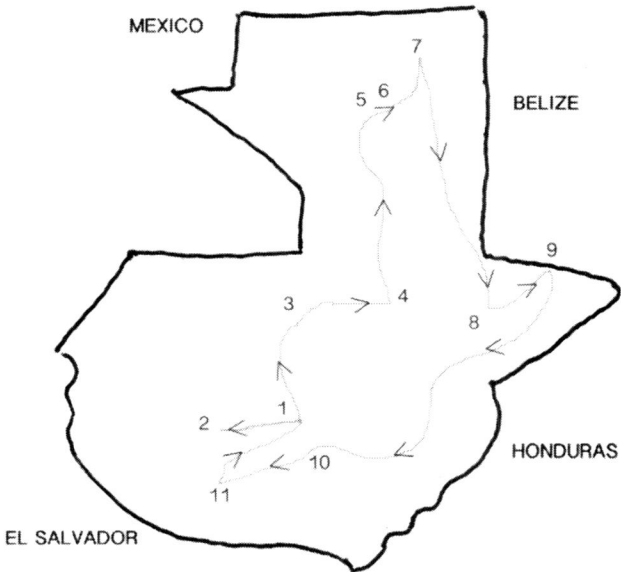

1	GUATEMALA CITY	7	TIKAL
2	LAKE ATITLAN	8	RIO DULCE
3	COBAN	9	LIVINGSTON
4	SEMUC CHAMPEY	10	ANTIGUA
5	FLORES	11	PACAYA VOLCANO
6	EL REMATE		

Guatemala lies at the junction of three tectonic plates and has a string of volcanoes. Four of them are still active. Lake Atitlan filled the hole left by a gigantic volcanic eruption eighty-five thousand years ago. Three more recent volcanoes now dominate the lake, giving it a spectacular surreal beauty.

We landed shortly before midnight. Exhausted, we crashed out in a hotel near the airport.

In the morning, woken early by the roar of planes taking off over our heads, we set off to catch the bus to Lake Atitlan, intriguingly described by Aldous Huxley as 'Really too much of a good thing'. Already waiting at the station were a sweet young couple from the city, off for a romantic weekend by the lake, and a wild-eyed young guy with a guitar.

Enlivened by our presence he began to strum his instrument, badly, and get friendly with us. He was one of the street urchins who make their living by hanging out with tourists. I joked around with him and the young lovers. It felt great to be speaking Spanish again. We turned down the kid's offer of a shot of rum, but he went ahead anyway, toasted us all and drank his breakfast booze mixed with a little orangeade.

The strumming got faster as he grew more animated. He paused to drink again and continued slamming the strings, laughing and singing. In the space of two minutes, he went from confident, cocky performer to slurred stumbling drunk. Then he slid off the bench and knocked over his drink as he sprawled on the floor. He made it onto the bus before it pulled out of the station and stayed lolling across the aisle while the bus filled up around him. He woke up, threw up and fell asleep again.

We spent our first day wandering around, getting the feel of the place. Guatemala is a poor country and there were few tourists. In the morning we had a huge breakfast of black beans, eggs, tortillas and fruit, washed down with a pot of good Guatemalan coffee. Our breakfast blowout had cost us a dollar apiece. We took a boat ride across the lake to San Pedro. It was a hot day so we went to a juice bar for a drink. I got into conversation with a couple of young tourists who were offended when I took them for Americans.

'Hey, we're not Yanks, we're Canadians!' the girl said indignantly.

It seemed like a good idea to change the subject. 'Where's the best place you've been in Guatemala?' I asked them.

'Semuc Champey,' they chorused and shared a radiant look that made me think we would do well to go there too.

'Where's that?' Sue wanted to know.

'Near Coban, in the middle, Alta Verapaz.'

Alta Verapaz, literally high true peace: it sounded good to me. We thanked them for their help, drained our drinks and went back to the hotel to check it out on the map.

From Atitlan we travelled west, further into the mountains and up into the cloud forest. We were headed for Fuentes Georginas, where piping hot water bubbles and pours out of the rock and into a natural rock-pool, eight thousand feet above sea level. There's just enough flat space for a basic restaurant and half a dozen little overnight chalets with fireplaces. The manager gave us paper, kindling and a big armful of logs.

'You'll need a fire,' he said. 'It gets cold once the sun goes down.'

In the afternoon, after a lengthy wallow in the hot swimming pool, we sat quietly outside the back of our chalet, looking into the lush vegetation. Soon the trees had birds flitting through them. Lots of brightly

319

coloured little yellow and red things, then a hummingbird – the first I'd ever seen – followed by a small flock of toucanets, green, yellow and black. What a treat! We were hoping to see a quetzal, the national bird which lives in the cloud forest, but we were out of luck.

When the sun dropped out of the sky, the temperature plummeted. I lit a fire and we went to swim in the pool again. The closer we got to the rock wall, the hotter the water became. I made it to the far side, but couldn't stay there for more than a few seconds. We had the pool to ourselves that evening and again in the morning. Relaxing in hot water is where I get my best ideas. If I'd been invited onto *Desert Island Discs,* my luxury item would've been a hot spring. Lying back in clouds of shifting steam, wrapped in sublime music, I wouldn't be looking to be rescued.

I'd been hoping that the minerals, dissolved in hot water, would help Sue's eczema. She feared they might aggravate it. In the event it seemed to have made no difference. Her skin was still bothering her.

We boarded a bus to Coban and soon discovered our driver was in competition with another bus – he'd been jumped at some roadworks.

The two drivers began to race each other. In Guatemala, drivers are paid a percentage of the fares they take. First at the bus stop wins the passengers. The race in which we were involuntarily participants appeared to have a lot of needle; an excess of machismo lies behind most quarrels between Guatemaltecos.

Both drivers kept taking increasingly stupid risks. Repairs were being made to the road after the landslides of the previous wet season and road works kept slowing our progress.

Whenever the traffic the other way was halted, the two drivers assumed the road belonged exclusively to them – only coming towards us, as we battled round a blind corner in second place, was a road crew in their minibus. The other bus driver slammed on the brakes, skidded on the dusty road and slewed sideways on two wheels before coming to a halt a few feet short of the minibus. We barrelled past, through clouds of dust, with fists waving and loud cheering.

'I can't take any more of this. We're getting off at the next stop.' Sue was adamant. 'I don't care if we've paid the full fare. We're getting off.'

I didn't argue. Tropical countries have certain similarities all around the globe: stately trees covered in giant perfumed flowers, pineapples that melt you with their sweetness and buses crammed with passengers, children and chickens, driven by reckless lunatics.

Coban, sitting on the edge of the mountains, at four thousand feet, looks north over the jungle plains of El Petén. It's the city of cardamom, coffee and orchids. Our little backpackers' hotel had fifty different orchids in its courtyard. We ordered coffee and got talking to a dark-haired Frenchwoman from Saint Pierre et Michelon, travelling on her own.

'Has it been a bad winter with you, Sara?' Sue asked. 'With us it got down to thirteen below. It was minus fifteen in the valley. Really bitter.'

'Ha!' Sara replied. 'That's nothing. On our island it went down to minus thirty-five.'

'Are you sure?' I asked, thinking this woman is

an absolute bullshitter. Minus thirty-five indeed! 'It didn't get anything like that cold, even in the mountains.' I added. I'd heard of the islands Saint Pierrre et Michelon, but I only had a hazy idea of where they were. Somewhere off the west coast of France, near the Ile de Re, I reckoned.

'Have you been to Semuc Champay?' Sue asked, diplomatically changing the subject. 'We're going tomorrow.'

'So am I. It sounds amazing.'

We talked about our travels, ate dinner together and had an early night in preparation for our dawn start.

Getting to Semuc Champey was a business, so we'd bought tickets for the tour the hotel offered. In the minibus with us were a driver, a guide, and ten youngish travellers of assorted nationalities. Most were doing a day trip, but Sara, Sue and I wanted to stay the night and return the following evening.

'No problem,' the guy in the hotel had said. 'A night's lodging by the river is included in the price of the ticket.'

We set off at six in the morning and drove into the mountains on a good road for some thirty miles. Abruptly, the driver turned sharply downhill onto a dirt track. We lurched up and down and around for another fourteen bumpy miles. In a jungle clearing, we stopped at a bar.

'Last chance for a visit to the bathroom or a drink before Semuc Champey,' our guide called out. 'This is where you're staying,' he told me. 'There's a couple of rooms here. Leave your bag if you want.'

We parked our luggage in our rooms in , a wood-framed plank-clad shack, up a long rickety flight of

322

stairs. After a quick wash and brush up we went down, joined the others and drove the last leg to the river.

Alta Verapaz is limestone country and the rocks are porous. Just above the lagoons of Semuc Champey, the river Cahabón plunges through a great cavern and travels along an underground tunnel before re-emerging into the light. Most of the river disappears. A small portion of it still runs into the old riverbed, the one that existed before the gravity-hungry river ate its way down to a lower level.

The old riverbed is now a limestone bridge, three hundred metres long, in which nestle a necklace of turquoise pools, each one a tropical dream conjured from some improbable high-budget advertisement.

To get the best view of the pools, our guide, René, took us up to the *Mirador*, the lookout point. We zigzagged up the rough wooden steps dug into the mountainside, ascending five hundred metres in a little over a kilometre.

Sue and I, panting heavily, were the last to the top. We must have been at least twice the age of the others. We slumped to the ground. For a minute or two we could do nothing more than gulp air into our heaving lungs. When we got our breath back we looked around and saw the climb had been worth the effort. The pools lay like a string of sapphires on the velvet carpet of the jungle canopy.

Above the pools at Semuc Champey

When everyone in the group was ready, we climbed down to the spot where the mighty river thunders into its underground pit. Then we walked down the limestone bridge, stripped off and swam in the blue pools, cupped in the palm of the mountains. It was fucking amazing.

The lowest pool empties into a waterfall above the point where the main river surges back into the light. René took the rest of our group down a rope ladder through the waterfall to a projecting rock. From there they had the option of fighting their way back up through the falling water on the swaying ladder or diving into the main river and swimming to a beach before the current took them onto the rocks downstream.

Until a few years ago, I'd have been up for the challenge. Now I was not far short of sixty, still with a dodgy shoulder and glad to be capturing this on camera from below rather than participating.

Two Norwegian guys followed René into the water. The others took the harder retreat, up the waterfall.

In mid-afternoon the minibus picked up the group to take the youngsters back to Coban.

The driver dropped us off at the jungle lodge and the sound of the VW receded into the distance. Once it had gone the place seemed deafeningly quiet: Just Sue, Sara and I, the three young guys who worked there and the tireless cicadas. We went down for a juice. Sara wanted to complain about her accommodation. The lads were drinking beer and playing the fool. There were no women around, I realised. Unusual.

A pick-up pulled up in front of the bar. Three short, stocky men got out. All of them wore baseball caps and had bellies that bulged over their belts. They made a big show of inspecting the new building going up on the next plot of land, then moved on to examine the toilets before disappearing from sight.

Remembering I'd left my money in the room, I walked out through the bar, along the path and was halfway up the stairs when I realised there was someone on our landing. Three people in fact. The guys from the pick-up were standing outside our room. They excused themselves and set off down the stairs. What was that about, I wondered. The room was still locked. Our stuff was untouched. 'Why would three men want to look at a double bedroom?' I asked myself. From my vantage point on the platform, I saw they were at the bar, having a drink. I checked the rooms from the outside, standing on the landing at the top of the stairs. There was a fist-sized hole in the mosquito netting in both rooms, perfect for slipping your hand in and unlocking the bolt that shut the door from inside. This had a very bad smell.

The men were nowhere to be seen when I came down. Was I being paranoid? It didn't matter. I couldn't take the risk.

'We're leaving,' I told Sue. 'We're going to put our essentials in a shoulder bag, walk down to Las Marias, the bar by the river, and get them to put us up for the night. We can pick up our rucksacks in the morning when we return with the hotel minibus. You're coming with us, Sara.'

'That's it!' Sara spat out the words as we headed downhill towards the river, 'Fucking Guatemala. I've had enough. I've been ripped off, hassled, shot at...'

'What?' Sue exclaimed. 'Who shot at you?'

'The police in Antigua. OK, they weren't actually shooting at me. They opened fire on an escaping thief, in a street full of people! Everyone was screaming and lying on the ground. I ran into a hotel.' She expelled her breath in a long drawn-out sigh. 'That's it for me. I've had enough adventure. I want to go home to Saint Pierre.'

I'm a map freak. I felt I ought to know the location of Saint Pierre. My ignorance was bugging me. 'So remind us where Saint Pierre is.'

'Saint Pierre et Michelon are in the North Atlantic: two little French islands off Newfoundland in Canada. There are six thousand people on the islands. We all know each other, pretty much. It's horribly cold and windy nearly all the time, but I miss it. Especially my family, I miss them much more than I thought I would.'

All the rooms at Las Marias were taken, but the staff cleared some attic space for us to sleep in, once I'd explained why we'd left our initial lodgings. The manager was sympathetic.

'There have been some problems there in the past.' he said. 'I'll drive you up to collect your bags'.

I offered to pay for his time and petrol, but he wouldn't accept any money for the help.

'Let me at least buy you a drink,' I said, on our return to his riverside bar. 'What will you have?'

'I'm a Guatemalteco. I'll have rum, of course.'

Guatemala isn't an expensive country. I thought I could afford to treat him to a really good drink.

'OK. Let's have a couple of double shots of the best rum you've got.'

The rum was twenty-five years old. We clinked glasses. He knocked back half of his in one deep swallow, I had a cautious sip. The drink was amazing; different flavours developing as I sluiced it around my mouth. I'd always thought of rum as something to be avoided, or knocked back with a grimace, but this drink was as full of character as a fine malt whisky or an ancient Armagnac.

'Wow, this is superb!' I exclaimed.

'Of course it is. Guatemalan rum is the best in the world,' he replied, topping his glass up with Coke…

In the morning Sue and I joined a group going to explore a series of partially submerged caves alongside the river. With our guide we were eleven: Sue and I, six Maltese students, and a large South African couple. Our guide wore a miner's headlamp; we held lit candles. We waded into the first cave, then swam, candles held aloft, through a succession of five or six caverns.

To reach the final pair, we had to climb up a rope ladder and to leave we had to squeeze through a narrow gap and descend a small waterfall. I hadn't known whether we'd enjoy it but it was a magical experience, full of fun and shadows, light and laughter. When we emerged into daylight it felt like we'd known each other for ages and were friends.

We'd carried inflated inner tubes with us on the walk up to the caves. Now we put them in the river, linked arms with the feet of the person behind and, led by our guide, floated off downstream like a giant processing caterpillar chain.

We stayed together until we'd safely navigated the rocky shoals. At this point we separated and carried on drifting down the green river at our own pace. I was peering into the luxuriant tropical vegetation on either side, still hoping to catch sight of a quetzal.

Back at the bar, Sara was being chatted up by a French guy. Seeing the eczema on Sue's arms, he asked what the problem was. She explained.

'I can give you directions to a Mayan herbalist in El Remate,' the guy said. 'She's very highly recommended.'

The following morning we said goodbye to Sara, who was returning to the capital, and got on a minibus for the six-hour trip to Flores, the first leg of our journey to El Remate.

It was an enjoyable ride to begin with. The scenery kept changing as we lost height. We were leaving the mountains and going down into the jungle. Then we breasted a rise and were flagged to a halt behind another minibus.

The road ahead ran straight for a mile, dipping down then rising to the next crest. There appeared to be some obstruction in the distance. Our driver went up to the first bus and came back looking worried.

'There's been an accident,' he said. 'The villagers have closed the road.'

I translated for Sue's benefit. 'What happened,' I asked the driver.

'A lorry hit two kids, brothers aged five and eight.'

'Are they OK?'

'No, they're both dead. Another boy is injured. The villagers are very angry. They've closed the road as a protest.'

'So what do we do?'

'Nothing. It would be a big mistake to try to get past their roadblock. We'll just sit here quietly and see what happens. Maybe they'll open the road in a while.'

We sat and waited. A few minutes later another vehicle halted behind us. Small groups of local people were converging on the scene of the accident. All the men carried Guatemalan machetes, fearsome steel blades, two feet long.

After a quarter of an hour or so, the minibus behind us turned round and left. The one in front did the same. This left us at the front of the queue. Our driver must have felt exposed, because he soon said 'I think we'll go back to the last junction and see if we can find a way round. Who knows, maybe they'll think of putting a roadblock behind us and then we'd be stuck.'

I was relieved to be driving away from a potential nightmare. You only have to read Elias Canetti's *Crowds and Power* to learn how quickly an angry crowd can be inflamed into a bloodthirsty mob. As far as the locals were concerned we were traffic, and traffic had brought tragedy to the village.

Five kilometres back up the road we came to a junction and turned down the dirt road towards Laguna Lachuá.

'Hey! Where're you going?' the driver of another bus shouted.

'Trying to get round the roadblock,' our driver replied.

'You won't make it. That's a really bad road.'

We turned round and sat waiting in a big clearing in the jungle. The sun was right overhead. Sweat splashed from my dripping face onto my damp clothes. After half an hour two police jeeps sped past, heading towards the scene of the accident. We waited a while longer then set off after them, hoping that they would have cleared the route. But when we arrived at the village the road was still blocked and there was no sign of the police.

'Maybe we should go back to Coban,' I suggested to the driver. Twenty minutes had passed with nothing happening except the arrival of more machete-wielding locals. They were gathering around a gesticulating man who had a lot to say.

I remembered something I'd read in the Lonely Planet guidebook. In 2000, a crowd of villagers had beaten a Japanese tourist and his Guatemalan driver to death. The tourist had taken photos of some children. Mayans don't like being photographed.

The tourist and his driver were unlucky enough to have turned up after rumours of child-sacrificing Satanists had swept through the area. We had the misfortune to have turned up just after two kids had been killed.

The Danish woman sitting in front of us got out her camera. I leaned forward and tapped her on the arm.

'I'd put that away if I were you' I said. I knew her a little. We'd met a couple of times in Coban. She was a good-looking redhead in her fifties, talkative and foolish.

'But it would make such a striking photograph.' Flaunting her excellent English, she laughed away my concern.

I held the camera hand of the garrulous Dane and hissed 'Listen, you stupid woman. No photos!'

'OK. Let go. You're hurting me.' She called to the driver, '*Vamos a Coban*. Let's go back to Coban.'

'I don't think we can turn back without aggravating the crowd,' the driver said nervously. 'I think we have to wait. The police will sort it out.'

We sat tight. The machete mob around the speaker began to drift off towards the scene of the accident. After a few minutes, a group of people appeared from the village and dragged the tree trunks and the branches off the road. Traffic started to come through from the other direction. A police car escorted us through the village. The driver mopped his brow with a big yellow handkerchief. We were all mightily relieved to be on our way.

In El Remate, by the shores of Lake Petén Itza, we found the Mayan herbalist the Frenchman had recommended. Maria was tiny and wrinkled. She had sparkling eyes and greying hair.

'I was the youngest of twelve children and the only girl,' she told us. 'I'm not a girl any more,' she admitted. She was sixty-seven, but could still bend down with straight legs, put her palms on the floor, then walk them forward until they were eighteen inches away from her feet. She showed us.

'Your blood is on fire,' she told Sue. 'I'll bring you some medicine that will cool you.'

In the evening, Maria turned up with a green paste, made from seven different plants, which she plastered all over Sue's body.'

'*Mira,*' she laughed, '*La mujer verde!*' 'Look, the green woman!

'How does it feel?' I asked.

'It stings, but then anything I put on stings at first – water, oil, the cream the doctor gave me...'

After showering off the paste, I rubbed her with the juice from a cactus Maria had left. It was soothing. 'I think it's helping,' Sue sighed, 'but it's too soon to say.'

The *ladino* lady who ran the hotel we'd stayed in on our first night in the country had told me that the Mayan people remain essentially apart from the descendants of the Spanish *conquistadores*.

'They have a way of thinking that is alien to ours,' she'd said. 'Don't forget, these people diverged from the mainstream of human history maybe twenty thousand years ago. They are very different from us.'

I wasn't impressed by her air of superiority. The native Indians of the Americas developed in their own way, it's true. The Mayans independently discovered agriculture several thousand years ago. Their crops included maize, beans, tomatoes, peppers and chillies... They kept turkeys and dogs, wove baskets, made pottery and worshipped implacable gods. Three thousand years ago, when migrating tribes roamed throughout Europe, the Mayans were developing city societies.

Templo 4 Tikal

The Mayan's greatest city, Tikal, first rose to prominence in the third century CE, long before the Anglo-Saxons invaded Britain. In its eighth century heyday, under the powerful Lord Chocolate, Tikal was the centre of the Mayan world.

Mayan society collapsed sometime around 900 CE. The survivors of the disasters abandoned all their great cities and returned to being the farmers they had been, the farmers they still are to this day.

Our trip to Tikal began at five in the morning. Light seeped into the sky as we drove north in the taxi we'd booked the previous day. We were at the site before sunrise and had the place to ourselves. Early morning was the optimum time to see the wildlife and the best time to walk around, before it got too hot. There were monkeys in the trees, parrots, macaws, ibises and bright woodpeckers. Royal turkeys, strutted about like peacocks. There were many other birds I couldn't identify.

For the next seven hours we strolled around, thunderstruck. The central area of the city covered several square kilometres. Many of the bigger structures had been excavated and restored, but most were still buried under the jungle that had hidden the city for a thousand years. We didn't get much beyond the Grand Plaza and the main buildings immediately around it, but we must have walked ten kilometres or more.

We climbed the massive forty-four metre Templo 4 and looked out over the jungle canopy to the tops of other great temples poking into the sunlight. There were monkeys everywhere. All day we looked at stunning plazas and pyramids, each in its own clearing, each surrounded by riotous foliage.

Suddenly jungle fatigue set in.

Back at our guest house all I wanted to do was lie down. Maybe I had a little heat stroke. My stomach was upset and I felt mildly delirious. I lay on my bed and pondered the rise and fall of the Mayans.

Was our civilisation going to go the same way? Were our complicated systems going to break down under the strains of overpopulation and environmental degradation? Would the survivors of our collapse remain as subsistence farmers for the next thousand years, as the Mayans had?

Perhaps that would be the best long-term hope, not only for humanity's survival but also for the hundreds or thousands of other species endangered by our activities. Our globalised assault on the planetary life-support systems is breathtaking in its vast scope and blind stupidity.

For the last few days in Guatemala, we based ourselves in the former capital of Central America. Antigua was founded in 1543 and destroyed by a massive earthquake two hundred years later. The ruins of its cathedral and thirty-odd churches are dotted all around the new town. Many old buildings have been restored, some churches too. Full of cobbled streets, plazas and colonial courtyards with fountains, brightened by bougainvillaea and jacaranda, Antigua is a pearl, lying in the shadow of a volcano.

The lovely Mayan family we stayed with in Antigua

In the tropics, the days begin as the sky lightens. We started the climb of Pacaya, an active volcano, at 6 a.m. We did it because we could – I don't suppose the chance is ever going to occur again. Pacaya isn't one of Guatemala's highest volcanoes, but it's over eight thousand feet. We weren't going to go all the way to the top; red-hot lava is pouring out of the cone and had been doing so for ten months.

We were a group of nine. You're only allowed on this volcano with a registered guide. Mountain rangers patrol the area, all in constant radio communication about the state of the slopes and the movement of the lava. Stout footwear was a requirement.

At first we could have been walking up any wooded hillside. The path was steep and we had to pay attention to our footholds. Sue kept going until the second rest. There she decided she'd ride the horse our guide had brought along. As we climbed, the trees thinned and the terrain began to open out. We had a great view of three volcanoes, all over twelve thousand feet, higher than anything in the Pyrenees. I was feeling strong for most of the climb, in good enough shape to handle an ascent like this. Then I hit an invisible barrier, my legs went wobbly and I had to stop and sit down for a few minutes. I took it steadily and plodded up to the grassy meadow where the youngsters and rider were waiting. They'd halted just on the edge of the lava flow. Above us, white smoke billowed from the cone of the volcano. Red veins of molten rock were slowly pulsing down its blackened slopes.

Alongside the lava, we sat down to eat the picnic lunches we'd brought. Sue and I finished ours with a big disc of delicious Guatemalan chocolate. I broke up the disc and passed it round. Lord Chocolate gave us the energy to do the final kilometre.

We set off behind our guide. White splashes of paint indicate our path. It's fairly well defined for the first five hundred metres across an old flow. Then quickly

336

it gets a lot hotter. All around us are places where the ground is smoking or smouldering.

Sue and I about to cross the lava

'*It was flowing here five days ago,*' *José, our guide, says. '*Keep to the path. Don't use your hands. It's still hot in places.*'

To demonstrate, he takes the top off his bottle and splashes some water into a fissure. The liquid vaporises instantly in a great puff of steam.

We carry on in Indian file walking slowly through a, sterile landscape. I feel as though I'm carrying the burden of the one ring to the heart of Mount Doom. Each step forward is harder than the one before. The heat is growing by the minute. The sensible part of me wants to run away and hide. We come to a halt, standing on a lava shelf, tilted away from the cone of the mountain. The temperature rises abruptly.

'A lifetime burning in every moment.'

This line from T.S.Eliot's 'East Coker', has echoed around my head for over forty years. Now, for the first time, I'm really feeling it.

Gingerly, I pick up a small chunk of lava. Last week it was deep down in the earth. Five days ago it was flowing on the surface. Now it's cold.

We all live on the slopes of a potential volcano. We like to think we stand on solid ground, but it's molten below. Massive seas of liquid iron swirl continually beneath the Earth's thin crust.

Volcanoes can lie dormant for a lifetime or erupt in an instant: any moment could be our last.

We're all travelling down the river of life, all being carried towards the waterfall of death. That's the deal, and there's nothing we can do about it.

It's not how long you live that matters most. It's what you do with life while you have it.

AFTERWORD

I'm looking over my few chapters and thinking about the hundreds I haven't included: sixty-odd years of living compressed into a few hours of reading...

Writing about your life experiences can be very interesting and instructive – I'd recommend it to anyone. You begin to understand yourself a little better as you discern tendencies, patterns and processes that weren't visible when you were up to your eyes (or out your depth) in the high drama of mid-life. What an extraordinary chain of events we can get tangled up in!

However far out you've pushed the boat of your life, there is always a route back to the heart of your own improbable existence. All of us have to find a way to live with ourselves and with everything that we have done. As my darling Sue says, nobody has a copy of the script. We're making it up as we go, while we're carried down the river of time.

I'm dying to find out what happens after life...

After living together for fourteen years, Sue and I were married in October 2015, the best move I ever made.

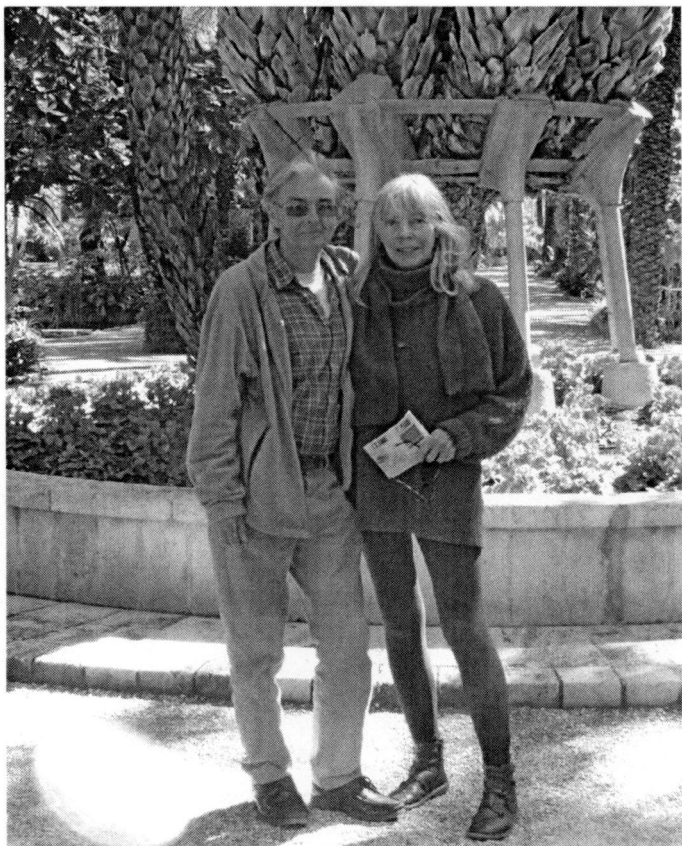

APPENDIX OF FOREIGN WORDS

<u>HINDI</u>:

Aacha	–	OK, Good
Bidi	–	Small Indian cigarette
Barfi	–	Indian sweets
Chai	–	Tea
Chalo!	–	Let's go!
Chapatti	–	Flat Indian bread
Charas	–	Hashish
Chillum	–	A conical hash pipe
Chowkidar	–	Caretaker
Dhaba	–	Eating place/ Restaurant
Dhal	–	Lentils
Dhanayabad	–	Thank you
Gaddi	–	People of Himachal Pradesh
Ghat	–	Waterside pier
Jhola	–	Shoulder bag
Lassi	–	A milk and fruit drink
Lungi	–	A rectangular cloth
Lathi	–	Long truncheon
Namaste	–	Hello
Paise	–	One hundreth of a rupee
Puja	–	Prayer
Rupee	–	Indian currency
Sahib	–	Sir, Master
Saddhu	–	Indian holy man
Shanti	–	Peace
Thali	–	Train meal, served on a metal tray
Tin	–	Three
Tis	–	Thirty
Tola	–	11.2 grams

CHICHEWA (MALAWI)

Mzungu — White man
Muli Bwanji — How are you?
Ndili Bwino — I'm fine.
Nsima — Maize porridge
Zikomo — Thank you.

SPANISH & CATALAN

Très — Three – Catalan
Deu — Ten – Catalan
Cava — Catalan champagne
Calçot — A type of onion for roasting
Romesco — A Catalan sauce
Soberano — Spanish brandy
Pebetero — The vessel used for the opening of the Barcelona Olympics
Ducados — Spanish black tobacco cigarettes
Miel Mel — Honey
Fuera! — Go away!
Adios Adeu — Goodbye
Vamos! Anem — Let's go!
Ladino — Of Spanish origin
Guatemalteco/a — Guatemalan man/woman

ACKNOWLEDGEMENTS & THANKS

I thank Sue Whatmough, now Sue Fielding, for her invaluable editing help.

Sue's books are '*NO COPY OF THE SCRIPT*' and '*HANGING ONTO HOPE*'. She is also a regular blogger under the name of *POT POURRI* for AngloInfo, the Worldwide Expat Network.

Thank you Lewe, for the extraordinary times we shared, and for what we accomplished on our many visits to Malawi.

Thanks also to Roger Fielding for putting me straight on certain family matters.

Judy Colman for her useful suggestions.

Susi Fielding for her boundless enthusiasm and support.

Smiles and Sally for sharing a good part of the journey.

Jess Maciver for her timely interventions.

John Newson for his help on proof-reading, and the feedback he gave me.

Frankie Bailey for her perceptive comments at a crucial stage of the work.

Myles Jackson, for his computing skills.

Dave Dukes, for being Dave, and for the back cover photo.

And thanks to all my friends, Facebook friends and readers who've been badgering me to get part 2 finished and published.

Lightning Source UK Ltd.
Milton Keynes UK
UKOW03f0759110417
298838UK00001B/10/P

9 781786 975133